Praise for the extraordinary gift of being ordinary

"Brilliant and accessible, *The Extraordinary Gift of Being Ordinary* gets to the very core of our human suffering and offers wise and helpful practices for taming our striving, comparing minds. The peace and contentment we long for arise naturally as we wake up from the limiting stories that habitually confine us, and begin to trust the truth of who we really are."
—TARA BRACH, PHD, author of *Trusting the Gold*

"In Zen, one of the highest accomplishments is to be ordinary. This means not to compare ourselves, but to be free to be authentic and real. In a wise and loving way, Dr. Siegel shows us how."
—JACK KORNFIELD, PHD, author of
After the Ecstasy, the Laundry

"This is an insightful, well-written, and extremely useful guide to finding happiness in the midst of imperfection. Chock full of practical exercises alongside easy-to-digest nuggets of wisdom, this book will help you let go of shame and negative self-judgments and instead embrace who you are with compassion."
—KRISTIN NEFF, PHD, coauthor of
The Mindful Self-Compassion Workbook

"It feels so freeing to just stop comparing myself to other people, even for a little while. Dr. Siegel's writing is compassionate, funny, and insightful. I've never been so glad to be 'ordinary.'"
—SUSIE F., Boston

"Dr. Siegel shows how the world lures us with the shiny object called happiness, then hooks us. We spend our lives pulling and tugging, only to get more deeply caught in cycles of suffering. But we can unhook ourselves and swim in a different direction—toward a more achievable level of well-being, fed by connection and compassion. This book is written from deep personal wisdom and vast clinical experience."
—JUDSON BREWER, MD, PHD, author of
Unwinding Anxiety

"Dr. Siegel's message—there's joy in ordinariness and even in failure—gave me a boost of self-acceptance to step forward in my career. Dr. Siegel gracefully dismantled my ego as if he were peeling layers of an onion. His book gave me the courage to endure failure, feel less preoccupied with other people's opinions, and celebrate the imperfections that used to keep me up at night."
—CODY R., Seattle

"Freeing us from toxic self-criticism and shame, this powerful book is an opening into deep self-acceptance, self-worth, and inner peace. Dr. Siegel's warmth fills every page, along with insights and practical suggestions from his decades as a world-class therapist. With many examples and lots of brief experiential practices, he brings together current science, soulful wisdom, and his own humorous and down-to-earth perspective. Really a gem, this is a book both for help in the darkest night and for general guidance along the long road of life."
—RICK HANSON, PHD, author of *Resilient*

"Deploying his rare mastery of mindfulness approaches, reinforced by decades of insight as a psychotherapist, Dr. Siegel offers reliable, effective, and simple guidance to escape what he aptly calls 'the trap of self-evaluation'—a trap all too familiar to many of us."
—GABOR MATÉ, MD, author of *In the Realm of Hungry Ghosts: Close Encounters with Addiction*

the extraordinary gift of being ordinary

also available

the extraordinary gift of being ordinary

FINDING HAPPINESS RIGHT WHERE YOU ARE

Dr. RONALD D. SIEGEL

THE GUILFORD PRESS
New York   London

Published by The Guilford Press
A Division of Guilford Publications, Inc.
370 Seventh Avenue, Suite 1200, New York, NY 10001
www.guilford.com

Library of Congress Cataloging-in-Publication Data is available from the
publisher.

ISBN 978-1-4625-3835-5 (paperback) — ISBN 978-1-4625-4854-5
(hardcover)

The following publishers have generously given permission to reprint or
adapt material from copyrighted works:

"Reclaim Your Brain" by Susan Pollak. Copyright © 2018 Susan
Pollak. Adapted by permission.
Teaching the Mindful Self-Compassion Program by Christopher Germer
and Kristin Neff. Copyright © 2019 The Guilford Press. Adapted by
permission.
"With That Moon Language" in *Love Poems from God,* edited by
Daniel Ladinsky. Copyright © 2002 Penguin. Reprinted by permission.
"The Cloud in the Sheet of Paper" in *Being Peace* by Thich Nhat
Hanh. Copyright © 1988, 2020 Parallax Press. Reprinted by permission.
"Positive Psychology and the Bodhisattva Path" by Charles Styron,
in *Mindfulness and Psychotherapy* (2nd ed.), edited by Christopher Germer,
Ronald D. Siegel, and Paul R. Fulton. Copyright © 2013 The Guilford
Press. Adapted by permission.

contents

Purchasers of this book can download select practical tools
and audio files at *www.giftofbeingordinary.com*
or *www.guilford.com/siegel4-materials* for personal use or use
with clients (see copyright page for details).

author's note

Individuals described in the illustrations and examples in this book are composites of real people, thoroughly disguised to protect their privacy.

preface

I'VE HAD THE PRIVILEGE of working as a clinical psychologist for nearly 40 years, seeing kids and adults from all walks of life, who came to therapy for everything from back pain to marital disputes. Despite this diversity, some years ago I noticed that there was one painful struggle almost everyone seemed to share: the relentless quest to feel better about themselves.

Some strove each day to be special or well liked, by getting good grades, looking attractive, making money, or being part of the in-crowd, while others strove just not to feel rejected or like a failure. Almost all were trying, with only periodic success, to live up to inner images of who they thought they should be—by being good, strong, or smart, or by accomplishing something. All this striving stressed everyone out and made them unhappy, since nobody succeeded for long. It also cut them off from sources of satisfaction that would have been much more meaningful, fulfilling, and reliable if only they weren't so busy judging themselves or worrying about how they compared to others.

I was stuck in it too. There I was, in my 60s, with a loving family and a good career, having practiced meditation and explored Western and Eastern psychology since I was a teenager. Still, my feelings about myself were constantly going up and down—often many times a day. You'd think that years of studying and practicing psychotherapy, along with years of serious engagement in contemplative practices designed to loosen the grip of self-preoccupation, would have made me stable and secure about who I was—but they hadn't.

The suffering I saw in my patients, and experienced personally, was so painful and pervasive I committed myself to seeing what could be done to help—for the sake of us all. So I started doing research for this book. My quest led me into a fascinating, and humbling, exploration of how we humans evolved to be so preoccupied with self-evaluation, why we can't win at this game, and what we each might do about it.

The assumption that we can find lasting happiness by being more successful, likable, attractive, intelligent, fit, or morally above reproach is so woven into our biology and culture that few of us notice it's not actually true. Sure, having success or otherwise thinking highly of ourselves feels good—it just isn't long before we hit a bump in the road, lose the feeling, and are left hungry for the next boost. But if we look closely at our thoughts, feelings, and behavior, we can actually see through the psychological and cultural forces that reinforce our constant striving to feel good about ourselves and find far more reliable pathways to well-being.

There are useful insights and practical antidotes to our suffering all around us—we just need to know where to look. We can find them in the fields of evolutionary, social, and clinical psychology, in neurobiology, as well as in ancient and contemporary wisdom traditions.

The more I worked with these insights and practices personally, with patients, and with students in courses and workshops, the clearer became the paths to freeing ourselves from the stress of striving to feel we're OK and the heartache of feeling not good enough. Everyone's road is a bit different, since there are so many ways we measure ourselves and struggle to not come up short. And since there are powerful biological and social forces that conspire to keep us trapped in endless self-evaluation, most of us need guidance, reminders, and continued practice to free ourselves.

That's why we might want to read a book about being ordinary. As it turns out, embracing our ordinariness is far more gratifying than endlessly worrying about being better or worse, above or below others or our inner images of who we should be. Practicing alternatives to self-evaluation, we can discover the joys of savoring the present moment, connecting more deeply to other people, experiencing gratitude for our lives, and tasting the wonderful freedom that comes from everything no longer being about us. Our happiness then no longer depends on praise or good fortune, nor on feeling proud, accomplished, or noble.

Breaking free from self-evaluative concerns is usually a gradual process. I still sometimes fear that it's just me—that my recurrent self-doubt comes from having been picked on in middle school, or because I really am weak or inadequate. But more and more, along with my patients and students, I'm able to see both the folly and the universality of the self-evaluation roller coaster—and step off it to enjoy instead the extraordinary gift of being ordinary.

acknowledgments

ONE OF THE THEMES of this book is that we're all interdependent, and who we are and what we do are just a small part of a much larger interconnected world. As the astronomer Carl Sagan put it, "If you wish to make an apple pie from scratch, you must first invent the universe." It's with appreciation of this reality that I'd like to thank a few of the many people who made this book possible.

Closest to home, I'd like to thank my loving, generous wife, Gina Arons. A psychologist herself, she spent countless hours helping me with the manuscript, not to mention decades gradually helping me relinquish some of my self-esteem concerns to enjoy the fruits of loving connection instead. I wouldn't be me, and this book wouldn't be in your hands, without her efforts on both fronts.

I'd also like to thank my daughters, Alexandra and Julia Siegel, who offered a younger-generational perspective on the themes of this book, as well as helping me, throughout their childhood and beyond, appreciate the joys and support of family—not to mention giving me excellent feedback whenever I've behaved in ways that might be interpreted as arrogant, critical, or disconnected.

I'd like to thank my parents, Sol and Claire Siegel, though they're no longer with us, for their lifelong loving support, and for imparting values that lead to far greater happiness than self-involvement ever could; and my brother, Dan Siegel, for his love and friendship ever since we were kids. My gratitude, too, to my extended family, who have supported and enriched my life in innumerable ways.

Outside of family, I'd like to thank all of the patients and students who, over many years, have trusted their care or education to me and have shared with me their honest experiences of being human. They've taught me so much more about the joys and sorrows of life, as well as the forces that perpetuate and alleviate suffering, than books and articles ever could.

Many friends and colleagues also contributed in myriad ways to this book. I'd like to especially thank Michael Miller, who carefully read a draft of the manuscript and offered valuable feedback as well as many illustrative quotes and examples. He has also demonstrated how powerfully freeing it can be to openly share self-esteem concerns with another honest soul.

I'd also like to thank other friends and colleagues from whom I've learned so much, and whose work and perspectives appear in the book, including Richard Schwartz, Chris Germer, Kristin Neff, Judson Brewer, Tara Brach, Rick Hanson, Dan Siegel, Charles Styron, Susan Pollak, Paul Fulton, Norm Pierce, Robert Waldinger, Trudy Goodman, and Terry Real. Other friends and colleagues have also helped clarify my understanding of the book's themes, including Bill O'Hanlon, Joan Borysenko, Chris Willard, Bill Morgan, Susan Morgan, Michele Bograd, Tom Denton, Larry Peltz, Nancy Reimer, Don Chase, Nikki Fedele, Laurie Brandt, Susan Phillips, Alisa Levine, Jan Snyder, Susie Fairchild, David Fairchild, Joan Klagsbrun, Linda Graham, and the late Michael Urdang. I'm grateful, too, to my friends Mary Ann Dalton, Cody Romano, Ilana Newell, and Ellen Matathia for reviewing early drafts of the manuscript and providing valuable feedback.

Many of the ideas in this book are based on scientific research. While scientific knowledge is built up over time from countless contributions, I'd like to particularly thank a few of the investigators and scholars whose work directly informed the book, including Steven Pinker, David Buss, Jean Twenge, Keith Campbell, Matthieu Ricard, Albert Ellis, Roy Baumeister, Mark Leary, Seth Stephens-Davidowitz, Frans De Waal, John Hewitt, Mitch Prinstein, Richard Wilkinson, and Kate Pickett.

Contemplative practices not only shaped my life, but have informed my understanding of psychology, well-being, and the folly of self-preoccupation. I'd therefore like to thank all the teachers who have helped develop and enrich my meditation practice, including Jack Kornfield, Joseph Goldstein, Sharon Salzberg, HH Dalai Lama, Chögyam Trungpa, Larry Rosenberg, Shunryu Suzuki, Ram Dass, and Thich Nhat Hanh. I'd also like to thank all of my friends and colleagues at the Institute for Meditation and Psychotherapy who have supported my practice and contributed to my understanding of the power of contemplative traditions for decades, including, in addition to many already mentioned in other roles, Sara Lazar, Jan Surrey, Tom Pedulla, Stephanie Morgan, Andy Olendzki, Inna Khazan, Laura Warren, Doug Baker, Dave Shannon, and the late Phil Aranow.

Many of my opportunities to refine the approaches and exercises in this book came from offering workshops or presentations to other professionals. I'd therefore like to thank the friends and organizers who have helped me develop those programs, including Ruth Buczynski, Michael Kerman, Richard Fields, Gerry Piaget, Linda and Larry Cammarata, Spencer Smith, Rob Guerette, Jack Hirose, Agustín Moñivas Lázaro, Gustavo Diex, Miriam Nur, Larry Lifson, Rafa Senén, Yolanda Garfia, Paul Ortman, Fabrizio Didonna, Shea Lewis, Sanford Landa, Hailan Guo, Rich Simon, and Jeff Zeig.

Finally, but very importantly, I'd like to thank the entire team at The Guilford Press who have seen this project through from being as a vague idea to a published book. My deepest appreciation goes particularly to my indefatigable friends and editors, Kitty Moore and Chris Benton, who believed in the project, hung in through many revisions, and spent countless hours creatively thinking about how to make the book as accessible and useful as it could be.

PART I

The Self-Evaluation Trap

ONE

are we doomed?

> Sometimes I lie awake at night, and I ask, "Where
> have I gone wrong?" Then a voice says to me,
> "This is going to take more than one night."
> —CHARLIE BROWN, *Peanuts* (CHARLES M. SCHULZ)

IF YOU ARE SOMEONE who reliably feels that you excel at what
you do, you're a good person, everyone likes you, and you're fully
and happily engaged in the present moment, this book is not for you.

This book is for the rest of us, who may have days when we
feel really good about ourselves, confident and perhaps even proud,
but sooner or later hit a bump or crash. It's for those of us who are
like the star of our own movie, with an ever-present narrator com-
menting on our performance: "Great job!" "What were you thinking?" "You look fantastic!" "That was really dumb." "You're a good
friend." "You need to work harder." "I can't believe you said that
. . . did that . . . wore that." While some of us manage to feel good
about ourselves longer than others, this book is for all of us who feel
not good enough more often than we'd like.

Undeterred by regular setbacks, we keep trying to hang on to
the positive feelings and avoid the pain of feeling inadequate. In
fact, it can become a full-time job. Many of us spend our days anxiously second-guessing ourselves: "Did I sound stupid?" "Should I
have written back sooner?" "Am I too selfish?" "Was I not assertive enough?" We read books and blogs about how to make a good
impression, succeed at work, and attract or keep a great mate. We

starve ourselves, buy new clothes, and work out trying to look better. We might even work ourselves to death for higher positions, more money, better grades, or social success—just to feel good enough.

All this self-focused evaluation and effort is not only stressful and exhausting, but can leave us lonely, confused, and plagued by self-criticism. We may sense that something's missing in our life and that our striving—even when successful—isn't really fulfilling. And when we fail, feel rejected, or don't live up to expectations, we get a horrible sinking sensation, feel ashamed, and just want to put our tail between our legs and hide. The stress of constantly trying to feel good about ourselves can wreak havoc on our bodies, giving us headaches, backaches, and upset stomachs. It can keep us up at night and leave us wondering why we're not happier, more loved, or more successful. It can stop us from trying new challenges. And it can alienate us from our friends, family, and coworkers—the very connections that could help us break free from our self-preoccupation.

Many of us imagine that healthy, secure, truly successful people don't struggle this way—our ups and downs are a sign of our inadequacy or insecurity. We imagine that they have positive, stable self-images and don't regularly compare themselves to others or to rigid inner standards. But it turns out that nearly everyone is preoccupied with self-evaluation and rides this sort of roller coaster.

Why? Because, I'm sorry to say, we humans did not evolve to be happy. The propensity to evaluate ourselves and compare ourselves to others, which was once useful for survival, is actually hardwired into the human brain. It traps almost all of us in unnecessary self-focused suffering, while cutting us off from the very pursuits that could actually make us happier and healthier.

So, are we all doomed? Luckily, not completely. There are reliable paths out of the self-evaluation trap. The challenge is that, because both our neurobiology and social norms reinforce our constant striving to feel good about ourselves, to break free we need a wake-up call. We need a way to recognize the thoughts, feelings, and behaviors that keep us trapped, and we'll need to try out new ones. It's absolutely doable—but it helps to have tools and a guide. And that's what this book is for.

Why pursuing good self-esteem is bad news

Hundreds of programs and countless books tell us how to improve our self-esteem—to create an enduring feeling that we're good, valuable, important, or successful. They suggest that if we could just think highly of ourselves, everything would be better. The only problem is, *it doesn't work*. That's because it's actually our relentless *trying* to feel good about ourselves that causes much of our distress. Explicitly or implicitly, we compare ourselves either to other people, or to some inner image of who we think we should be, all day long. After all, how do you know if you're smart, athletic, kind, honest, or successful if you don't compare yourself to someone else, real or imagined? While some of us are more outwardly competitive, and others more concerned with living up to inner standards, almost all of us judge ourselves incessantly.

The belief that we can be happy if we do well in these comparisons is so completely woven into our brains, into our relationships, and into our culture that we might not even notice it's a belief. We also might not see its costs, even though for thousands of years the world's wisdom and religious traditions have been trying to tell us that self-preoccupation and social comparison are a huge source of suffering.

One particularly pervasive cost is the relentless pressure of feeling judged. Since feeling inadequate is so painful, we desperately cling to whatever boosts our self-image, fearing that if we relax our efforts we'll miss out, slip up, or fall behind. It can start the moment we wake up: "Damn—didn't get enough sleep again. Hope it doesn't show at work." "Why do I always stay up so late binge-watching TV?" Then we check our phone: "No word from my boss. I wonder if she didn't like my proposal." As the day unfolds, the judgments continue. "Glad I had the oatmeal. I'm doing better with my diet." "But I don't exercise enough." "At least this new shirt looks cute."

And when we interact in real time with others, the inner judge really gets going: "Why did I say that?" "I wonder what she thought of me?" "I sounded pretty good in that meeting!" "Was I too self-centered?" "I wish I had more confidence." "Do I look like I'm trying too hard?" Always performing, we rarely get a break to feel really content or at peace.

Why are we so insecure? Why do we keep needing to prove ourselves? Why can't we just succeed at our goals and feel good about ourselves as we imagine others do? There are two main reasons.

One is that everything always changes, so what goes up eventually comes down. Can you recall the last time you did a great job, got positive feedback, or felt really special? Remember the feeling? How long did it last? What came next? How did *that* feel? Olympic gold medalists don't stay on top forever, successful entrepreneurs are sooner or later surpassed by competitors, youthful bodies age, and even saints occasionally sin.

The other reason we can't win is that we keep changing our yardsticks. Remember how you felt when you got your first job? How long did it take before you felt like you needed something more? Remember the feeling of your first apartment? How long was it before you wanted to have a nicer place?

Because everything changes, including our measures of success or even adequacy, it's impossible to consistently feel good enough. And worse, constant self-evaluation keeps us focused on ourselves, leaving us lonely, distracted, and fearful, unable fully to enjoy the present moment.

Good news

What's the way out? It's finding the proven paths to well-being that have nothing to do with evaluating ourselves. Trying to win at that game is not only impossible, but it stresses us out, messes up our relationships, and holds us back from taking risks. The alternative paths help us embrace our ordinariness, make friends with our imperfections, and connect with other flawed human beings. We can then feel more love and gratitude, worry less about how well we're doing, and actually relax and enjoy our lives.

Because our self-evaluative habits are so tenacious, most of us need to address them on several levels. We need a *three-H* approach of working with our *heads, hearts,* and *habits*: challenging our ingrained ways of thinking; learning to work creatively with the pain of failure, rejection, or shame; and experimenting with new behaviors that support more sustainable and meaningful sources of well-being.

Everyone's path will be different, since there are so many ways to become trapped in self-evaluation. Some of us get addicted to self-esteem highs, the feeling that we're smarter, kinder, more attractive or popular than the average bear. Others of us rarely feel good enough, or struggle with shame. And as we'll soon see, we all judge ourselves using different criteria.

Because we tend to be like fish in water, not even noticing how preoccupied we, like everyone around us, are with self-evaluation, a good first step is to try to lift our heads out of the river long enough to see the pervasiveness of our self-judgment and its often hidden costs. Viewing this clearly can be disturbing, but it's totally worthwhile for the freedom it can bring.

Fear and loathing

Our efforts to avoid sinking, not-good-enough feelings limit us in a million ways. Have you ever been afraid to approach an attractive person for a date, apply for a long-shot job, or even just start a conversation at a social event for fear that the rejection would hurt too much? Have you ever avoided playing tennis with a better athlete, taking a tough class, or speaking in front of a group where your insecurity might show? Have you ever felt alienated or disconnected, keeping your real feelings to yourself because you felt vulnerable or ashamed?

Then there are all the times when our performance anxiety actually gets in the way of our performance. William Masters and Virginia Johnson, the famous sex researchers, described how our "internal spectator" interferes with sexual functioning. This spectator isn't just observing, but it's judging our performance and comparing it to what "should" be happening (other animals don't seem to have this problem around sex). The same thing happens when we choke under the pressure of public speaking, lose our concentration because of test anxiety, or toss and turn with insomnia because we're afraid that we won't feel rested, look good, or perform well the next day.

Then there's anger. How many conflicts could be avoided if we weren't worried about our self-image? Researchers studied the interactions that preceded schoolyard scuffles in Great Britain. Turns out they were usually arguments over *who is superior* or *who was right*. But of course, it's not just kids: "I'm sure *I* didn't leave the dishes in the sink." "*You* started it. *You* raised your voice first."

Conflicts at work? They almost always stem from someone feeling put down, devalued, or unrecognized: "But it was *my* idea!" At home? I don't care to count the number of times I was a less-than-optimal partner because I felt bad about myself, often for being a less-than-optimal partner a moment before. And reactions to feeling devalued or disrespected in intimate relationships can easily spiral. Couple therapist Terry Real says he has lectured for some 20 years about "normal marital hate" and not a single time has anyone asked, "What's that?"

One problem, many symptoms

One of the great privileges of being a psychologist is that I get to hear about other people's psychological difficulties and see the commonalities in our self-inflicted suffering. And a remarkable number of everyone's concerns center around struggles to feel good about themselves.

I once worked with a cardiac surgeon, Arjun. He was an accomplished professor at an elite medical school facing retirement. Rather than looking forward to it, every time he thought about leaving his position his heart raced and his hands got clammy. He had entered academic medicine because being "just a surgeon" operating on patients wasn't enough—he felt inadequate compared to the doctors who were breaking new ground.

Now Arjun was terrified of slipping into oblivion—despite all his accomplishments he feared being forgotten as younger doctors moved up. He got depressed whenever he saw a new physician present something interesting at a conference. What a great reward for a lifetime of hard work.

I also worked with Henry, a talented administrative assistant in the chemistry department at a local college. While he reliably got good performance reviews, he spent his whole career feeling awkward, never knowing the right thing to say, imagining that the professors looked down on him. "To them I'm just a secretary." No matter how much positive feedback he received, he never felt comfortable at work.

Or consider Beth, an attractive woman in her 50s who nonetheless started to hate her body. She tried to avoid mirrors because she thought she was ugly and seeing her reflection actually made her feel nauseous. Even getting attention on dating apps didn't shift her beliefs about her looks.

Arjun's, Henry's, and Beth's stories show that although others may see us positively, and might even be envious, it's easy to still feel inadequate.

Over the years I've seen successful achievers who needed to achieve more and more to keep feelings of failure and inadequacy at bay, underachievers who avoided challenges for fear of failure, and perfectly capable people who, despite doing fine at their jobs, felt like imposters. And then there were all the folks stuck in destructive habits—like drinking, spending too much, and eating disorders—seeking temporary distraction and relief from the pain of feeling not good enough, only to then feel ashamed about their habit.

Happily, I've also seen people from all walks of life find paths to well-being that are much more sustainable than trying to buttress their self-image. Arjun's fears of losing importance faded when playing catch with his 6-year-old grandson. One day he got hit in the head with the ball (luckily whiffle), and his grandson rushed over to help. "It knocked some sense into me. I realized it felt great to just be loved as Grandpa." Henry experienced fulfillment volunteering in a soup kitchen. "I feel better helping people who are down and out. The other volunteers are great, it makes me not care what the professors think, and the soup's not bad." Beth found community and acceptance in a singing group. "Everyone's just into the music and happy to see each other. So now I just have to worry about remembering the lyrics, which I should be able to handle until dementia sets in."

We can all find antidotes to our self-evaluation concerns—if we look for them. We can learn to savor the present moment and to see the folly of constant judgments about success, failure, and self-worth. We can heal the hurts of past disappointments and injuries and begin enjoying our ordinary humanity. We can develop the courage to take risks, to embrace what we have in common, to experience gratitude, and to develop deeper, more loving connections to other people.

Sound good? It is. But to free ourselves from the torment of self-evaluation, we need to not only see its costs, but also to look carefully at the particular building blocks we've been using to try to sustain good feelings about ourselves. Trigger warning: This will probably be embarrassing.

What's your poison?

One observation has stood out over my many years of hearing tales of triumph and defeat, of self-evaluation ups and downs: We each get hooked on different criteria for measuring our adequacy, worth, or success. What's super-important to one of us may be irrelevant to someone else, and vice versa. Seeing this in action can help us take our own particular ups and downs less seriously.

Consider Don, for example. Despite being an enterprising guy who started his own online business in his 30s, he struggled with feeling not good enough his whole life. No accomplishment relieved his feelings of inadequacy for long. He dated great women but always feared that they'd see his flaws and leave him. He became an accomplished artist but was distressed that he couldn't consistently be the absolute best.

Don read plenty of books about how to be successful. Most of them suggested goal setting, so he created a scrapbook, which he brought to one of our early sessions. My heart sank as he showed me the pictures of a luxury car and an executive mansion in the suburbs. I sat there thinking, "This therapy is going to take a while."

So I decided to take a little risk. Since he seemed to trust me, I thought that hearing about my concern du jour—which I had a hunch would seem foolish to him—might help him to see the arbitrary nature of his own self-esteem preoccupations.

At the time, my 10-year-old flat-screen TV had stopped working. Being a frugal guy who fancies himself an intelligent problem-solver, I Googled the symptom and determined that it had a blown power supply. I found a YouTube video, bought the replacement capacitors on eBay for $9.95 (including shipping), and got set to prove to myself, and the world, how clever I was. I carefully took everything apart (photographing each step), removed the faulty parts, but then couldn't get the solder to melt properly and ruined the circuit board trying to install the new capacitors. A moment later I discovered a loose bolt on my soldering gun and realized that because I hadn't thought to check it, the TV, and my self-esteem, were now both goners. I felt like a failure hauling it to the dump and hated shopping for a new one. My wife had to put up with my foul mood for longer that I want to admit.

Since I assumed that Don wouldn't have thought twice about just buying a new TV, I thought it might help him to see that we can get hooked on *anything* as symbols of our worth, success, or adequacy—including clever frugality. I told him the story. "You're shitting me!" he said. "Why did you waste your time? New TVs are so much better anyway, and they're so cheap now."

It helped. Once he got over the worry that his therapist might be insane, Don became curious about why symbols of financial success became so important to him (and why clever frugality was so important to me). He even started to ask himself, "What really matters?" The question eventually led him to put more energy into his marriage and friendships and spend less time stressing at work, hoping to be a winner and afford that house in the suburbs.

What defines you?

Now for the embarrassing part. I invite you to try an exercise that can clarify the criteria *you* use to feel good, or not so good, about yourself. Mercifully, you don't have to tell anybody what comes to mind when you try it. You'll probably find it helps to illuminate your particular self-evaluative concerns:

Exercise: What matters to me?*

Here's a list of some common criteria people use to evaluate themselves. Try reading it slowly, pausing at each item, giving yourself time to reflect. Consider whether you have ever found yourself going up or down emotionally, comparing yourself to others or some inner standard, or thinking highly or poorly of yourself based on any of these concerns (remember, go slowly so you can reflect on each item):

SKILLS AND TALENTS

Who's smarter? Am I smart enough?

Who's more educated? Am I educated enough?

Am I creative enough?

Talented enough?

Do I have good taste?

Am I good enough at sports? Who's better than me?

ACCOMPLISHMENTS

Who earns more money? Do I earn enough?

Am I respected enough? Do others get more respect?

Who has the better-looking, better-behaved, or more successful children? Are my kids doing well enough?

Who has the better-looking, better-behaved, or more successful partner? Is my partner good enough?

Am I successful enough at work?

GROUP MEMBERSHIP

Do I come from a good enough family?

Did I go to a good enough college?

Who has more friends, or is more popular? Am I popular enough?

Am I part of the in-crowd?

Who gets more attention? Do people pay enough attention to me?

How do I feel about my race, ethnicity, gender, or sexual orientation? Am I proud? Ashamed?

---

*Audio available at *giftofbeingordinary.com* and *guilford.com/siegel4-materials.*

RELATIONSHIPS

Am I a good enough friend?

A good enough parent?

Am I a good enough child?

Am I a good sibling?

A good coworker?

VALUES

Who's nicer? Am I nice enough?

Honest enough?

Am I as generous as I should be?

As caring as I should be?

As forgiving?

Am I socially aware enough? Are others more attuned than me?

PHYSICAL QUALITIES

Am I attractive enough?

Who's thinner? Am I thin enough?

Who's taller? Am I tall enough?

Am I sexy enough?

Do I look young enough?

Who is stronger or in better shape? Am I fit enough?

Among those of us who are invested in spiritual or psychological development, even sillier items might show up on the list:

Who is more enlightened?

Who makes fewer social comparisons? Is less driven by ego?

Who is less concerned with self-evaluation? Am I too preoccupied with myself?

Personally, I get hooked to some degree by almost all of these concerns. Assuming that I'm not entirely alone, and you also notice that you compare yourself with others, or judge yourself, in several of these areas, do you always come out ahead? (I once asked a group of therapists, "Who here always wins?" A guy raised his hand and I thought, "Avoid him at lunch.")

Indeed, most of us go up and down emotionally, sometimes feeling that we embody the qualities that matter to us, and other times feeling that we don't. To investigate this further, I invite you to try another little exercise (this one is usually less disturbing):

Exercise: Riding the self-evaluation roller coaster*

Take a moment to reflect on which of the many possible building blocks of self-worth you just considered felt particularly alive to you—intelligence, wealth, beauty, kindness, popularity, honesty— whatever stood out. Now recall a time when that attribute or quality was affirmed—either you accomplished some goal, did well at something, or were praised or appreciated by others. Just notice the bodily sensations of feeling good about yourself. Exaggerate a bit the body posture that reflects this feeling. You might try putting your hand over the area where you feel the sensation to identify it more clearly. Close your eyes and savor the feeling for a few moments—since unfortunately, it won't last.

Next, recall a time when the opposite happened—when the very same attribute or quality was disaffirmed or negated. You failed to reach a goal, did poorly at something, or were criticized or rejected. Notice now what happens in your body when you feel the collapse. Exaggerate a little the body posture that reflects this feeling. Try putting your hand over the area where you feel this sensation. Close your eyes again for a few moments to really feel the collapse—don't worry; it won't last either.

See how different a boost, or positive self-evaluation, feels from a collapse? How pleasant the first one is and how unpleasant the

---

*Audio available at *giftofbeingordinary.com* and *guilford.com/siegel4-materials*.

second? Notice, too, any impulse to move away or distract from the painful feelings? It's no wonder, given how good one state feels and how bad the other feels that we spend so much of our lives trying to feel good about ourselves.

To make matters worse, most of us aren't just hooked on one criterion. We believe that to really be OK, we have to do well on many, if not all fronts. We have to be intelligent, interesting, successful, honest, kind, fit, creative, sexy, *and* rich—just to be good enough.

The pain of social comparison

It's not always obvious to us that most of our judgments about ourselves are indeed based on comparisons either with others or with inner images or standards. For example, if I like to think of myself as intelligent, I'm making an implicit comparison with others. The same holds true for any other quality I might consider—generosity, popularity, honesty, sense of humor, fitness, creativity, wealth—you name it, it's based on social comparison.

Of course, we care about comparisons only on dimensions that matter to us. My patient Don didn't particularly care about being cleverly frugal—and was surprised to hear that it was so important to me.

The philosopher Bertrand Russell lamented how our yardsticks often stretch, leaving us perpetually feeling inadequate: "If you desire glory, you may envy Napoleon, but Napoleon envied Caesar, Caesar envied Alexander, and Alexander, I dare say, envied Hercules, who never existed."

We'll see in the next chapter that this propensity for social comparison is so universal and powerful partly because it's rooted in our neurobiology. For now, just noticing how often you make comparisons, how intense they are, who or what you use as reference points, and the fact that you're not alone in the habit, may help you take your evaluations less seriously.

But isn't a positive self-image essential for happiness?

At this point you may be thinking, "There's got to be another side to this argument! Don't we need to think highly of our ourselves to get ahead in life? Isn't it necessary for happiness?"

On the surface, this makes a lot of sense. You've probably noticed—in yourself or others—plenty of ways that negative thoughts about ourselves can lead to trouble. We might give up because we expect to fail. We might assume that we'll be rejected once others really get to know us. We might desperately try to prove our value by groveling for approval or trying too hard to conform. And we've all encountered (and may have been) people who compensate for feeling inadequate by being defensive, acting superior, seeking status, posturing in grandiose ways, or being a less-than-optimal partner.

Indeed, there is also some evidence that people who feel good about themselves often are living lives that have gone reasonably well—they've been able to earn a living, have more stable relationships, and stay out of trouble. But we easily confuse the causal arrow: It's not that positive self-evaluations *make* your life better, it's that a frequent side effect of life's going well is to also feel better about yourself. In fact, it turns out that particularly high self-esteem is linked to problems like arrogance, conceit, overconfidence, and aggressive behavior—so it's not exactly a formula for a good life.

There's another way

Despite our predispositions to compare ourselves to others, we don't actually need to spend our lives preoccupied with self-evaluation. We don't have to be driven by thoughts of what others think of us or feel like failures if we don't reach certain benchmarks. We humans also evolved instincts for love, connection, gratitude, and cooperation that can free us from the pain of self-evaluation and social comparison. Love can fill us with a warmth that makes our self-image irrelevant; connection with others can dissolve our concern with individual success or failure; gratitude can free us from preoccupation with unfulfilled longings; and cooperation allows us to accomplish much more, and have more fun doing it, than self-preoccupation ever could. We've all tasted this. Just recall a moment talking with a close friend when you felt deeply connected, a moment of appreciation and contentment in nature, or the good feeling of being part of a team.

I wrote this book because painful self-evaluative concerns regularly take over my heart and mind, despite years of personal and professional psychological work, and I know how much they hurt. I also did it because so many of my patients suffer similarly. I'm happy to report that like Arjun, Henry, and Beth, many other patients are becoming less possessed by these worries, as, thankfully, am I. We're having more moments of feeling like regular vulnerable human beings, living ordinary lives, connecting more deeply with one another.

I invite you to join us. What would today, or even the next hour, be like for you if you were freer of self-evaluative concerns? If you felt lovable just as you are? If you didn't have to choose your clothes so carefully, stay late at work to prove you're diligent, or make sure your partner noticed that you made the bed or took out the trash? How would you like to feel connected with whomever you met, realizing that we really are all very much equals in this life together? The remainder of this book offers tools to make this a reality.

The adventure will be challenging and rewarding. I'm regularly dismayed to see how often I still go up and down emotionally with every self-evaluative boost and collapse, and how much of my daily energy can go into trying to maintain the highs and avoid the lows—despite taking these ups and downs less seriously. Yet the more I practice letting go of this game, the happier I become. I enjoy trying to help my patients because I care about their well-being, rather than proving I'm competent as a psychologist. I have fun finding interesting projects that allow me to team up with colleagues, giving us opportunities to connect, rather than looking for ways to get noticed professionally. I like being more attuned to my wife's feelings and sharing my own honestly with her so we can feel closer, rather than trying to rack up accomplishments in the outside world, or even rack up good-guy credits in our relationship. All of these shifts leave me feeling more ordinary, and much happier.

Neurosis is the manure of *bodhi*

There's a principle we can borrow from Buddhist psychology to help guide us in this effort: *Neurosis is the manure of bodhi*. *Neurosis* is our habit of causing ourselves unnecessary suffering, *manure* is both shit and fertilizer, and *bodhi* is awakening. We can use this principle, that there's a way to use our pain to become wiser, to grow from our losses and disappointments, big and small. Why not? Our neuroses are so ubiquitous, we might as well get something useful out of them.

In the coming chapters, we'll look at the myriad ways that we cause ourselves unnecessary suffering by adding self-evaluation to almost everything we do. The more clearly we can see ourselves doing this at work or school, in our families, in the bedroom, when we interact online, and in our daily choices, the easier it'll be to take our evaluations less seriously.

We'll also learn how to get up close and personal with each negative judgment or self-evaluative collapse—having the courage to feel our pain—so we no longer need to fear it. Using proven tools such as mindfulness and self-compassion, you'll be able to watch and soothe your reactions to each new rejection or failure: ruminating over mistakes ("I never should've said that"), wanting to undo what happened ("I wish I'd prepared more"), distracting yourself ("What's on TV?"), or undoing the pain of a crash by finding a new boost ("Let's see if anyone liked my post").

Then, instead of going down the usual path of seeking an uplift, you'll practice using each disappointment as an opportunity to gain insight into the dynamics of the self-evaluation roller coaster, to increase your awareness of our shared predicament:

o What unreliable self-esteem building block is this collapse highlighting?

o What illusion is it exposing?

- o How would it feel to give up this support?
- o Who might I be without it?
- o What are the pros and cons of being that person?
- o Are there more reliable paths to well-being that I can pursue?

You'll also practice using each new disappointment as a chance to connect to past collapses, so that you can gradually drain the pool of accumulated sadness, hurt, and shame that they may have left behind.

Instead of being a problem, each new crash will become an opportunity to be less concerned with evaluating yourself and to move toward more sustainable bases for well-being—opening your heart, connecting more deeply with other people, embracing our common humanity, loving more, and discovering what really matters to you. It'll be another chance to transform your head, heart, and habits. This is *neurosis is the manure of bodhi* in action.

Sooner or later, of course, a new self-image boost will come along, and you may get hooked on that for a while. But fear not—it won't last long—and there'll be an opportunity to learn from the next collapse too.

This book is designed as a step-by-step guide to this adventure. In the following chapter, we'll explore the roots of our concerns with self-evaluation. Next, you'll learn skills for both catching your troublesome instincts in action and reexamining your beliefs about who you are (Part II). You'll then see how to recognize all sorts of crazy pursuits you might use to feel better about yourself, including unnecessary achievements, being liked or admired, moral superiority, status symbols, and even romantic love (Part III). The remainder of the book offers techniques to heal past hurts and break free from our addiction to self-evaluation, replacing it with compassion, wise perspective, celebrating being an ordinary human being, and lovingly connecting to the world outside of ourselves.

Since we all get hooked on different sorts of self-evaluation and use different criteria to cobble together our self-image, some topics and exercises will likely resonate more for you than others. Please feel free to focus your attention on these, returning more than once to practices that speak most to you. (You'll probably find that themes that might be less relevant to you apply to your family and friends. Just be careful if you choose to tell them about your insights!) Treat the chapters ahead like a Swiss army knife or drawer of kitchen utensils—a collection of tools to help you work with different ways you might get trapped in painful self-judgments, with each tool being more useful at different moments.

This journey is a bit counterintuitive, and can be challenging, but it's well worth the effort. Just think of how wonderful a day would be without worrying so much about how well you're doing and what others think of you, instead simply enjoying life. What a delight, and what a relief!

TWO

it's Darwin's fault

All animals are equal, but some animals
are more equal than others.
—GEORGE ORWELL, *Animal Farm*

WHEN WE START PAYING attention to our self-evaluative concerns, it can be shocking to notice how often we judge ourselves or make comparisons to others. It's easy to feel like a self-centered wretch, preoccupied with self-judgment, competition, and social comparison, or chronically insecure, looking for approval or feeling inadequate. The good news is that it's not our fault. Our brains actually evolved to do this. Even better, it turns out that we don't need to give in to our more primitive instincts. Instead, we can break free by reinforcing our hardwired capacities for love, connection, and cooperation, making our lives richer, happier, and more meaningful as a result.

Take Juanita's experience. She had been a fashion model. Ever since she was little people were drawn to her for her looks. The attention felt good, but now that she was getting older, she got fewer jobs and turned fewer heads. Eventually she left the industry.

It was a painful transition, but ultimately one she was grateful for. "I always had to be the prettiest woman in the room. If I gained a few pounds, I went into a funk. I didn't give it up easily—every wrinkle, every pound, every time I wasn't the center of attention, it hurt. But now I can finally walk into a room and just enjoy connecting with friends or getting to know new people. While I miss the attention sometimes, I'm actually a lot happier."

Human (and animal) nature

I once had the chance to visit Kruger National Park in South Africa. Guided by experienced naturalists, we got to see lions, elephants, giraffes, rhinoceroses, and other remarkable creatures in their natural habitat.

It didn't take long to notice a pattern. In species after species, we'd see a dominant male surrounded by a group of reproductively promising females. Then somewhere in the distance, there would be a group of younger males, engaged in the species-specific equivalent of playing basketball. They'd be intensely involved in some competitive activity, heightening their skills in the hopes of one day dethroning the dominant male and taking his place. Meanwhile, the females would compete for the attention of the king or other males with good prospects—doing the species-specific equivalent of runway modeling.

The naturalists pointed out that these dramas had high stakes. They determined whose DNA was going to be passed on to the next generation. Anyone who didn't join in the competition was likely to miss out on opportunities for procreation, and that might mean the end of their genetic line. Over time, through natural selection, all of these different species evolved to care a great deal about social rank and desirability.

As it turns out, these instincts aren't confined to big game. Birds have "pecking orders," as do fish, reptiles, and even some crickets. And, of course, so do we humans. Those on top have lots of privileges unavailable to those below, including greater reproductive success and more resources to care for their children. In neighboring Swaziland, this was actually enshrined into law—the king had 14 wives and 36 well-cared-for offspring.

These hierarchies create a lot of stress as animals constantly jockey for position. As the well-known neuroendocrinologist Robert Sapolsky concluded after years of primate study hiding behind blinds of vegetation in Africa, "it turns out that it's very bad for your health to be a low-ranking male in a baboon troop."

Of course, as the smart monkeys, we may think that we've evolved beyond all this. But a quick glance at all the rich and powerful men cycling through trophy wives, and the expectant brides comparing the size of their engagement rings, shows us we're not far from our mammalian roots.

There's another powerful evolutionary legacy that dovetails with our status concerns. Back on the African savanna, being rejected by our troop was a death sentence. We needed one another to find food, to hunt, and to alert one another to danger. On top of this, human babies needed to be cared for by adults to survive. So we evolved a very strong aversion to being rejected. This shows up today in our preoccupation with popularity and acceptance, as well as our concerns about being lovable. Our feelings of well-being can easily soar or crash based on whether we feel that other people like or want us. Just think of how it feels to be invited—or not—to the party. Did you ever sit home on a Saturday night wondering if the other kids were getting together without you? Wouldn't you still prefer to be on the guest list—even if you don't want to go?

The inner primate

Evolutionary psychologists have spent the past several decades trying to discern which aspects of human nature are universal instincts that evolved because of their survival value. Their findings shed a lot of light on our concerns with self-evaluation and social comparison.

These psychologists don't suggest that the instincts they identify are somehow *good,* or that just because they occur in other species, cross-culturally, and can be measured in laboratories, we should blithely indulge them. Rather, they suggest that we treat many of these instincts the same way we try to treat our attraction to doughnuts. We're drawn to rich sweets because for our ancestors fat and sugar were associated with important nutrients. But nowadays, most of us over the age of six realize that eating them all day long isn't a reliable path to well-being.

What other troublesome universal instincts do evolutionary

psychologists identify? Concerns about social rank, dominance, group acceptance, and access to sexual mates play an outsized role in human activity across cultures, leading to a lot of conflicts and pain—no surprise to anyone who reads or watches the news.

While these instincts show up in other species in outward behavior, in humans they also show up regularly in our thoughts and feelings. In fact, our relentless self-evaluative thoughts and feelings of adequacy or inadequacy are fueled by our brains' instinctual preoccupation with social rank, dominance, likability, and mating success.

Binh, for example, wasn't very strong, had a delicate build, and hated being one of the weakest kids in his class. He got picked on by the bullies and struggled in gym. Even as an adult, the first thing he thought in new social situations was almost always "Am I the skinniest guy here?" When he wasn't, it was easier to strike up a conversation and more fun to meet new people.

What have you noticed personally? Have animal instincts caused distress in your life or the lives of people you know? The more clearly we can see our own inner primate in action, the less we need to believe in, identify with, and act on its instincts.

Let's start with *dominance*: Have you ever found yourself wanting to be big, tall, powerful, or highly accomplished? Ever ostracized someone, acted like a bully, or gravitated toward successful or powerful people to stay on top? Next *sex*: Are you attracted to men with cross-culturally desirable traits, who are taller, with broad shoulders, a taut waist, deep voice, and a strong chin, or with signs of wealth, authority, respect, or self-confidence? Have you wanted to be more this way yourself? Or are you attracted to women who look younger, have full lips, smooth skin, clear eyes, lustrous hair, good muscle tone, or more curves? Have you wanted to look more this way yourself? Finally, how about *likability* or popularity? Have you longed to feel wanted or accepted by others? Do you ever fear rejection?

I enjoy leading meditation retreats for psychotherapists. Living in nature, without the distractions of TV or Internet, we spend much of the day in silence. The mind becomes more sensitive, and we develop clearer awareness of thoughts and feelings.

Once, after a couple of days together, I asked the group to notice how often their mood shifted as they compared themselves to others. A brave psychologist, Elaine, spoke up:

"Since I got here, I've been comparing my body to the bodies of all the other women. Compared to some I feel good, next to others bad. Guess I'm not very evolved." I asked if anyone else had experienced something similar. Every other woman in the room raised her hand, along with several men. We really *do* have a lot in common with other primates.

While alarming, this is also excellent news. It means it's not our fault—we are not alone or crazy. We, like everyone else, were born this way. So instead of feeling ashamed of our competitive, sexual, and other instincts, we can recognize them for what they are and learn to work with them creatively rather than being enslaved by them. Happily, as it turns out, our brains also evolved other instincts that can help us do just that.

Also wired for love

Many of the instincts that organisms have evolved aren't useful for them as individuals but are very useful for their species and genetic heritage. Take, for example, our impulse to take care of our children or watch out for other family members. Doing so doesn't necessarily enhance our personal chances for survival. But it very much increases the chances that our genes will live on, since our children, and our siblings' children, share our genetic makeup to different, predictable degrees. This observation led to a famous wisecrack by the biologist J. B. S. Haldane, who was once asked if he would lay down his life for his brother: "No, but I would for at least two brothers or sisters, four cousins, or eight nephews or nieces."

While not exactly a heartwarming answer, this is actually the good news from evolutionary psychology. Our brains didn't only evolve with instincts to compete for scarce resources, raise our social status, and spread our genes through successful reproduction. They also evolved with instincts to cooperate and take care of our fellow humans, which we can fortify.

In addition to our proclivity to look out for our families, evolutionary psychologists identify an instinct called *reciprocal altruism*. Sharing in foraging societies makes sense because everyone is kin— they all share genes to some degree. But even among genetically distant people, we're inclined to share in the expectation that they'll share with us in the future when we have less. If I give you some of the wildebeest I killed today, you'll give me some of your gazelle next week. Many studies show that we, along with many other social animals, have this biologically rooted sense of fairness that helps us establish cooperative relationships.

Despite other similarities, we humans differ from most other animals in the amount of time we care for our young. Babies arrive without a lot of independent survival skills. This intensifies our parental instinct to look after our kids and also gives babies a strong instinct to turn toward adults for nurture and protection. These instincts show up throughout our lives as powerful desires to love and be loved.

While our longings to be accepted or wanted can preoccupy us with worries about inadequacy and rejection, our capacity to love can also lead us to pathways to well-being that are much more reliable than social status or mating success. In fact, as we'll see later, the single best predictor of physical and mental well-being is the quality of our caring relationships.

Feeding the right wolf

It would seem that as long as we have our competitive instincts and biologically based concern with social status, our self-evaluative difficulties aren't going to disappear anytime soon. But might we harness our cooperative instincts, our capacity to care for others, and our desire to be part of the group to temper them? Might there be a way to reinforce our instincts toward love, cooperation, and caring and become less caught in our instincts to improve our social rank, mate for reproductive success, or defend our honor?

There's a well-known story often presented as a Cherokee legend (though its origins are unclear) that suggests a path forward:

An old man is teaching his grandson about life. "A fight is going on inside me," he said to the boy. "It is a terrible fight and it is between two wolves. One is evil—he is anger, envy, sorrow, regret, greed, arrogance, self-pity, guilt, resentment, inferiority, lies, false pride, superiority, and ego." He continued, "The other is good—he is joy, peace, love, hope, serenity, humility, kindness, benevolence, empathy, generosity, truth, compassion, and faith. The same fight is going on inside you—and inside every other person, too."

The grandson thought about it for a minute and then asked his grandfather, "Which wolf will win?" The old man replied simply, "The one you feed."

Our challenge is how to feed one wolf more than the other, to find fulfillment in love and connection rather than pursuing effervescent, competitive highs. Safe, caring connection not only feels good but supports physical and emotional well-being, in part because our threat-response system evolved to relax when we're in trusting relationships. And feeling safe in this way frees us to thrive. An important step, which we can take right now, is to notice that the caring, connected, loving wolf is indeed very much alive inside each of us. Sorry to mix animal images, but this wolf is another aspect of our inheritance as primates.

Let's start with our instinct for *cooperation*: Do you ever try to understand others' perspectives, take into account their needs, let them take the lead, or support them even if you feel envious? Next *nurturing*: Have you ever taken care of a child or pet, cared for a friend in need, or gone out of your way to help someone in pain? Now *kindness and compassion*: Have you given away or shared something that you value, just to give another person joy, or volunteered your time to be helpful? *Fairness*: Have you ever negotiated with an eye toward both parties feeling satisfied, rather than just coming out ahead yourself, or restrained yourself even though you could get away with something? Finally, *connection*: Have you ever apologized or admitted your faults to reconnect, forgiven someone, or reached out to less popular or successful folks just to make them feel included?

Chances are, you've done a lot of these things with regularity.

The loving, caring wolf is very much alive within you. Notice how good it feels when these instincts are activated?

Cultivating the caring wolf is what rescued Juanita from having to be the center of attention. After feeling repeatedly distressed about each new wrinkle and pound, she started to get it that hanging on to youthful beauty was a losing proposition. Her pain led her to ask, "What really matters? What should I do with my life?"

The answer that came to mind was that she longed for more moments of loving connection. She was tired of struggling to keep feelings of shame, inadequacy, and failure at bay by being the center of attention. So Juanita took on the project of exercising her caring wolf instead—with her head, heart, and habits. She tried deliberately paying attention to the ways that she wasn't so special but was actually quite ordinary, much like everyone else (shifting her thinking). She scrounged up the courage to feel more fully the pain of her body changing, and use the pain to connect more honestly to friends and family who were struggling themselves (working with her heart). And she went out of her way to be helpful when she could, experiencing the joys of generosity (changing her habits). Growing older wasn't going to be a picnic, but these shifts all felt like steps in the right direction.

Binh found a similar path to becoming less preoccupied with his physique. Thinking about his predicament, he realized that his brain, like everyone else's, evolved to feel that being big and strong was super-important. (It's a powerful instinct—the word for *leader* in most foraging societies means "big man.") But the current consequences of his build were mostly in his own mind—he could still have a decent job, friends, and love in his life. Armed with this knowledge, he was able to revisit the times big guys knocked the books out of his hands and the humiliating moments in gym, now having the strength to feel the hurt, anger, and fear that used to overwhelm him. And he developed a new strategy for meeting people. When he entered a room, instead of sizing everyone up (literally), he deliberately thought, "How might I connect?" "Might anyone here be having a hard time like I used to have?" "Can I be helpful?"

The rest of this book will provide tools for disengaging from our hardwired preoccupation with social comparison, popularity, and mating success—changing our heads, hearts, and habits to connect instead with more durable pathways to well-being. We'll see how nurturing our caring instincts can not only help us get along with one another but can be a powerful antidote to our competitive concerns and feelings of shame, inadequacy, and self-doubt, while helping us heal the hurt of past rejections and failures.

For now, just be on the lookout for the caring aspect of human nature in yourself and others—the loving wolf. As you go through your day, notice when you and other people act altruistically, tending to the needs of others. Pay attention to stories of generosity, fairness, and forgiveness in the news (they may not be the lead, but they're there). Just seeing human decency, and taking the time to appreciate it, can reinforce our caring instincts.

Given the strength of our competitive instincts, energizing our loving wolf, calming the competitive one, and stepping off the self-evaluation roller coaster will require good tools. One of the most powerful is mindfulness practice. It can help us transform our habitual reactions, get perspective on our concerns with social comparison and self-judgment, and support our efforts to embark on a different path—one on which we let go, enjoy the moment, celebrate our ordinariness, and safely connect with others. The next chapter shows how you can cultivate mindfulness to move beyond your more problematic instincts and become the best primate you can be.

PART II

The Essential Toolkit

THREE

the liberating power of mindfulness

You can observe a lot by watching.
—YOGI BERRA

BY NOW I EXPECT you're beginning to agree: Despite our ability to transplant hearts and land robots on Mars, we humans remain struggling primates motivated by all sorts of biologically based instincts that were once important for survival and reproduction but now trap us in painful self-evaluative concerns. While, luckily, we also have other instincts that help us care for and get along with one another, these aren't always online. Given our biology, how might we get beyond our stress and worry about keeping up and being good enough? How might we learn not to stake our happiness on something as unreliable as thinking highly of ourselves, but to energize our other instincts instead so we can find more peace, love, connection, and meaning in our lives, liberating us to savor the present moment?

Of the many tools that can help set us free, some of the most powerful are mindfulness practices. Many different cultures have developed versions of these, in part because people all over the world, and throughout history, have been plagued by the same tendencies that currently torture us and get in the way of our well-being. These practices can help us transform all three *H*'s—our heads, hearts, and habits.

Mindfulness practices can help us notice the craziness of our endless self-evaluative thoughts: "I'm a failure—I gained two pounds." "I liked my job until you got a better one." "Why didn't more people text me on my birthday?" They strengthen our capacity to embrace emotions, so we can handle it when our heart sinks if we don't get invited to the party, and so we don't have to numb ourselves by visiting the fridge every time we feel dejected. And they can help us pause and choose new ways to respond to failures, to use disappointments as opportunities for insight into how we look for happiness in the wrong places, as well as using them to connect to others who are struggling, rather than just seeking some new success or reassurance.

Mindfulness practices can even help us reconsider our sense of who we are, which, as we'll see, can powerfully support our efforts to escape the self-evaluation roller coaster. In fact, in several of the cultural traditions that developed mindfulness practices, their principal purpose was gaining liberation from self-preoccupation. They were designed to help us experience life's ups and downs less personally, without believing that each one makes us winners or losers, lovable or unlovable, saints or sinners, worthy or inadequate.

I went on my first silent mindfulness meditation retreat as a young man because I was depressed. It's a long story, involving my lovely college girlfriend, me in Connecticut, and her former boyfriend on the West Coast. All you need to know is that she moved to California.

While there were several upsetting features to this situation, one was definitely my self-esteem collapse. "How come she wants him more than me?" "Wasn't I good enough?" The retreat was powerful. I watched these thoughts coming and going, each one followed by a wave of pain. Eventually, they started to seem more and more like just *thoughts,* rather than concrete realities. And instead of being sunk in depression, I connected with the underlying hurt, longing, shame, anger, and fear: "I wish you were here in my arms again." "I'd like to kill you—and him." "How will I live without you?" It wasn't easy, but by the end of the retreat I was definitely not depressed. I had a lot of emotions, and noticed a lot of thoughts coming and going, but I didn't feel so stuck anymore. And I was inspired to investigate the role of my broken self-image in my broken heart.

Mindfulness is a tool for freeing our hearts and minds. We'll be using it to support interwoven approaches to escaping self-evaluation traps and feelings of inadequacy throughout this book. This chapter will give you what you need to begin making mindfulness a part of your life.

What exactly *is* mindfulness?

Mindfulness describes an attitude toward whatever is occurring in consciousness at the moment—it's *awareness of present experience with loving acceptance*. While most of us know what it feels like to be aware or pay attention, loving acceptance can seem foreign. One way to understand it is to bring to mind the image of an adorable little puppy—let's call her Daisy. Imagine her face, her fur, her body (close your eyes and picture her for a few seconds before reading further). What feeling arises as you imagine her? Is it a sense of harsh, critical judgment? (If so, give me a call.) Unless we've had the misfortune to have been attacked by a puppy in the past, most of us feel something akin to the universal sound of compassion: "Awwwww." Even if Daisy pees and poops at the wrong time, even if she doesn't listen to instructions, we'll think: "She's young, she needs love, she needs training." And that's precisely the attitude we want to cultivate toward our own hearts and minds when we practice mindfulness. It's the attitude of the caring, loving wolf that we visited in the last chapter.

This is important because as you'll see when we try a little mindfulness practice in a moment, the mind *does* pee and poop at the wrong time and *doesn't* listen to instructions. The attitude we'd have toward that puppy is the attitude we want to maintain in these moments when our mind is unruly. It can require some practice to cultivate, since many of us are much more adept at beating ourselves up than we are at loving and accepting ourselves.

We can be mindful of whatever is arising in consciousness. This attitude not only can illuminate how our mind works, freeing us from automatic self-evaluation preoccupations, but also can help us heal past injuries—including those accumulated from rejections and failures.

Learning to be mindful

Here's a little riddle: What do swimming, making love, and eating a gourmet meal have in common? Some people say that they're all sensory experiences—which is true. Others say that they're all pleasurable, which might also be true, depending on whom we're making love with and how we feel about the water. But there's another answer that's relevant to our discussion—talking about them is very different from doing them. So, before we go any further talking about mindfulness practices, I invite you to experience one:

Exercise: Mindfulness of breath

This exercise can be done sitting, standing, or lying down, though most people will start by sitting. It can be helpful to have an erect spine, since this posture supports alertness. You might imagine a string tied to the top of your head gently pulling up toward the ceiling, allowing your spine to be straight without being tense. (Please read the rest of these instructions and then give them a try, or else do this as a guided meditation using the recorded instructions at *giftofbeingordinary.com* or *guilford.com/siegel4-materials*.) It's best to do this practice for 15-20 minutes to really taste its effects:

Start by closing your eyes and feeling the sensations in your body. If all is going well at the moment, you'll notice that you're already breathing. In fact, the breath is happening by itself. Allow the body to be relatively still, as this will make it easier to attend to sensory experiences.

All that we're going to do for the first part of this exercise is to pay attention to the sensations of the breath in the body. See if you can notice the various sensations of the inbreath and the sensations of the outbreath.

To develop some continuity of awareness, try following the breath through its full cycles, from the beginning of the inbreath to the end of the outbreath and on to the next.

Now it would not be unusual for thoughts to enter the mind. That's OK, they're our friends. In fact, the brain evolved to think. While we're not going to try to stop our thoughts, we aren't going to follow them as we usually do either. Instead, as soon as you notice that your attention has been hijacked by a chain of narrative thought and has left the sensations of breathing behind, gently and lovingly return your attention to the breath.

This is where the puppy image comes in. We can think of mindfulness practice as being like puppy training. We try to accept whatever arises in our awareness, with love and care, as we gently train the mind to pay attention to sensations—in this case the breath—occurring in the present moment.

See if you can cultivate an attitude of interest, or curiosity, in whatever sensations arise. Should you feel some discomfort—say an itch or an ache—that's actually a very special practice opportunity. If this occurs, instead of doing what we'd normally do—scratching the itch or adjusting our posture to relieve the ache—turn your attention for a little while to the unpleasant sensation, leaving the breath in the background. Just stay with the sensations of physical discomfort and see what happens to them. (No need to be stoic—if you're very uncomfortable, go ahead and scratch or shift postures—just try the experiment first.)

Continue this practice for 15-20 minutes, allowing whatever occurs to occur.

What happened? While everyone is different, and every meditation session is different for a given individual, here are some typical observations:

"MY MIND WAS VERY BUSY—I COULDN'T STOP THINKING."

One of our most important survival mechanisms is our capacity to think. It allows us to analyze the past, strategize, and plan for the future. It's therefore not surprising to discover that the mind is very busy thinking much of the time. That's OK. Rather than trying to stop our thoughts, in mindfulness practice we cultivate what cognitive scientists call *metacognitive awareness*—the ability to observe thoughts as just thoughts. This can be a novel experience, since most of the time when we're living in our thought stream, we don't actually see thoughts as thoughts, but we believe that they reflect reality and define who we are.

The more we practice gently bringing our attention to sensations in the here and now, the more we see thoughts as mental contents that come and go—like clouds passing in a vast sky. This helps us not believe in them so much, which can be an enormous relief.

After all, it's mostly our thoughts that torment us. Take a moment right now to bring to mind something that you're upset about. If it weren't for the thought, would you be in distress here and now? Probably not. Unless you're reading this in a war zone, or have just had surgery, it's likely that it's your thoughts that are causing you distress. In fact, even if you're in physical discomfort, unless it's severe, the thought that it'll last forever probably creates more distress than the sensation itself.

Gaining this perspective on thoughts can be very helpful when dealing with distress around rejection, shame, or feeling not good enough, because here especially it's our thoughts—our interpretation of what's happening—that creates our suffering. Being mindful of our thoughts can also help us see the role of our instincts in our experience—we can begin to notice how many of our thoughts reflect the no-longer-very-useful concerns of our inner primate.

When Aaron first started practicing mindfulness, he was alarmed that his mind was "like a sewer." Not only were the thoughts nonstop, but they were mostly about sex and dominance. "I can't stop thinking about all the women I've ever wanted to date, and all the times I've felt put down." It took a while for him to learn to let these thoughts come and go and to realize that he was just tuning in to his evolutionary inheritance—he wasn't a terrible person.

"THE ITCH (OR ACHE) WENT AWAY BY ITSELF."

The more we practice mindfulness, the more skilled we become at tolerating discomfort. Seeing pain come and go on its own, as well as practicing sitting with it, makes us more comfortable with being uncomfortable. And being able to feel our emotions—including painful ones—is necessary to heal past hurts. On my retreat I was amazed by (1) the intensity of the waves of hurt, anger, sadness, and longing that came up, and (2) the fact that I could stay with these experiences and allow them to arise and pass.

This capacity to *be with* emotions opens a path to freedom, including freedom from the self-evaluation roller coaster. Recall the exercise in Chapter 1 where we sat with the physical sensations of feeling good and then bad about ourselves? If, through mindfulness practice, we become less afraid of the painful sensations of a disappointment or rejection, we'll feel freer to risk it. We won't feel as compelled to hold on to highs and ward off the lows. You'll learn how to use mindfulness and other practices to work with difficult emotions in later chapters.

"I'M NO GOOD AT THIS."

Is it any surprise that most of us turn mindfulness practice, like everything else in our lives, into a measure of our ability or worth? And that when our minds are frisky, or sleepy, or restless, we give ourselves a bad report card?

The biggest obstacle to benefiting from mindfulness practice is having the expectation that we should be able to focus our minds at will, which is based on the mistaken notion that we're somehow in charge of our consciousness. Especially once you begin to practice regularly, you'll come to see that the mind is indeed quite unruly. The Buddhist monk Bhante Gunaratana put it well:

> Somewhere in this process, you will come face to face with the sudden and shocking realization that you are completely crazy. Your mind is a shrieking, gibbering madhouse on wheels barreling pell-mell down the hill, utterly out of control and hopeless. No problem. You are not crazier than you were yesterday. It has always been this way, and you just never noticed. You are also no crazier than everybody else around you.

Shivani's first forays into mindfulness practice were rough. As a teacher and a mother of two young boys, she was always tired and never had enough time in her day. When she tried to sit still and follow her breath, her mind immediately went to her to-do list. She was wasting time—simultaneously failing to get things done and failing at meditation. Stressed out and frazzled, she nonetheless kept at it.

Shivani eventually found that if she could sit for longer periods—a half hour or so—her mind actually began to settle. Instead of just racing from thought to thought, she began to notice feelings arising and passing and to notice when she was holding tension in her neck and shoulders. She saw how frequently she judged herself harshly, thinking, "I'm just not cutting it at work *or* at home," "I'm a lousy meditator." It began to dawn on her that this constant self-pressuring was nuts—she was pedaling as fast as she could and needed to take some time to let go, let be, and open to her inner experience. As she practiced stepping out of the thought stream and bringing her attention to the sensations of the moment, her self-evaluative chatter became quieter. Rather than just believing it, she became curious about the critical, judgmental voice that had become her constant companion.

Narrative and experiential self

Cognitive scientists identify two types of self-reference, which they call *narrative* and *experiential* focuses. Narrative focus creates comparisons with others and self-evaluative highs and lows. It involves our judgments as we talk to ourselves about ourselves and consider our enduring traits. When in narrative focus, I think "I'm smart" or "I'm dumb," "I'm strong" or "I'm weak," courageous or timid, kind or mean, generous or greedy, attractive or not—you get the idea. And these shifting judgments about ourselves—which often come from feedback we receive or we imagine receiving from others—create our self-evaluation ups and downs.

Experiential focus is different. It's moment-to-moment awareness of what's happening in the mind-body. We taste experiential focus when we practice mindfulness. Our attention goes to the sensation of an inbreath, then to a sound in the street, then to an itch, back to the outbreath, on to a feeling of sadness, and back to the inbreath. Experiential focus is centered on sensations, including the bodily sensations that underlie emotions, as well as awareness of images and thoughts that pass through the mind. However, unlike in narrative focus, in experiential focus we don't believe our thoughts so much—we just watch them come and go.

In a now classic study, researchers randomly assigned people either to eight weeks of mindfulness training or to a control group that received no training. They taught both groups to respond to a list of adjectives with either a narrative focus (reflect on what the adjective means about you as a person) or experiential focus (just notice your moment-to-moment reactions to hearing the adjectives). They then put both groups of subjects in a functional MRI scanner to see what was happening in their brains when they responded to adjectives with one focus or the other.

It turns out that when people are involved in narrative focus, there's usually activation of a part of the brain called the *medial prefrontal cortex (mPFC)*. While it has many functions, the mPFC is particularly active when we're thinking about our traits, the traits of people like us, and our future aspirations. It helps us create a narrative that links our subjective experiences over time.

The researchers found that the meditators, compared to the control group, were much better able to reduce activation of the mPFC when they moved into experiential focus. This meant that mindfulness practice actually trained their brains to be better able to step out of narrative focus—to step out of the approach that gets us caught in social comparison and self-evaluative highs and lows. It was an effective antidote to our hardwired instincts to compare ourselves with others, to worry about dominance or submission, desirability or rejection.

Developing a regular mindfulness practice

There's an old story about a tourist who's lost in Manhattan. He's getting frantic, late for a performance. Luckily, he spies a guy in a tuxedo with a violin case. He runs up to the musician and says, "Help me, please, how do I get to Carnegie Hall?" The musician stares at him and becomes pensive, looking him up and down. The tourist gets agitated, wanting an answer. Finally, after a long pause, the musician speaks: "Practice, practice."

Like most skills, mindfulness practices are dose related. If we do a little bit of practice, we develop a little mindfulness. If we do more, we develop more. Since mindfulness is a valuable skill for getting beyond our self-evaluative concerns, and for activating the caring inner primate, it's worth putting in some time to cultivate.

There are many ways to practice. We can simply try to pay attention to sensory reality when doing daily activities like walking the dog, showering, or eating lunch. We might pay attention to the sensations of our feet contacting the ground, the droplets of water caressing our body, or the taste and texture of our food (this is called *informal* practice). But to experience more profound shifts in our consciousness, it's usually necessary to take some time out of our day to do *formal* meditation practice, like the breath awareness training described earlier. It's helpful to try to develop a routine—to do it every day, or most days, at a particular time. It can also help to join a meditation group, or have a meditation buddy, to compare notes on your experiences. Some people find apps like Headspace, Calm, or Insight Timer helpful. You can also listen to a variety of mindfulness practices on my website, *DrRonSiegel.com,* and can find more detailed suggestions about how to establish a mindfulness practice in my book *The Mindfulness Solution: Everyday Practices for Everyday Problems.* While longer periods will be more powerful, even 15 minutes of meditation a day can begin to increase our awareness.

Here's an application of mindfulness practice that I personally find very helpful for breaking free from self-evaluation concerns. It involves approaching fluctuations in our feelings about ourselves mindfully and can help us be less caught in our judgments throughout the day:

Exercise: Mindfully riding the self-evaluation roller coaster

As you develop your mindfulness practice, see if you can notice every time that a self-evaluation comes to mind, either during formal meditation or during the rest of your day.

Whenever a thought or feeling of "I'm doing a good job," "They like me," "That didn't go well," "They don't like me," or a comparison with another person occurs, see if you can notice the sensations in the body that arise with it. Just try to observe the inner report card, the constant judgments that you're doing well or poorly, or that you're somehow better or worse than someone else. See if you can bring an attitude of *awareness of present experience with loving acceptance* to the bodily sensations that accompany each thought or feeling.

When negative judgments show up, instead of distracting yourself or trying to make them go away, experiment with bringing loving attention to any hurt that arises—lovingly care for yourself as you would care for a distressed puppy.

While this exercise is helpful, I also find it disconcerting, since I often notice self-evaluative or comparative judgments happening nonstop. But I also find that by staying with the bodily sensations associated with each high and low, I'm less possessed by the judgments and can take refuge in an experiential rather than narrative focus. And the more I practice mindfulness with a loving attitude, the better I'm able to tolerate the discomfort of crashes and the more I trust that they'll pass. Of course, some days are easier than others— the trick is to be as kind to ourselves when we're caught in the folly of our self-evaluative dramas and judgments.

In the coming chapters, you'll learn how to use mindfulness practices to see how we construct our stories about ourselves, to explore the amazing variety of our self-evaluation traps, to develop the courage to fully experience past injuries and feelings of inadequacy, to overcome addiction to self-esteem highs, to develop loving compassion for ourselves and others, to safely connect with other people, and to embrace our profoundly liberating ordinariness. As you'll see, they're versatile tools!

For our next step in this journey, let's look at some of the transformative insights that come from doing mindfulness practice regularly, including how, by helping us become grounded in an experiential focus, they can transform the way we see ourselves. You may discover that you're not who you think you are.

FOUR

discovering who we really are

"Who are you?" said the Caterpillar. This was not an encouraging opening for a conversation. Alice replied, rather shyly, "I—I hardly know, sir, just at present—at least I know who I WAS when I got up this morning, but I think I must have been changed several times since then."
—LEWIS CARROLL, *Alice's Adventures in Wonderland*

WHILE DISTRESSING FOR ALICE, changing a lot is good news for us. Because, as we'll see, all of our self-evaluations, and the comparisons we make with others, are based on an unexamined notion that *we* are somehow solid, coherent, stable, independent selves, who can be winners or losers, good or bad, lovable or not, better or worse than other people. One of the wonderful gifts of observing our minds carefully is realizing that this is an illusion—an insight that can help free us from the stress of trying to be good enough or needing to come out on top.

During a weekend mindfulness retreat Stacey attended to deal with her stress, she had an unexpected revelation along these lines. "It was weird at first. I started thinking less about how well I was doing in my life and experiencing my consciousness more as a *process*—a stream of different experiences unfolding over time. It made me not worry so much about me."

Or consider this. Making small talk after a meditation session, a student asked her teacher, Trudy Goodman, a seemingly simple question: "How was your meditation?" Trudy paused for a moment and then answered, "Well, a part of me was trying to attend to the breath. A part was fantasizing about the future. Then there was a part of me judging myself for fantasizing. We better ask the committee!" If there's no single "me" in there, then who is it that is good or bad, proud or ashamed, a success or failure, worthy or not of love?

Getting to know the committee

Norman Pierce is both a psychologist and a minister. He once pointed out that historically, polytheism, not monotheism, has been the norm. Ancient Greeks and Romans had their pantheons of gods, each representing a different facet of our humanity. Catholic traditions revere various saints, each embodying a different virtue or aspect of our nature. Tibetan Buddhists have a collection of enlightened bodhisattvas that play similar roles, and Hindus have thousands of gods, each with a different personality.

Why? Because as Trudy noticed, when we look carefully at our experience, we don't find one continuous integrated "me," but rather many different parts continuously arising and subsiding. At different times one or another set of feelings, thoughts, or attitudes is running the show.

The more closely we look, the more apparent these multiple selves, parts, or self-states become. Just consider how we view the world, and how we behave, in different moods. My wife can attest that Angry Ron is a different person than Sad Ron, who bears little resemblance to Frightened Ron, Arrogant Ron, Compassionate Ron, or even Hungry or Sleepy Ron. Our attitudes, thoughts, and behaviors are in fact so different in these different states that practically the only things gluing them together are a name, shoe size, and Social Security number. Who is the real *Ron*? Which of these is the good one, the bad one, the success, the failure? The more we can notice how unstable "we" are, the less we'll believe in our self-evaluative judgments.

Many of us are ashamed to admit to not being a coherent, stable self. We imagine that only very immature people, or those with serious character flaws, are unstable in this way. And while it's true that some people, in some moments, have so little memory of their other selves or self-states that they make foolish decisions (like quitting a job during an argument with the boss, or diving into an extramarital affair in a flash of lust), and there are even disorders in which people completely forget what they did in another state (so-called dissociative identity, or multiple personality disorders), almost all of us are more unstable than we like to admit.

Often these different selves, parts, or states are in conflict. We say things like "Well, a part of me would like to take the job, but I'm afraid that it'll be too stressful" or "A part of me would like to go to dinner, but I think I should stay home and finish my work."

Many cultures describe this experience of different selves using the language of *possession*—which is how it feels when one or another part takes over. Even if we don't think that external entities like spirits take control, we all know what possession feels like: "I don't know what possessed me to say *that*—it was really a dumb thing to do."

Identifying these multiple selves, states, or parts can help free us from thinking that we are, or need to be, only one way or another. This can be particularly useful in lightening our self-evaluative concerns. Seeing our different parts can also help us not identify with any particular state. I'm neither my angry part nor my compassionate part—rather, these are all part of a changing kaleidoscope of experience that's neither good nor bad, a winner nor a loser, worthy or not.

I have a little shadow that goes in and out with me

The psychiatrist Carl Jung noticed that we tend to identify with some parts of ourselves, which he called our *persona,* and reject others, which he called our *shadow.* If in order to feel good about myself I need to see myself as generous, intelligent, and hardworking (my persona), I'm going to have a hard time with my greedy, stupid, and lazy parts (my shadow). If I need to see myself as tough and confident, I'm going to have a hard time with my vulnerable, insecure

parts. We all tend to hide, and may completely block out of awareness, the parts of ourselves that don't fit the image we want to por-
tray to ourselves and others. We can feel like imposters—imagining
that others in roles like ours don't have these unwanted parts.

Not surprisingly, the list of parts we eschew is the inverse of
the attributes we use as the basis for our positive self-evaluations.
For example, we might reject the parts of us that aren't very bright,
creative, or worldly. We might not want to admit to feeling rejected
by the in-crowd, having vulnerable feelings like sadness and longings for love, or having "primitive" instincts like anger or lust. And
of course, for meditators and those on spiritual paths, we particularly
like to hide our competitive feelings and preoccupations with status
or self-image.

As long as we try to hold on to some parts while banishing others, we're going to be stressed, needing to be ever vigilant that the
shadow parts don't reveal themselves. This can wreak havoc in relationships, since we tend to get particularly upset with others when
they highlight or activate parts of ourselves we've disavowed. If I
need to think of myself as fair and generous, and my wife points out
that I'm being selfish, I'll probably get upset—and take it out on her.

Another result of trying to keep our shadow from showing is
posturing to emphasize our favorable attributes. How often do we
try to get people to notice our strengths? How often do we maneuver
to make others think that we're kind, honest, smart, hardworking,
popular—whatever the opposite of our particular shadow might be?
This then has the unfortunate side effect of activating other people's
competitive impulses—so that they then feel the need to prove their
own positive attributes and hide *their* shadows. It can be exhausting.

Dr. Richard Schwartz developed a form of psychotherapy
called internal family systems (IFS), which helps people integrate
their various parts. He points out that we all have vulnerable, hurt
parts, which he calls *exiles,* that we tend to keep out of awareness. I
remember a horrible moment at summer camp, around age 12, after
a particularly large, tough kid moved into our bunk. He was soon
dominating everyone in true simian form. One day he singled me
out for ridicule and declared triumphantly that he was better than
me at *everything.* He dared me to name one thing at which I was

better—and while I thought to myself "I'm smarter than you, you big ape," I didn't dare say anything.

I recall walking to the dining hall for dinner feeling painfully small, weak, and vulnerable. As years went on, that vulnerable part went further and further into exile. I'd do almost anything to keep it from showing. I became quite invested in its opposite—wanting to look competent and successful. It took me many years to become more comfortable with that exiled part—and we're still not always on speaking terms.

Ironically, I'm also pretty uncomfortable with my competitive parts that developed to protect the vulnerable ones. I'm not proud of all the times I raised my hand in class to show off that I knew the answer (yeah, I was one of those kids), or when just last week at dinner I overdid it, tenaciously asserting *my* understanding of Middle East tensions (it was important to be right).

It's said in Zen traditions that the boundary of what we can accept in ourselves is the boundary of our freedom. Our goal is to become more comfortable being a collection of various parts, warts and all, rather than reaching some state of perfection. Paradoxically, as we learn to accept the warts, and even judiciously let them show, we become happier and kinder.

In fact, accepting all of our parts is what allows us to thrive. Perhaps you've heard a version of this popular European fairy tale:

> The kingdom is in trouble. Either the crops are dying, the women are infertile, or there's a plague—and the situation is grave. The king, desperate for a solution, summons his three sons. Two of them are gallant knights on sturdy steeds, displaying all the signs of masculine dominance, while the third is a skinny, bumbling, vulnerable loser. The king decrees: "If one of you can restore the kingdom, I will abdicate the throne and you will become king." The virile brothers gallop off purposefully to the East and the West in search of an answer, while the third son wanders off and promptly falls into a well. There, stuck at the bottom, unable to climb out, he encounters a slimy, ugly frog. With nowhere to go, and no way out, the hapless young man tells the frog of his plight. The frog turns out to be a wise and compassionate sage and offers

him a golden ring with magical powers, which enables him not only to climb out of the well, but also to save the kingdom from ruin.

Fairy tales catch on because they resonate with universal psychological experiences. Imagine for a moment that the king and two virile sons represent our strengths—the parts we rely on to feel good about ourselves. They're handsome, strong, and healthy. The third, vulnerable son is our shadow or exile—the part that we're ashamed of, that we try to hide or deny. One way to understand the story is that the "kingdom" (our heart and mind) isn't doing very well because we're cutting off and denying important parts of ourselves. These are usually our tender, hurt, vulnerable parts, though they might also be our assertive parts, parts we developed to protect our vulnerabilities, our sexual parts—whatever we're ashamed of and trying to hide or suppress. It's by accepting and honoring these split-off parts that we find health, wholeness, and vitality.

Our salvation comes from where we least expect it—at the bottom of a well. In this way, the deep, loving acceptance of mindfulness can be profoundly healing. We can use it to reconnect with the parts of ourselves that were injured in past failures or rejections, gently draining the pool of pain we all carry around from moments when we didn't feel loved or successful. Reconnecting with these parts can free us from self-evaluation concerns as we become less invested in appearing one way or another to ourselves or anyone else.

Eddie, now a college junior, had banished his tender side years ago. Not very strong, nor good at sports, he was regularly harassed by his older brothers in elementary school. Determined to fight back, he took up karate in middle school, became a varsity wrestler in high school, and was a weight lifter in college. Nobody was going to mess with him now.

But keeping his vulnerabilities at bay had its costs. His girlfriend complained that she didn't really know him and threatened to break up: "You never tell me what's bothering you when you have a bad day. All you do is play video games." He got horribly anxious before class presentations, afraid that his voice would tremble. After a bout of painful stress-related heartburn his doctor referred him to the college counseling center.

It wasn't easy to be honest with his therapist, but Eddie eventually began to open up, both to her and to himself. He began to realize that beneath his tough exterior was this young, vulnerable kid, afraid of being picked on again. The more comfortable he became acknowledging this exiled part of himself, the less he had to keep up a front—with himself, his girlfriend, or the other kids at school. As he became less afraid of his tender side, he found he could relax, his heartburn diminished, and to his great relief, his girlfriend decided to stick around.

Cogito ergo sum

Archaeologists speculate that humans didn't have anything like our conventional sense of self until some 40,000 to 60,000 years ago. That's when the Middle to Upper Paleolithic transition happened— our *cultural big bang.* Paleontologists think our great-great-great-great-great-great-great (etc.) grandmother Lucy and, later, *Homo habilis, Homo erectus,* and our Neanderthal cousins all pretty much operated on automatic—feeling hunger, thirst, cold, heat, or sexual arousal and responding reflexively, like most other animals do today.

This is a very different kind of consciousness than ours. As the psychologist Mark Leary points out, it's "unlikely that cats or cows or butterflies think consciously about themselves and their experiences as they sit quietly, graze, or flit from flower to flower. 'I wonder why my owner feeds me this dry cat food.' 'Am I better than the other cows in my herd?' 'Which flower garden should I flit to next?'"

Our group, *Homo sapiens sapiens,* arrived on the scene around 200,000 to 300,000 years ago. While we began burying our dead early on, it took tens of thousands of years before we started behaving (and presumably thinking) like modern humans. It was only during the cultural big bang that we suddenly began making sophisticated tools, adorning ourselves with beads and bracelets, creating representational art, and planning for the future by building boats.

Although it's impossible to know exactly when language as we know it started, we began *acting* as though we were thinking about ourselves during this period. Our narrative self, with all of its often painful judgments, appears to be a relatively new invention.

Constructing our identity

René Descartes famously suggested in the 1600s, "I think, therefore I am" (*cogito ergo sum*). (Were he alive today he might say, "I have a to-do list, therefore I am" or even "I'm on Facebook, Instagram, and Twitter, therefore I am.") The thoughts that I'm an American, a husband, a father, a psychologist, a nature lover, or an old guy—not to mention the judgments that I'm good or bad at these roles—are all based on words. My identity, career, reputation, and plans are all solidified with language. This realization, which in philosophy is sometimes called *constructivism,* can be experienced directly by training the mind through mindfulness practice to step out of the thought stream.

It's a worthwhile pursuit, because the more clearly we can observe our minds *constructing* rather than simply perceiving ourselves and the world, the less we believe in our constructions, the more flexible our attitudes become, and the less prone we are to go up and down or get stuck in one or another idea about ourselves.

By looking closely, we can actually see our minds creating our identity out of building blocks. Let's take a few moments to see how this works and how it can help free us from our worries about ourselves.

The construction project begins with sense contact—we see, hear, smell, taste, and touch as our sense organs connect with the world. But the mind doesn't stay at this level for long. It immediately organizes these sensations into perceptions. Look at the following shape:

What might it be? Most people say "a face," some "a bowling ball." The interesting thing is that either way, our minds are filling in a lot of missing information based on assumptions and past experiences—and doing this instantly. There's actually no nose or mouth. And if it's a bowling ball, it's for a two-toed sloth.

Because they're so strongly colored by our past experiences, beliefs, and assumptions, our perceptions are pretty unreliable. Just consider conflicting eyewitness testimonies in court. This led one cognitive scientist to quip, "If I hadn't believed it, I wouldn't have seen it" and the poet Anaïs Nin to observe, "We don't see the world as it is. We see it as we are."

The unreliability of perception is easy to observe even in less charged arenas. Consider this drawing:

Which did you see first, the duck or the bunny?

It gets weirder. Immediately after organizing sensations into perceptions, our brain adds a feeling tone. We experience our perceptions as pleasant, unpleasant, or neutral. And almost simultaneously, the mind forms dispositions—impulses to hold on to pleasant experiences, push away the unpleasant, and ignore the neutral.

It's these likes and dislikes of perceptions, with their attendant dispositions, that play a big role in constructing our identity, personality, and sense of self. We see this most obviously in adolescents. If you ask a teenager, "Tell me about yourself," you will be told, "I really like hip-hop," "I hate books," I love sports," "I don't like big parties." Kids construct their identities based on what they like and don't like, buttressed by self-evaluative thoughts: "I'm really good at tennis," "I can't draw," "I'm great at math," "I'm a terrible swimmer."

Now, we may think that as mature adults we're beyond this, but we, too, cobble together identities based on what we like and don't and how we appraise our abilities. If you drive a Prius or Tesla, I bet I can guess how you feel about pesticides, national parks, and gun control, not to mention who you voted for in the last election. If you've achieved a lot academically, I bet I can guess whether being smart matters to you.

The more clearly we can see our minds constructing reality and our sense of self this way, the better our chances of not getting caught in particular views of ourselves, others, and the world around us. And the less we're caught in these judgments, the freer we become from worries about how well we're doing or how we compare to others.

"And I, sir, can be run through with a sword"

There's a famous Zen teaching story about a sadistic general whose troops are attacking a town, killing able-bodied boys and men, raping women, burning crops, and destroying buildings. This general really wants to vanquish the population, and he catches wind that the residents revere their Zen master. He gallops his horse up the hillside, right into the main hall of the temple. There, sitting on his meditation cushion in the middle of the room, is the master. The general raises his bloody sword above the Zen master and says, "Don't you realize that I could run you through with this sword without blinking an eye?" The little old man looks up and says, "Yes, and I, sir, can be run through with a sword without blinking an eye." At that moment the general becomes flustered and leaves town.

Now, it's not always going to work as a military strategy. But this story speaks to one of the powers of mindfulness practice discussed earlier—its ability to help us tolerate pain. It goes beyond that as well. Somehow this Zen master wasn't concerned for his welfare. He wasn't caught up in ideas of his own importance.

This story has implications for how we deal with emotions, including the emotions associated with self-evaluation highs and lows. Let's try another little practice that illustrates how this works:

Exercise: Identifying emotions in the body*

It's best to do this exercise with your eyes closed, opening them briefly to read each instruction. Start with a few moments of mindfulness practice, sitting upright and tuning in to the sensations of the breath.

Next generate a little feeling of sadness—you may be able to just imagine feeling sad, or perhaps it'll help to conjure up a sad thought or image. Don't pick anything overwhelming, but rather try to generate just enough sadness to feel it clearly. Stay with the feeling for a little while. Where exactly in the body do you notice the sensations of sadness? Gently place your hands over this area. What do these sensations feel like?

Now generate some fear or anxiety—you may be able to find this already present in your body or may need the help of a thought or image. Again, aim for a moderate level. Stay with this feeling and note where in your body you notice it. Again, touch the area. What do the sensations of fear or anxiety feel like?

Next generate some anger. (If you're a nice person who doesn't easily get angry, try imagining someone in the *other* political party, whichever that is for you.) In the same way, stay with it for a little while, notice where you feel it, touch the area, and then note what the sensations feel like.

(I won't ask you to do lust, but you get the idea.)

We can see from this practice that emotions have three possible components: a bodily sensation, a thought, and an image. If we can see emotions being constructed this way, rather than getting caught in our narratives, we're less likely to be captured by them.

Take anger, for example. Let's assume I have a friend to whom

---

*Audio available at *giftofbeingordinary.com* and *guilford.com/siegel4-materials*.

I've been very generous who does something selfish that hurts my feelings. Living in my usual thought stream, I'd think, "I can't believe you did that to me after all I've done for you." Every time I have that thought the sensation of anger will intensify, and every time the sensation intensifies it'll generate another angry thought.

Approached mindfully, with an experiential focus, things unfold differently. Anger arises, and the sensations are felt in the body. Back and neck muscles tense, heart and respiration rates increase. With mindfulness practice, I can tolerate them, like other painful sensations, more readily. This is both because I've practiced being with other forms of physical discomfort and because I have an understanding that all experience is in constant flux, so these sensations won't last forever.

Indeed, thoughts may arise, but they're taken as mental contents coming and going—I don't believe in them as much, so they don't grip me as strongly nor generate such strong feeling. Images may also arise on the screen of awareness—perhaps a vision of decapitating my former friend (or something milder)—but I let these come and go too.

With mindfulness, the whole experience feels less personal. We're simply not identified with the anger in the same way. We come to notice that all experiences in consciousness, this included, are in a way impersonal. They're the result of a brain that, as the neuroscientist Wolf Singer put it, is like "an orchestra without a conductor."

The combination of having a greater capacity to experience painful sensations without feeling compelled to fix or alleviate them, not believing in or identifying with our thoughts, and experiencing mental contents as ever-changing impersonal events, helps us develop what psychologists call *affect tolerance*—the ability to feel strong emotions without being overwhelmed or swept away by them. We develop the capacity to pause, breathe, and allow space for feelings without being compelled to act on or avoid them.

One of the reasons that Shivani, the busy teacher with two young boys introduced in the last chapter, stuck with mindfulness practice was it allowed her to be less reactive emotionally. Whether in her classroom or at home, when things went wrong, it was usually because she had difficulty controlling her reactions to painful feelings. When a kid in her class with attentional problems interrupted her lesson, she felt humiliated, thinking "I'm just not engaging enough," "I've never been any good at discipline"—and yelled at him. The same thing would happen when her oldest son taunted his brother.

The more she practiced mindfulness, the more Shivani could notice and tolerate feelings of humiliation when they arose, the less she found herself automatically yelling, and the better the atmosphere became both at school and at home. She became less self-critical and more compassionate toward herself, her student, and her child.

Being able to tolerate strong emotions in this way allows us to choose whether or not to express or act on them. It also helps us bear the pain of shame, rejection, feeling unworthy, and other self-evaluation collapses, so that we don't have to expend so much energy trying to avoid these feelings and can use them instead to heal our past hurts. Also, the more we can open to our inner kaleidoscope of thoughts, feelings, and sensations, the less we try to control them. This open-hearted, flexible attitude then makes it easier to connect safely with other people, which, as we'll see, is another great antidote to self-evaluative concerns.

Getting beyond "me"

Despite their diversity, the world's religions generally all agree on one thing: self-preoccupation is a problem. It interferes with connecting with God, being touched by the Holy Spirit, accepting Jesus as our savior, knowing Allah, reaching nirvana, finding the natural way of the Tao. It also gets in the way of lovingly opening to our own pain and to others' suffering. To the extent that we're caught up in talking to ourselves all day long about our desires and our image, we're blocked from spiritual development.

Almost all religious traditions therefore differentiate between a small, self-interested sense of self (often called "ego") and a larger "true self" that is connected to, or indistinguishable from, God, Allah, Brahman, Tao, Mother Earth, or Great Spirit.

Comparative religion scholars point out that almost all traditions have as their inspiration a liberating self-transcendent experience on the part of a sage. These experiences involve feeling connected to the whole world, losing a sense of separate self or personal
identity, and feeling peace, love, joy, and wonder as a result. In fact,
the English word *ecstasy* comes from the Greek meaning roughly "to
stand outside of oneself."

While self-transcendent states are often referred to as *mystical,*
there is nothing necessarily supernatural about them. Although in
many cultural traditions they've been understood in religious or
spiritual terms, they can equally easily be understood as simply seeing reality clearly and opening our hearts. What we sense in these
states is the interdependence of all things, experiencing ourselves
and the world as a modern biologist or physicist would describe
them—as a unified, constantly changing whole. When we grasp this
experientially, however, it goes from being an abstract intellectual
notion to a deeply moving, awe-inspiring realization.

Einstein, who was decidedly secular and scientific in his understanding of the universe, saw self-transcendence as our most important project:

> A human being is part of the whole called by us universe. . . . We
> experience ourselves, our thoughts and feelings as something sepa-
> rate from the rest. A kind of optical delusion of consciousness. This
> delusion is a kind of prison for us, restricting us to our personal
> desires and to affection for a few persons nearest to us. Our task
> must be to free ourselves from the prison by widening our circle of
> compassion to embrace all living creatures and the whole of nature
> in its beauty. The true value of a human being is determined by
> the measure and the sense in which they have obtained liberation
> from the self.

The techniques offered for self-transcendence differ from one
tradition to another, but they all involve moving away from our
habit of thinking about our own desires and opening our hearts
to love other living beings. Whether through prayer, prostrations,
ecstatic dance, mindfulness practices, yoga, or koans, almost all of

the world's religions have developed exercises designed to foster self-transcendent awakenings.

The insights that arise during these experiences lead to remarkably consistent advice about the foolishness of pursuing happiness through status, popularity, or achievement, or otherwise trying to feel good about ourselves. They almost all suggest cultivating humility instead. We can taste self-transcendence ourselves with a simple exercise:

Exercise: The joys of self-transcendence*

Begin with a few minutes of following the breath to settle the thought stream a little and bring the attention into the present moment. Just be with the rhythms of the breath and other sensations in the body.

Once the mind has settled a bit, imagine for a moment that you're a deeply wise and compassionate person. (Don't worry if you don't usually think of yourself this way. We all have the potential within us. Just enjoy the fantasy that it's been awakened.) You're able to watch your own desires come and go, while having an open heart, feeling compassion for others who are driven by their cravings for achievement, recognition, wealth, success, righteousness, popularity, respect—all of the things that make our self-esteem soar, however briefly. You watch your own and other people's moods going up and down with good and bad fortune, with changing self-evaluations, but your moods don't last so long—you understand how transient our gains and losses are, how what goes up must come down.

Seeing the fluid nature of both success and failure, you're not gripped by either. Rather, you live in the present moment and feel connected to both other people and timeless realities, like the cycles of nature, birth, and death. And since you're able to see the world as it is clearly, you feel compassion for yourself and everyone else who regularly experiences ups and downs.

Just let yourself enjoy being this wise, compassionate, open-hearted being for a few minutes (you might close your eyes to savor the experience). As you go through your day, see if you might periodically reconnect with this way of seeing the world.

---

*Audio available at *giftofbeingordinary.com* and *guilford.com/siegel4-materials*.

In the pages that follow we'll look at techniques drawn from both ancient wisdom traditions and modern psychology to get beyond our own self-preoccupation and feel the freedom self-transcendence can offer. We'll even see what it might feel like to be so open-hearted and connected to others and the wider world that we no longer feel like a separate self.

Most of us have tasted this way of being accidentally. Have you ever had a moment of closeness with a friend, lover, or family member where you felt completely relaxed, safe, and at home? Have you experienced a warm, loving feeling when caring for a pet, child, or someone in need? Have you had a moment in nature where you were absorbed in its beauty, or had the feeling of being engrossed in music, or had a sense of awe entering a cathedral? These are all moments where we're not focused on ourselves, or how we compare to others, but are connected to something larger. The more we learn to get out of our own way and open our hearts, the more we open the door to these sorts of transcendent experiences.

Ironically, we'll see that rather than diminishing us, transcending our usual self-preoccupation brings enduring strength and satisfaction. It allows us to be more effective in the world and accomplish our goals more readily. We feel more love for others, and more at home in our own skin.

The problem is, many of our biologically based instincts pull us in the opposite direction—they incline us to get stuck in competitive concerns, craving, and trying to feel good about ourselves. Instead of connecting us to others and the wider world, they leave us continually asking, "What does this say about me?" "How will this make me feel?" These impulses are so deeply wired in our brains and so strongly reinforced by those around us that it can be challenging to overcome them. Becoming free therefore requires both learning to work with the instincts that trap us in self-preoccupation *and* cultivating the self-transcendent attitudes that make life richer and more connected. The process goes more smoothly if we can be kind to ourselves about our self-preoccupation, remembering that it's only natural.

Julian grew up in a poor neighborhood. After studying creative writing in college, he did well in the corporate world. He was bright, articulate, and hardworking, with excellent people skills. He made sure that his efforts were noticed, so that almost as soon as he settled into a position, he was promoted.

But it all felt strangely empty. When he turned 40, he asked himself, "Is this all there is?" "Why do I care so much about getting ahead?" "How come I feel lonely and like an imposter, even though everyone seems to think I'm so great?" After some soul-searching, he realized that he missed the idealism of his youth, the way writing used to make him feel so alive, his passion for social justice, and the joy of exploring ideas with his professors and classmates. And he missed the warmth he felt growing up in his big family. But he felt tethered to his job. The money, the position, the nice office, traveling, his parents' pride—why did it all matter so much?

Julian realized that he had to understand the pull of these things if he was going to escape it and find a way to feel alive again. There were many facets: "Every promotion felt so good—I didn't feel like the poor kid anymore." "Who's going to date me if I don't have a good job?" "It would break my parents' heart if I wasn't a success anymore—none of the other kids made it." While he decided to stay at his job, Julian found a way to come alive again. He was able to shift his focus from pleasing everyone and proving himself to connecting more honestly to his friends, reconnecting with family, getting involved politically, and starting to write again. His favorite stories were the ones about escaping self-evaluation traps.

In the next few chapters, we'll take a deeper dive into examining the sorts of forces that kept Julian climbing the corporate ladder and that keep almost all of us trapped in trying to feel good about ourselves one way or another. I invite you to consider which realms activate you, since we're all vulnerable to different concerns. Our goal will be to catch these instincts in the act of running our lives. We'll also see how crazy and self-destructive these forces are, so that we can learn to take them less seriously. This last part of the project will be easy, since a little reflection will reveal that most of us are quite insane when it comes to worrying about our status and self-image.

PART III

Catching Ourselves in the Act

FIVE

the failure of success

There is perhaps nothing worse than reaching the
top of the ladder and discovering that you're on
the wrong wall.

—JOSEPH CAMPBELL

ONE OF MY FIRST patients was the most financially successful—
he had just sold his oil trading business for $30 million cash. He
kept using that expression, "$30 million cash." I kept imagining the
overflowing wheelbarrow.

Despite this formidable accomplishment, he was bereft. He had
spent his entire adult life building the business, and now that he had
sold it, he was adrift with little sense of meaning or purpose. His
relationships with family and friends were a shambles, and he had
few interests outside of oil trading.

As a newly minted psychologist, I thought, "This is great. We're
going to get into the meaning of life." I had long-standing interests
in spiritual journeys and life-span psychological development and
was eager to explore his potential with him.

As often happens when a therapist has a clear idea of where
therapy should go, we weren't connecting very well. Nonetheless,
since he was in a lot of distress, he kept coming to see me. Then suddenly, on the third or fourth visit, he seemed transformed. Instead of
being downtrodden and disconnected, he was full of energy. When
I asked him what had happened, he said, "I just came up with a
business plan by which I could parlay my $30 million into a $50

million company—and if I could do that, I'd feel like I had finally succeeded." There was no irony in his voice. It was the last time I saw him.

Watching my patient struggle with feelings of inadequacy because he had sold his company for *only* $30 million was a real wake-up call for me personally. If $30 million wasn't enough for him, fulfilling my fantasies of getting a higher position or earning more money might not work for me either.

But why *didn't* the $30 million work for him? Why don't our achievements reliably make us feel good about ourselves? One reason is *narcissistic recalibration*—our propensity sooner or later to take our accomplishments for granted and need more and more to keep our self-appraisals afloat.

I can't get no satisfaction

Most of us feel proud of our achievements at first. When we learned to walk as toddlers, or successfully put multicolored plastic rings on a post in size order, most of us felt pretty good about ourselves—and enjoyed showing off to anyone willing to watch. Remember how it felt to be able to catch a ball, ride a bike, or go to the store alone? How about graduating from grade school, high school, or college? Having your first girlfriend or boyfriend? Getting a job or a driver's license? Or perhaps getting married, renting an apartment, owning a car, buying a house, or having a child? Most of us work hard for these milestones and feel buoyed up when we reach them.

The problem is, we humans (like all creatures) *habituate to everything*. We become accustomed to having what we have, and our feelings about ourselves then go up or down from our new normal. I frequently offer trainings to mental health professionals, all of whom worked hard for their advanced degrees. I ask them, "Who woke up this morning feeling worthy and fulfilled because you have your professional degree?" Everybody laughs. Occasionally, one newly minted therapist raises a hand, looks around dejectedly, and asks, "Why is everybody laughing?" Ouch.

Closer to home, one of my daughters graduated from medical

school several years ago. When she started her internship, she sent my wife and me a picture of her new hospital ID with "MD" after her name. That evening I saw a psychiatrist friend and told him about the picture. His heart sank, reflecting on how quickly his first hospital ID lost its luster. Ouch again.

Check this out in your own life. Has the glow of any of your accomplishments or personal milestones worn off? Do you still feel proud about being picked for the team, graduating high school, getting into college, owning a car or house, or having your current job? It's not that we wouldn't feel horrible if we lost any of these things—it just doesn't take long for us to take them for granted and to need something more to feel good about ourselves.

Running on the hedonic treadmill

So why do we still imagine that the next achievement is going to create a lasting change in our self-assessment? That this one will do the trick? It's because our emotions react to *changes* in our circumstances, and we make the mistake of thinking that emotions will last.

Instead of lasting, we find that self-image boosts are particularly subject to what psychologists call the *hedonic treadmill*. "Hedonic" comes from the same root as "hedonism"—having to do with pleasure. And treadmills are human hamster wheels—contraptions on which we run and run but never get anywhere.

Even though we might be otherwise intelligent creatures, it's easy not to notice how many of the things we pursue are subject to the hedonic treadmill. Have you ever had your income go up—perhaps because you got a new job or a promotion? Remember how good it felt to be able to buy the things you wanted, be financially more secure, and maybe even feel proud of your newfound affluence? What happened? As studies of lottery winners attest, it usually doesn't take us long to return to our previous level of happiness.

The same is true for fame or notoriety. I once met a British psychiatrist who toured with famous rock bands. The musicians would routinely fall apart with too many drugs, crazy schedules, and wild sex, and his job was to put them back together. I asked him if there was truth to the popular idea that rock stars crash and burn, become drug addicted or commit suicide, more often than ordinary folks. He said, "Absolutely—happens all the time." They often start out as normal people of modest means. Suddenly they become rich, everybody thinks they're wonderful, and thousands of adoring fans will do anything (including sexual favors) just to get a little of their attention.

"At first, the rock stars are ecstatic with their new lives," he explained. But before long, they become accustomed to fame, and it stops working. It becomes ho-hum—just another gourmet meal, private jet, fancy hotel, adoring crowd, and night of drug-enhanced sex. To make matters worse, they develop a new comparison group. Instead of comparing themselves to regular people, they now compare themselves to other rock stars. And not everyone can be Mick Jagger.

The rock star's dilemma highlights another way that the hedonic treadmill works. It's not just that we become accustomed to our new level of success; we develop new standards. My patient's first million probably felt pretty good, but now $30 million wasn't enough. My psychiatrist friend once felt pretty good about becoming a physician, but now he notices how much more surgeons are paid. Sadly, as long as we're looking for achievements to make us feel good about ourselves, we're doomed to always need more and more just to feel good enough.

This next exercise, which works with the *head* component of our three *H*'s, can help. There's nothing quite like seeing how previous successes have failed to sustain us to help free us from compulsively pursuing new ones.

Exercise: Tracking the failure of success

Try filling in the following chart, either by completing it in writing or just thinking about what would go on each line. In the first column, note achievements, successes, or personal milestones that made you feel good about yourself at different points in your life. In the second, rate how important they were for you on a scale from 1 to 5, where 1 = mildly and 5 = very. Finally, in the third column, note about how long the accomplishment sustained you before you found yourself looking for something else to give you a boost. (Adjust the age ranges to fit your situation and draw your own table if you need more space or print out the one available at *giftofbeingordinary.com* or *guilford.com/ siegel4-materials*.)

TRACKING THE FAILURE OF SUCCESS

Accomplishment	Importance (1-5)	Duration of boost
Age 1-5		
Age 6-12		
Age 13-18		
Age 19-30		

Accomplishment	Importance (1-5)	Duration of boost
Age 19-30 *(continued)*		
Age 31-40		
Age 41-50		
Age 51-60		

Accomplishment	Importance (1–5)	Duration of boost
Age 61–70		
Age 71–80*		

*Hopefully we quit trying to boost our feelings about ourselves with successes after 80, but feel free to continue the chart if necessary.

What did you notice? How long did your greatest successes last? Have you experienced narcissistic recalibration, in which you became accustomed to a given success and it then lost its power to help you feel good about yourself?

You can see what my chart looks like on pages 70–71.

As I completed my chart, I was struck by how short-lived the effects of my accomplishments have been. While I certainly appreciate having good relationships with my wife, kids, and others, feel good about being a psychologist, and am happy when my body functions well, all I need is a bit of failure to see that a lot of the achievements that previously floated my boat don't work anymore. Once I

Accomplishment	Importance (1–5)	Duration of boost
Age 1–5		
Walking	5	Maybe 3 weeks?
Riding a bicycle	4	A few months?
Becoming articulate	5	Still hooked on this 60 years later
Age 6–12		
Going to first grade	3	2 weeks?
Having a girlfriend in fifth grade	5	6 weeks until it ended in disaster
Breaking windows with the tough kids	2	30 minutes—until we got caught
Age 13–18		
Getting in with cool kids	4	2 months
Having a high school girlfriend	5	3 years of intense self-esteem ups and downs
Getting a driver's license	4	2 months
Getting into a selective college	3	3 months
Age 19–30		
Having a college girlfriend	5	3 years of intense self-esteem ups and downs
Graduating college	3	2 weeks
Getting into graduate school	4	2 months
Becoming a licensed psychologist	4	2 months

Accomplishment	Importance (1-5)	Duration of boost
Age 31-40		
Getting married	4	2 months (that's the self-evaluation high—appreciating the relationship is another matter)
Having children	4	30+ years of self-image ups and downs (again, appreciating the relationships is another matter)
Establishing a professional practice	3	35+ years of self-evaluation ups and downs
Age 41-50		
Professional advancements	3	2 months each
Feeling good about my kids' successes	3	A week or so at a time, renewable
Taking care of my family's needs	4	A few hours, but renewable
Age 51-60		
Writing books	4	1–2 months each time
Speaking professionally	3	1 day after each event
Hobnobbing with well-known folks	4	A few hours each time
Age 61-70		
Staying reasonably fit physically	3	For a few hours after I exercise (if no body parts break)
Having a good marriage	4	Renewable, until the next argument (again, appreciating the relationship is another matter)
Being articulate	2	Still hooked!

become accustomed to a success, I habituate, it loses its power, and it no longer keeps my heart from sinking when a new disappointment comes along. I find myself longing for new achievements to get that good feeling again and ward off the pain—but they're not always available.

What goes up must come down

As though this wasn't bad enough, fate is fickle. Sometimes a rock star is popular for a few years, but then teenage pop idols come along. We may have a great job or business, but then conditions change and we lose it. Perhaps we're fortunate enough to have investments, but then markets sour. As I mentioned, even gold medalists are unlikely to win the Olympics again in 4 or 8 years. Not only does continued success lose its power, but we also have to deal with downturns. And having our position sink is even more painful than habituating to success.

But sink it will. Have you noticed any changes in your body since you were 20? Have you welcomed and embraced them all? Sometimes when I'm discussing this topic in groups I'll ask, "Who here is going to die?" Usually about 20% of the hands go up. We don't like to think about death, no less illness, aging, or disability. Yet we can look forward to them all. Sorry, but it's true.

Even if we're able to keep our self-appraisal afloat for a while with shiny new accomplishments, and even if we're unusually lucky at warding off setbacks, eventually we all deteriorate. Most of us will eventually peak in our jobs and in our physical and mental capacities. Sinking is inevitable. It's pretty wild to visit a nursing home and be told that the incoherent old lady in the wheelchair "was once a well-known nuclear physicist."

While hard to face, the more directly we can see this reality, the better our chances of enjoying our lives—since seeing how this all works will help free us from being so caught up in pursuing accomplishments just to feel good enough. And luckily for all of us, there are lots of more fulfilling and reliable pathways to well-being that we can put our energies into instead.

What really matters?

If you've been an achievement junkie, you might be thinking at this point, "So if I don't try to win at the game of life, what will I do instead?" While it might conjure up memories of late nights in the college dorm, one way to answer this is to ask, "What does it all mean?"

There are several ways to inquire. One is just to reflect, "What really matters to me?" Or, as the poet Mary Oliver asks, "Tell me, what is it you plan to do with your one wild and precious life?" You might imagine your tombstone or obituary and ask yourself, "What would I like it to say?" Maybe the answer is "He was a good [father, son, husband, or friend]." Or perhaps, "She loved learning and had insatiable curiosity." "They wanted to make a difference in the world." "She strove to know God." "He knew how to have a good time." It can be helpful to consider your aspirations in different domains such as work or study, relationships, personal growth, and leisure.

Another way to find what really matters to you is to recall the moments in your life that have felt most meaningful, that you cherish. What were these? An intimate moment with a friend? The birth of a child? A sunset? Playing the piano? A meditative experience? Are there common themes to the meaningful moments? Perhaps connecting with others, with nature, or with spirituality? Artistic expression? Discovery? Play?

Inquiring about what really matters, you may discover that even though there isn't a single, stable, coherent self to be found, you can identify values and activities that feel meaningful to you. As we'll see, these turn out to be much more rewarding than trying to keep our self-esteem afloat, and escaping self-preoccupation frees our resources to pursue them.

Shifting your goals

I invite you to use your insights into your values and the unsustainability of positive self-appraisals to approach some activities differently—to work with the *habit* dimension of the three *H*s. It can make anything you do more fun:

Exercise: Leaning up against the right wall

Take a few minutes to consider things you pursue to feel good about yourself. These can be any of the building blocks of a positive self-image we explored in Chapter 1—money, fitness, intelligence, honesty, popularity, job advancement, looking good. They can be items from the chart we just completed. First list (in your mind or in the table below) these pursuits.

Next to each one, jot down a word or phrase that identifies how it makes you feel good about yourself. Then reflect on how you might go about working toward the same goal, engaging in the same project, but with a different aim—for a purpose other than feeling better about yourself.

For example, I like to teach workshops for other mental health professionals. And it's definitely true, I get a boost when more people show up to hear me or when they tell me that they liked my presentation (I also reliably get a collapse when fewer people show up or they don't seem engaged). But I can also do the same teaching with a different aim—with the wish to genuinely help participants to help their clients. I both become a better presenter and enjoy the process a lot more when I deliberately try to let go of my self-evaluation concerns and focus on being helpful instead.

See if the same is true for you. Fill in the table below with some of your accomplishments, the boosts you get from them, and the alternative aim that you might work toward (I filled in the first line with my example). For more space, print the table available at *giftofbeingordinary.com* or *guilford.com/siegel4-materials*.

LEANING UP AGAINST THE RIGHT WALL

Accomplishment	Self-evaluation boost	Alternative aim
Present at conference	Feel liked, respected, smart	Focus on clinicians' and patients' needs

Accomplishment	Self-evaluation boost	Alternative aim

From *The Extraordinary Gift of Being Ordinary* by Ronald D. Siegel. Copyright © 2022 Ronald D. Siegel. Published by The Guilford Press. Purchasers of this book can photo-copy and/or download enlarged versions of this material from *giftofbeingordinary.com* or *guilford.com/siegel4-materials*.

The next time you're trying to accomplish something, see if you can focus on the alternative aim—it'll likely make you more skillful and make the project much more enjoyable.

A friend of mine, Amanda, recently told me about her experiment doing this. She liked to share her blog posts on Facebook, but she struggled. "Whenever I write, this imaginary critic shows up on my shoulder. If the writing seems good, the critic smiles. My heart beats a little faster, I sit a little taller, and I think, 'Hey, I'm pretty good at this.' Then I post it." But the good feeling doesn't last. "I keep checking for likes or comments—and my mood goes up and down with each bit of positive or negative feedback."

Amanda was tired of all these ups and downs. One day, it dawned on her that there must be a better way. While she couldn't entirely escape her wish that others like her work, she could more deliberately focus her attention on what really mattered to her. Sometimes she just wanted to play with a fun idea; other times she was after a political or social change, like when she wrote about a racist exchange that horrified her in the supermarket. So she turned off notifications on her phone and put herself on a *checking diet*—she would only check responses to her posts once a day. The more she focused on what she really wanted to accomplish with the post, the less she cared about how many likes she got, and the more fun writing became. The self-evaluative chatter didn't go away completely, but blogging went from being fraught to being more of a joy.

Swimming in Lake Wobegon

> There's one way to find out if a man is honest: ask him; if he says yes, you know he's crooked.
> —MARK TWAIN

Because of the near impossibility of consistently feeling good about ourselves through achievement, most of us try other approaches as well. Social psychologists tell us that the most popular one is lying—to ourselves and others.

This particular form of deception is called *illusory superiority,* or more colorfully, the *Lake Wobegon effect.* Named in honor of a fictional town where "all the women are strong, all the men are good looking, and all the children are above average," it describes our remarkably pervasive tendency to overestimate our achievements and capabilities in relation to others in order to feel better about ourselves. Across an astonishingly wide range of skills or accomplishments, most of us like to think we're above average.

You can't make this stuff up. It's well established by high school:

o In a large study, 70% of high school students rated themselves as above the median in leadership ability, 85% rated themselves as above the median in ability to get along with others, and a full 25% rated themselves in the top 1%.

It continues in college:

o College students were asked to rate themselves and "average college students" on 20 positive and 20 negative traits. Typical students rated themselves as better than average on 38 out of the 40 traits.

It extends to graduate school:

o 87% of MBA students at Stanford rated their academic performance as above the median.

And even afflicts professors:

o 96% of university professors think that they're better teachers than their colleagues.

Our self-evaluations are just as inflated outside of school:

o In one study, 93% of American drivers rate themselves as above average for safety.
o A study of 1,000 Americans asked them to say whether they themselves or certain well-known individuals were more likely to go to heaven; 87% thought that they themselves would indeed be chosen. The next most endorsed person was Mother Teresa, who 79% thought would gain entry (she may have been good, but apparently not as good as us).

As though all of this wasn't enough, there's another important area where we consistently overestimate our abilities: objectivity. Most of us think that our capacity to evaluate ourselves accurately is better than average!

My favorite observation in social psychology, the Dunning-Kruger effect, helps predict when our self-evaluations will be most inflated. Researchers have found repeatedly that across all sorts of human domains and activities, *actual competence is inversely proportional to perceived competence*. This means that people who are truly skilled at things tend to underestimate their ability, while those who are less skilled tend to overestimate their ability. Let that be a warning the next time we're thinking how talented we are.

Too clever for our own good

Social scientists tell us that our desire to prop up our self-evaluations can create all sorts of other distortions as well. If, for example, we encounter someone who is more talented than us in some area, we assume that he or she must be extraordinary (because there's *no way* that we could be below average). If we're told by experimenters that we did better than average on a test, we conclude that we're smart or skillful. But if we're told that we did poorly, we surmise that the test was unfair or excessively difficult, test conditions were bad, or we were just unlucky.

Even our ethics are subject to spin. When we behave immorally, we tend to attribute this to external conditions: "Everybody does it" or "I was just following orders." In group activities, when the outcome is positive, we overestimate our contribution; but when the outcome is negative, we underestimate it. (Which explains why it's easy to feel that our contribution to successful projects isn't acknowledged sufficiently.)

Here's a brief experiment from the data scientist Seth Stephens-Davidowitz you can try to see the pull toward deceiving ourselves and others. Just answer the following questions:

1. Have you ever cheated on an exam?
2. Have you ever fantasized about killing someone?
3. Were you tempted to lie on #1 or #2?

THE PRICE OF SELF-DECEPTION

These attempts to fool ourselves to keep our self-image intact are addictive—they feel good in the short run but exact a cost over time. They rob us of the honest self-assessment that we need to make informed choices about when and how to tackle challenges. They also keep us on guard and stressed, because our distorted judgments and opinions are constantly threatened by facts.

But perhaps the most painful cost of living in Lake Wobegon is what happens when our delusions collapse. Many of us flip from illusory superiority to harsh self-criticism. Rather than simply concluding that we're more like other people than we had supposed, we suffer a collapse and conclude that we're losers or failures, and feel ashamed, not fit to be part of the human family. This is made worse by messages we hear from others that being ordinary or average isn't good enough—we're all supposed to be special.

Getting out of the water

There's a surprising antidote to these habits. It involves realizing that we're all actually in the same boat, all struggling in the same ways, all lying to ourselves to various degrees—but don't have to. We can support one another in fighting back, by embracing our ordinariness and our membership in the human family.

We'll look at several ways to do this later, but for now you might try the following thought experiment. Since this exercise requires using your imagination and activating your loving wolf nature, it will be most effective if you prepare with a few minutes of mindfulness practice first. Just attend to your breath, notice what's happening in your body, and allow thoughts to come and go.

Exercise: Just an ordinary day

Imagine that you've woken up one day and the world has magically transformed. Today, we're all just part of the human family, and nobody is superior or inferior to anyone else. We're different shapes and sizes, of course, and have different skills and talents, but none of that makes us feel better or worse than others. There's no special advantage to being one way or another, since there's enough of everything to go around, everybody is inclined to share, and we're all lovable just as we are.

As you go about your business, you're savoring the present moment, not comparing yourself to others, but just enjoying their company. When there are tasks to be done, people all pitch in and are grateful for each other's help.

How do you feel as an ordinary person on this ordinary day?

What might you do today, in the real world, to make your day a bit less focused on self-evaluation or social comparison, and more focused on all pulling together for common goals? What might make you feel more connected to others, more part of the human family?

Deliberately making this shift helped Julian (the fellow at the end of the last chapter who felt empty in his corporate job) come alive again. In addition to focusing on connecting more to family and friends and taking up writing again, he committed to approaching his relationships with clients and coworkers differently. He deliberately thought before each encounter, "Do we have a common goal here?" "Is there a way I can share the wealth?" "How might I support my colleague?" "What will help my client feel more satisfied?" Often it didn't take much—sending an email highlighting someone's accomplishment, negotiating a contract that gave up a little profit today but nurtured a relationship. Making this shift not only made Julian feel more warmly connected to people at work, but it actually *increased* his success. Coworkers wanted to include him in new projects and clients sought him out.

Personally, I've come to love the practice of embracing ordinariness and common humanity. It's embarrassing to admit, but I got hooked on thinking I was special at an early age. I was a quick learner and soon got attached to the idea of being one of the smartest kids in the class. (In other ways I was pretty dense—I somehow didn't get that showing off for the teacher really pissed off everyone else.) At first it was fun, relatively effortless, and made my other insecurities go away. I imagined it made the teachers like me. But nobody stays on top for long, so I soon got stressed out trying to *stay* special. In fact, as I reflect on my life, angling to be the smart kid has been ridiculously stressful—tarnishing far too many encounters with competitiveness.

But when I'm able to recognize what a sad, crazy habit this has been and focus instead on being kind and supportive, joining others in our common goals, it's wonderful. Sometimes all I need is a moment to shift focus and notice what we have in common. Not only do I relax, but all my interactions become more playful—I get to really enjoy the other kids' company. And we have an easier time getting things done. Trust me, given my early training, if I can do this, anyone can. As we'll soon see, there are lots of approaches that work—we just need to experiment to find those best suited to each of us.

But as we go forward on this path, we'll face a number of obstacles. Some involve messages that pull in the other direction, reinforce our instincts to build ourselves up, hide our insecurities, or otherwise make us think we need to be special in some way to be loved or accepted. Some are as old as humanity, while others are more recent. One of the newer ones involves seeing everyone else's carefully curated successes and great times on social media. Facebook and Instagram are enough to stir feelings of envy, inadequacy, and alienation in anyone. Let's take a look at how these influences conspire to keep us trapped, whether they might be hooking you, and if so, how you might escape their grasp.

SIX

resisting selfie-esteem

WHAT DO GANG MEMBERS, pregnant teens, drug addicts, abusive parents, and unemployed workers have in common? According to psychologists in the 1980s, it was low self-esteem. In response, the forward-looking governor of California and members of the legislature created the California Task Force to Promote Self-Esteem and Personal Responsibility. The idea was that feeling good about yourself could be a kind of "social vaccine" that could prevent all sorts of problems. They even thought it might help balance the state budget, on the assumption that people with high self-regard earn more and would therefore pay more in taxes.

The project didn't exactly pan out as expected. After spending over a quarter of a million dollars, the task force found that associations between social ills and self-esteem were either mixed, insignificant, or entirely absent—and there was no scientific evidence that poor self-esteem actually caused *any* social problems.

But that didn't dampen the enthusiasm of the task force. They went on to recommend and implement all sorts of self-esteem enhancement programs. Then, as often happens, a trend that started in California eventually engulfed the nation and, to a lesser degree, the world.

Sadly, as we'll see, the net result of this has been to lock all of us ever more deeply into self-preoccupation and social comparison.

Everybody's doing it

By the early 1990s schools throughout the United States came to see positive self-regard as a prerequisite for learning. Parents were told, "Don't be afraid to tell your child over and over again how bright and talented they are." Schools offered courses called "Self-Science: The Subject Is Me" and gave out participation trophies. Thousands of schools adopted "building self-esteem" as part of their mission statement. And they haven't stopped. Searching Google for "school mission statement self-esteem," I just got 2,360,000 hits.

Sadly, the movement quickly expanded beyond schools to infect adults. Management consultants told entrepreneurs that they should create organizations where "everyone feels great about themselves," while farmers were told that there was one skill that would determine their success, and it wasn't information about "weeds, seeds, breeds, and feeds," it was knowing how to "develop and maintain a positive self-image."

Thousands of books today continue to promote good self-esteem (my Amazon search just returned over 100,000 titles). Whether it's little ones (*Be a Winner: A Self-Esteem Coloring & Activity Book*), adolescents (*Self-Esteem: The Teen Girl's Journey to Self-Worth, Body Image, Mr. Right, and Being Your Whole You*), or adults reaching for the top (*Ten Days to Self-Esteem: The Leader's Manual*), we're all being taught how to think highly about ourselves.

Too much of a good thing

Kim Jong-il, the late "dear leader" of North Korea, apparently had very high self-regard. His official biography states that he was born on top of the highest mountain in the country, a glacier opened to emit mysterious sounds, and a double rainbow appeared at the time of his birth. He learned to walk at 3 weeks, spoke by 8 weeks, and wrote 1,500 books as a university student. Stalin, Mao, Hitler, Idi Amin, and Saddam Hussein also claimed to be very special people, apparently thinking very highly of themselves.

There is a debate in the psychology field about exactly how

inflated self-regard works. Clinical psychologists assume that people who present exaggerated pictures of their worth or abilities are compensating for hidden doubts and injuries—using self-image boosts to ward off the pain of rejection, criticism, shame, or failure. That's certainly what seems to be going on in my own psyche when I'm trying to build myself up, and it's what I see in many of my patients. It's also not hard to notice that when we're able to connect in a safe, caring way to our underlying hurts and feelings of inadequacy, our need to puff ourselves up diminishes.

Social psychologists see it a bit differently. They create tests to reveal people's inner feelings, and the tests suggest that narcissists *really believe* they're better than everybody else. For example, on a test that reveals which words and images go together in our minds, narcissistic subjects hit the key for "me" readily in association with words like *good, wonderful, great,* and *right* (they don't, by the way, associate "me" as readily with words like *kind* or *compassionate*— more on this shortly). As a clinician, however, I suspect that the test isn't sensitive enough—it's just not detecting the hidden insecurity beneath the self-aggrandizement.

But it's also possible that there are different types of inflated self-evaluation. Some narcissistic folks may be compensating for underlying feelings of inadequacy, while others are just deluded. Either way, on objective measures, it turns out that people who think highly of themselves are no smarter, more attractive, or otherwise superior to those with lower self-regard—they just think they are.

The consequences of these delusions aren't pretty. Having high self-esteem doesn't necessarily lead to becoming a totalitarian dictator. But in children, it makes it more likely that they will be uninhibited, willing to disregard risks, and prone to engage in sex at a younger age. Bullies also tend to be surer of themselves and have less anxiety than other children. Adults with high self-esteem are no better. In video games designed by political scientists to simulate real-world geopolitical conflicts, the more certain players were of themselves, the more often they lost. Overconfident "leaders" often launched rash attacks leading to reprisals that were devastating for both camps (let this be a warning to us all when we step into the voting booth). We may be able to see these tendencies in our own hearts and minds with a bit of reflection:

Exercise: The benefits of humility

Take a few moments to recall a time when you were feeling pretty good about yourself. Maybe you had success at school or work or had a new romantic relationship. When you felt successful, did you notice yourself feeling superior to others who were less fortunate? Perhaps judgmental of others who had less success? It can be embarrassing to notice this, but many of us indeed get a bit colder when we're on top—a bit less aware of the suffering around us. If you recall such a reaction, please be nice to yourself about it. We're all vulnerable to becoming callous when we're on a self-evaluation high. But the next time it happens, see if you notice its cost.

Next consider the benefits of humility. Recall a time when your self-appraisal came down a notch. Maybe you failed at something, had a disappointment, suffered a rejection, or felt ashamed. While we can certainly get preoccupied with our pain and withdraw from others, sometimes our crash allows us to relate more compassionately to the suffering of those around us. See if you might take your next crash as such an opportunity—a chance to consider all the other people in the world who may be similarly in pain, feeling bad about themselves. Imagine reaching out to them, giving them a hug, and letting *them* know that *you* know how it feels.

As I expect you've gleaned by now, my own self-appraisals go up and down with remarkable regularity. And while I'm wired like everyone else to prefer the ups, I've come to notice that the downs are more valuable. When suffering from disappointments, I wake up and notice the suffering around me more vividly. I think, "I can't believe I'm feeling this bad about not being included on the project—it must really be hard for my friend who lost his job." Or "Here I am feeling sorry for myself that I pulled my calf and can't jog for a few weeks—how do all the people with serious disabilities or illnesses handle it?" Sadly, when I'm experiencing good fortune, just as the studies suggest, I'm less attuned to the suffering around me.

The take-home point? Instead of scrambling for a new boost right away, see if you might take a few moments to welcome your next disappointment as a chance to open your heart to everyone else who might also be hurting.

Seeking fame and fortune

OK, so perhaps enhancing self-esteem doesn't actually lead to success or to becoming a better person, but does it really make us unhappy? Probably, yes. There's growing evidence that Americans, at least, have become more materialistic, self-centered, and narcissistic (qualities research consistently shows contribute to unhappiness) since the proliferation of self-esteem enhancement programs. While correlation doesn't prove causation, rather than making us happier and more productive, the self-esteem movement might well be adding to our misery.

As we'll see, younger people have been affected the most by these developments. But whatever your age, as you read these next few pages, see if you notice any ways that you've been influenced by society's growing self-preoccupation—and try to identify where, and from whom, you may have gotten the message. Noticing this will help you ward off unhelpful impulses to build yourself up when they threaten to take over your heart and mind.

More than ever before, young adults are dreaming of winning the lottery, becoming influencers, and getting rich by age 30. They're increasingly believing that the path to well-being is through accumulating self-esteem boosts.

In one of the largest surveys of its type, the Pew Center for People and the Press reached out to hundreds of young adults, asking millennials, who were raised when the self-esteem movement took off, about their generation's goals in life. The results, and the contrast with the generation before (in parentheses), were striking: 81% (vs. 62%) said they wanted to get rich; 51% (vs. 29%) to be famous; but only 10% (vs. 33%) said they wanted to become more spiritual. The big increases belong to self-esteem boosts.

It's pretty grim on the other side of the Atlantic too. A poll in Great Britain asked teenagers what was "the very best thing in the world." Their top three answers were "being a celebrity," "good looks," and "being rich."

A historian at Cornell University went back and analyzed personal diaries over 100 years. In the 1890s, young women typically resolved to take more interest in others and refrain from focusing only on themselves. Their goals were to contribute to society, build character, and develop mutually fulfilling relationships. By the 1990s, their goals were to lose weight, find a new hairstyle, or buy new clothes, makeup, and accessories.

Sorry, these trends, whether or not definitively caused by the self-esteem movement, don't bode well for our collective future. But there's good reason to look at them. Our chances of breaking free from toxic messages that trap us in self-evaluative concerns are much improved if we can recognize them.

Mirror, mirror, on the wall—who is the fairest one of all?

At the same time that our goals have shifted toward wealth, fame, and external appearances, our opinions of ourselves have skyrocketed. This is the Lake Wobegon effect on steroids. In 1951, only 12% of 14- to 16-year-olds agreed with the statement "I am an important person." By 1989, 80% did. In 2012, 58% of high school students expected to go to graduate or professional school—twice the number in 1976. Yet the actual number attending remained unchanged at 9%. A full two-thirds of high school students expect themselves to be in the top 20% in job performance. Clearly a lot of people are going to be disappointed.

In some cultures, fitting in with the group is valued. Religious traditions worldwide point to the perils of thinking of yourself as better than others. This is definitely not the case in post-self-esteem-movement America. How many of us feel comfortable saying that we're "average" in ability? Perhaps we're OK being average in some areas, but only if we excel in others. This idea that "average" isn't good enough is a setup for misery—since we all can't always be at the head of the pack, and we recalibrate the scale regularly as we move up. And, as we'll see, it can rob us of the surprising joy of embracing our ordinariness.

How did this happen?

Social psychologists have made a cottage industry out of trying to explain these developments. In addition to the self-esteem enhancement movement, the emphasis on rugged individualism, particularly in America, has contributed. Being "true to yourself" and "looking out for number one" go hand in hand. In fact, the very idea that we all have a "genuine self" inside waiting to be discovered or reach its full potential is quintessentially American.

This contrasts sharply with some other cultures. Desmond Tutu, the South African theologian, says that in many African languages you can't answer the question "How are you?" in the first person singular. The answer is either "We're doing well" or "It's a difficult time for us." They're on to something: it turns out that being part of a "we" is actually a great antidote to worrying about being special or even good enough (more on this, too, shortly).

Comparing my inside to your outside

> Woke up this morning after another fitful night. Feel exhausted, have the runs, expecting a bad review from my boss. Girlfriend probably wants to break up with me. Discovered a bunch of new zits—despite the special new cream.

Not your typical social media post. Instead, on Facebook and Instagram everyone we've ever known is having a fantastic time in the Caribbean, eating great meals, getting promoted, looking gorgeous, and partying nonstop.

Google searches tell us more about people's *real* thoughts and feelings. You probably know that if you type a phrase into Google, it will attempt to complete it with the words most people type in next. Just now I tried "Is it normal to want to . . . ?" and Google returned (1) be alone, (2) kill, (3) be single, (4) cheat, (5) sleep all day. Following up on the second most common rejoinder, I typed "Is it normal to want to kill . . . ?" And Google returned (1) your boyfriend, (2) your ex, (3) cute things, (4) your brother, (5) your family.

On Facebook, the most common phrases people use to describe their husbands are "the best," "my best friend," "amazing," "the greatest," and "so cute." In anonymous Google searches, the most frequent words that people type along with "my husband" are "mean," "annoying," "a jerk," and "gay."

There are so many ways that we lie on social media to try to look good and feel good about ourselves that it's impossible to catalog them all. The highbrow *Atlantic* magazine and lowbrow *National Enquirer* have similar circulations and similar numbers of Google search inquiries. Yet the *Atlantic* has 27 times more Facebook likes. The most popular pornographic film on the web is apparently *Great Body, Great Sex, Great Blowjob*—with more than 80 million views. Yet it has only a few dozen Facebook likes, mostly by porn stars. All of this has led data scientist Seth Stephens-Davidowitz to conclude:

> In Facebook world, the average adult seems to be happily married, vacationing in the Caribbean, and perusing the *Atlantic*. In the real world, a lot of people are angry, on supermarket checkout lines, peeking at the *National Enquirer*, ignoring the phone calls from their spouse, whom they haven't slept with in years. . . .
>
> In Facebook world, a girlfriend posts twenty-six happy pictures from her getaway with her boyfriend. In the real world, immediately after posting this, she Googles "my boyfriend won't have sex with me." And, perhaps at the same time, the boyfriend watches "Great Body, Great Sex, Great Blowjob."

The net result of all this self-aggrandizing propaganda is we're all left feeling inadequate because we compare our actual experience to other people's curated social media presences. Combined with addicting us to self-evaluation boosts whenever we get a like or new follower, our time on Facebook or Instagram traps us ever more deeply in feeling like we're just not good enough—we're less successful than everybody else and missing out on all the fun. This naturally makes us even more desperate for boosts.

We long for the perfect selfie to post (which explains why *selfie* was the 2013 word of the year and my Google search today returned 10,100,000 videos about "how to take a great selfie"). Increased communication over Zoom and FaceTime has led to an explosion of *Zoom dysmorphia disorder*—people seeking cosmetic procedures to correct what they see as defects in their faces onscreen. And if you happen to be dating, you can enjoy your feelings about yourself going up and down all day long checking Match, Tinder, or Bumble.

Disturbing as all of these reactions are, they have a silver lining. If you're feeling inadequate comparing yourself on Facebook and Instagram to everyone you've ever known, worrying about your image on Zoom, or being stressed out visiting dating sites, you're not alone. It's not a sign of your inadequacy, but rather the natural result of modern technology colliding with our baser evolutionarily crafted primate nature. And we're all in this together.

Fortunately, there are antidotes to the social-media-intensified addiction to feeling good about ourselves, which we'll explore shortly. But for the time being, you might just try to be aware of the ups and downs that you experience perusing social media, and if you find that it's making you miserable, consider reducing your screen time. Also, every time your heart sinks because nobody liked your post, you see someone else's success, or someone didn't swipe right on a dating app, try taking a moment to reflect on all the other people in the world looking at social media experiencing similar pain this very moment. You may feel less alone.

Self-control, not self-esteem

Roy Baumeister, arguably the world's foremost researcher on self-esteem, concluded in a review of the scientific literature, "After all these years, I'm sorry to say, my recommendation is this: forget about self-esteem and concentrate more on self-control and self-discipline." The self-esteem movement seems to have backfired. Rather than creating a culture of contented, productive citizens, we've trained ourselves to expect that rewards will come without effort and to feel deeply disappointed and ashamed when our achievements don't match our (often inflated) expectations. Being "normal," "average," or, God forbid, "ordinary" feels like failure in a world where stardom, celebrity, and wealth get all the attention.

What can we do about our predicament? If we're involved in raising or educating children, we might think twice about trying to raise their self-regard. This doesn't mean never praising kids for their accomplishments. But it does mean trying to develop a new habit—emphasizing values such as working hard if you want to reach a goal, being considerate of others, and noticing that we all win some and lose some and have times when life goes our way and times when it doesn't. It also means addressing their hearts in a different way—soothing the pain of their disappointments by letting them know that we, too, feel bad when we don't succeed or get what we want. We might even try to inoculate them against the toxic aspects of social media, which not only addicts us to self-evaluation boosts but also sets us all up for endless comparisons between our insides and other people's advertising copy.

How can we keep these cultural influences from possessing us as adults? In addition to reconsidering the pursuit of high self-regard and reevaluating our relationship to social media, we can keep an eagle eye for all the messages we get that we should strive to be on top. The more clearly we see these messages, the more we have a chance to swim against the current. You might try this little thought-changing project over the next few days:

Exercise: Swimming against the current

As you go through your week, try to be aware of each time you find yourself getting caught up in messages that reinforce self-evaluative concerns. These might involve moments of praise, when other people tell you how wonderful you are. Or they may be moments of criticism or rejection, when other people don't seem approving or interested in you.

You might hear inner voices, like "I'm special, I deserve more" or the opposite, "I'm not good enough." Observe the feelings that arise with each judgment.

Note the times that you either feel ahead of the pack or like you're not keeping up. Try to be particularly attentive to assumptions you might carry about how competent, good, likable, or special you should be—in whatever realms matter to you. See if you can use disappointments, rejections, failures, or moments of shame to illuminate illusions about how you *should* be that trap you.

The more plainly we see these forces at work, the less we're likely to get caught by them. And the less we get caught by them, the happier and kinder we're likely to be—both to ourselves and to others.

Another way we can push back against demands to always be above average is to regularly remind ourselves that we're all in this together and embrace our common humanity. In this arena, it's nice to *not* feel so special and to know that we're not alone in our pain.

Of course, there are situations where something important is riding on competitive success and we need to do our best. But there are lots of other times when it really would be OK to be average, or just to enjoy the activity without judgment. How would your life be different if you didn't have to be special or above average in these moments? If you felt lovable and worthy just as you are, and didn't have to prove yourself? How would your life be different if you used your time and energy to follow your interests and focus on what really matters to you? Here's a little exercise to taste this joy of being ordinary.

Exercise: Choosing ordinariness

Bring to mind a few of the challenges you've faced over the past week. In which of these did you feel compelled to do especially well? In which did you try to be nicer, smarter, stronger, more generous, cleverer, funnier, more thorough, more attractive, or otherwise better than average? In which activities did you strive to live up to an inner image of how you *should* be?

What would've been the consequence of being ordinary or average in those situations? Would you have made less money, been less well liked, or otherwise missed out? Would that have really mattered, beyond a temporary dip in your feelings about yourself? Would you have been doomed to self-criticism?

Now focus on the activities in which, upon reflection, it clearly doesn't matter to have competitive success or meet some standard. Perhaps it's time with friends, being helpful to others, or pursuing an interest just for fun. Is it easier to be average, ordinary, or just good enough in those endeavors?

Finally, do you ever have moments of simple engagement—perhaps eating an ice-cream cone, watching a movie, or feeling the cool water on your body when swimming—when you're simply present without judgment? (The more comfortable we can be with ordinariness, the more frequent these become.)

In the coming days, allow yourself to notice all the situations when it might be just fine to be ordinary, to be exactly as you are, and try it out.

When Inna chose ordinariness, she stayed in on a Saturday night to clean her aquarium—a hobby that had brought her comfort and joy ever since she was a teenager. For Zev, it was playing catch with his kids and taking care of himself by going for a long run. Cindy spent an afternoon reading a novel. Ordinary people, freed up to enjoy doing ordinary things, not proving anything to themselves or others.

This approach can be a great antidote to the social media roller coaster. Antoine just turned 40 and was back in the online dating scene after breaking up with his boyfriend of the past 4 years. His feelings about himself were shifting wildly—an exciting guy would respond to him, and he'd feel like he was hot stuff; he'd be ghosted, and he felt the same way he did sitting home alone in the 9th grade. He'd see his ex post about doing something cool, and wanted to curl up into a ball and disappear.

The highs were great, but the lows were awful. "What's wrong with me?" "How come I don't have any confidence?" "Will I ever feel loved again?" He began to see how he'd been a specialness junkie his whole life, chasing after the feeling that he was better than others at sports, his job, being popular—pretty much everything. And clearly, in this dating world, it was impossible to win consistently.

So Antoine experimented with letting go of the fantasy of being special, of fulfilling some ideal. He experimented with letting his friends and family know how insecure he felt and tried to deliberately remind himself that he was just another struggling human being like everyone else. He got into the habit of asking himself, "What would I do now if I wasn't trying to prove myself?"—and doing it. The answers varied: going for a walk, straightening up his apartment, cooking dinner, calling a friend. While it made him feel vulnerable, he also started feeling warmer inside, less afraid of the next left-swipe rejection, more open, and more connected to his friends, family, colleagues, and even strangers. Maybe he didn't have to be a winner to be content.

We'll experiment with more ways to discover the joys of actively embracing our ordinariness in coming chapters. But first, let's turn our attention to some older social forces that can hold us back, keeping us stuck in self-evaluative concerns. These influences began long before the self-esteem movement and social media. A particularly pervasive and troublesome one, first named in 1899, has deep roots not only in humans but also in other species—even peacocks get trapped by it. Let's see if it ever hooks you.

SEVEN

conspicuous consumption and other status signals

We buy things we don't need with money we
don't have to impress people we don't like.
—WILL ROGERS

I FIRST LEARNED ABOUT luxury vehicles when I was 8 years old. Standing on our driveway in suburban Long Island, my father, always eager to teach, declared, "That's a Cadillac. It's a status symbol. People buy them to show other people that they're rich enough to afford them."

My dad was unusual. He had taught economics and looked at the world through a social scientist's eyes. So it seemed perfectly normal to us both for him to follow up with "In 1899 Thorstein Veblen wrote a book called *The Theory of the Leisure Class*. He was the first economist to use the term *conspicuous consumption*. Veblen noticed that once people have enough money to meet their material needs, they start to buy things just to show other people that they can buy them, in order to raise their social status."

It took me years to understand that this wasn't how most dads spoke to their 8-year-old kid. But I'm grateful for his insights. They're an inspiration for this book. While I certainly get hooked on all sorts of other social comparisons, my feelings about myself go up and down quite regularly, and I can feel rejected or ashamed as quickly as the next guy, at least the conspicuous consumption trap never really captured me. (Though this observation is bait for another trap: It's easy to see the folly of other people's self-image building blocks and feel quite sophisticated and aware because *I'm* not caught up in *those*.)

Conspicuous consumption is everywhere. Our brains are wired for it, and we're surrounded by advertisements that prey on our sense of who we are and how we want to be seen. As a result, millions of people spend beyond their means or get stuck working crazy hours, compelled to buy status symbols for themselves or their loved ones. Whether it's name-brand sneakers, designer handbags, trend-setting jeans, the latest iPhone, or luxury cars (Cadillacs no longer cut it— now you need a Jaguar, Porsche, or Lamborghini), conspicuous consumption is everywhere.

I'm particularly amused by the categories invented by airlines to capitalize on our status concerns. One day I was waiting to board a jet. They began with the first-class customers. OK, they paid a lot more for their seats, so they get to go on first. Next they invited the "Executive Platinum Plus" passengers to board, followed by plain old "Platinum," then "Gold," "Silver," and finally me—one of the remaining eight proletarians allowed to slink on to the plane at the end. Yes, the chances of holding on to carry-on bags are greater if you board sooner, but beyond this they were selling status—a feeling of privilege for loyal customers. The high-ranking passengers even got to line up in the *preferred* side of the gate area. Thank God, despite my lowly standing with the airline, I had a Preferred Rewards Platinum Honors debit card from my bank—so I could still show my face in public.

It's only natural

I once flew business class to Asia, and despite knowing better, I actually felt special for a few hours, all the while also feeling ridiculous for feeling special. Speaking of flying, I was comforted to learn that not only is conspicuous consumption universally human, but even birds get trapped in it.

Ever wonder why male peacocks have such enormous, colorful tail feathers? Growing those feathers requires a lot of biological resources, hinders the birds' movement, and attracts predators. So why did they evolve? How have giant feathers possibly contributed to peacock survival?

It turns out that the feathers are actually a form of conspicuous consumption. They signal to the peahens, "I'm so extraordinarily strong and healthy that I can afford to put all of these resources into my tail feathers and nevertheless survive."

The grey shrike, a bird that lives in the Negev Desert, is even more like us. Before breeding season, the males collect edible prey such as snails and useful objects like feathers and pieces of cloth—90 to 120 such items in total. They then hang them on thorns and branches in their territories to show off their wealth. Females scan the collections and choose males with the most impressive objects, avoiding the males without resources (no wonder the dating scene is so painful).

Why do we do it?

As with the peacocks and grey shrikes, our desire to communicate social standing through material displays is designed to help us pass along our DNA. Males show off, and females gravitate toward show-offs to enhance reproductive prospects. It's therefore not surprising that historically, fishermen told tales about fish they caught, male farmers bragged about the size of their vegetables, and male hunters boasted about the large animals they killed. (Unfortunately for our preoccupation with such things, growing gender equality hasn't freed us yet. In a recent study of over 3,000 subjects from 36 countries, women still placed a higher value on good financial prospects in choosing a mate, while men placed a higher value on appearance, whether or not they lived in a more gender-equal society where women had greater earning capacity.)

At least the fishermen, farmers, and hunters were showing off that they could provide needed resources. But many of our contemporary status symbols, like the peacock's feathers, signal our status or prowess precisely because they're so useless, wasteful, or rare that only the wealthy or powerful would have resources to spend on them.

My friend Gustavo grew up working class, was overweight as a kid, and for years felt that he just wasn't making it. When he finally started earning money in his 30s, he bought expensive clothes, got a sports car, hung out at trendy bars, and even befriended a celebrity or two. None of this alleviated his feelings of inadequacy for long. "I kept wanting fancier stuff and cooler vacations. It wasn't until I was spending a third of my salary on credit card interest that I knew I had to cut back—I felt like such a fool."

Gustavo got lucky when he hit 40. He started dating a woman who was engaging, psychologically attuned, and spiritually inclined. With her encouragement, he started meditating and getting more in touch with his emotions. It wasn't pretty at first. "I had so much sadness and shame left over from when I was a kid. I felt embarrassed about being poor, and as if that wasn't bad enough, fat." As he stopped trying to undo his pain with status symbols, he started to enjoy being more fully present. "For the first time in my life, I appreciated the simple stuff—the birds outside, evenings with friends, cooking at home instead of going out to some fancy place." He sold his sports car and got his finances in shape. "I feel like an idiot that I fell into the consumer trap. But I'm so glad I escaped." He and his girlfriend eventually married, quit their jobs, and now travel the world teaching meditation—happily living frugally while refraining from creating social media posts that would make their friends working in cubicles envious.

This isn't to say that we all need to sign up for voluntary simplicity to be content. It's possible to flourish at many different levels of consumption. But rich or poor, examining our relationship to what we buy and how we choose to live can help us act in a way that's not so focused on getting others to like us or enhancing our self-image.

The many faces of conspicuous consumption

On the other side of the coin, some of us, uncomfortable with the hierarchical nature of conspicuous consumption and wary of the influence of marketers, show off in other ways. We wear older, utilitarian clothes without fancy brand names, drive decidedly nonluxury cars, and don't want to be seen eating at a fancy restaurant or staying at an expensive hotel (this has been my adaptation—not a surprise given my early education). But these acts of *conspicuous frugality* also trap us in social comparison—we just flip the scale and get to feel superior to people who sport corporate logos.

You might want to try this little exercise to become more aware of both sides of the conspicuous consumption game.

Exercise: Recognizing conspicuous consumption (or frugality)

Take a moment to reflect on your spending habits. Have you ever had thoughts of how others might view you if you had a particular item of clothing, car, house, apartment, or other possession? What role have these thoughts played in your choices? Have you ever considered what others might think if you ate at a particular restaurant, stayed at a particular hotel, or went on a particular vacation? Have you ever worried that people would think you're not classy enough? Too extravagant? Too cheap? How do your spending decisions make you feel about yourself?

Have you ever felt comfortable, or even proud, showing off a possession or activity to one person, but felt ashamed of it in front of someone else?

Next let's examine the choices that have had the most emotional impact. In the first column below, make a list of things you've acquired or done that secretly (or not) made you feel good about yourself because they showed off your status, privilege, virtue, or talent in some way. (If you need more space, go to *giftofbeingordinary.com* or *guilford.com/siegel4-materials*.)

In the second column, note the feeling associated with the act, and in the third, what self-regard criterion (what attribute that matters to you) it involved.

Act of conspicuous consumption	Feeling	Self-regard area affected
1.		
2.		
3.		

Next list any choices you may have made to prove to others how *unhooked* you are on showing off, how especially free from status concerns you are (like driving an old car or eating at the local dive). Again, in the second column, note the feeling, and in the third, the self-regard criterion your choice touched.

Act of conspicuous frugality	Feeling	Self-regard area affected
1.		
2.		
3.		

Perhaps some of your choices are actually not tied to concerns about status. These are worth examining too—especially since they show us a path to freedom. When do you spend money motivated by other interests? What are the things you buy or do mostly because you enjoy their aesthetic beauty, usefulness, or how they enrich your life? Note these choices and the feelings they bring up.

	Purchases that don't affect self-regard	Feelings generated
1.		
2.		
3.		

From *The Extraordinary Gift of Being Ordinary* by Ronald D. Siegel. Copyright © 2022 Ronald D. Siegel. Published by The Guilford Press. Purchasers of this book can photo-copy and/or download enlarged versions of this material from *giftofbeingordinary.com* or *guilford.com/siegel4-materials*.

Personally, I was humbled doing this exercise. I noticed that, despite my father's early tutelage, a great many of my spending deci-sions are connected to self-evaluation concerns and land on the first two lists, though conspicuous frugality is more my thing. I even discovered that I'm capable of feeling good and bad about myself simultaneously, both for seeming too high and too low class (feeling cool and sophisticated because I've traveled somewhere while feel-ing ashamed about being so privileged). The more clearly I see my conspicuous consumption and conspicuous frugality, the less power they have and the freer I am to focus on other, more sensible reasons to buy (or not buy) things.

Class signaling

Social psychologists tell us that we make judgments about other people's social class within a few minutes of meeting them. Criteria change over time, but our signaling continues. A hundred years ago, affluent white people prized untanned skin to show that they didn't have to work in the fields; today they go to tanning parlors, risking melanoma to signal that they have the leisure time to be outside in the sun. Having big muscles once meant that you were a laborer; now it means you have the time, resources, and discipline to work out. How does social class enter into your self-image and the social comparisons you make?

Exercise: My social class autobiography

Try to recall the first time you became aware of your economic or social class—when you first noticed that other people had more or less than you or your family. (My earliest memory was when my mother went back to work as a teacher and my parents hired a housekeeper/nanny to watch me at home. She came and went on the bus, while we had a car. I felt uneasy about the difference.)

Now allow yourself to reflect on the later stages of your life and the times that social class distinctions brought up feelings. See if you can recall a few of the more poignant moments, whether you felt above or below others, more or less privileged, and your emotions in each circumstance. (I've felt uneasy in both positions—guilty and fearing envy in the higher position; afraid of being looked down on in the lower position.)

Now let yourself recall signals you may have sent out to hide or distort your social class (perhaps trying not to give away your position or trying to act at home when you felt out of place).

While we can't make class differences disappear, being mindful of our judgments and seeing how they influence our self-image can loosen their grip, making it easier to get along with one another.

The alternative, staying stuck in social class concerns, causes a lot of unnecessary suffering. In my career as a psychologist, I've seen many patients who grew up in economically disadvantaged families and through education or business success wound up surrounded by wealthier people. I've been struck by how enduring, and painful, their feeling of not fitting in, and being less-than, has been.

Joe's parents had a high school education, prized hard work, and saved to send him to a parochial school. He had a knack for

academics, worked hard, and eventually became a college admin-
istrator.

The problem was, while he loved the world of ideas, he felt
out of place socially. Most of the faculty, fellow administrators, and
students were from more privileged backgrounds, and he was always
noticing references he didn't recognize and mannerisms that set him
apart. He felt a twinge of shame each time, imagining they'd look
down on him if they knew where he came from—as though he was
an imposter, faking it.

After years of trying to fit in, Joe finally told a colleague, "You
know, my dad was a carpenter, and nobody else in my family went to
college. A lot of times I feel more comfortable with the maintenance
guys than with you people in administration." Finally saying it out
loud shifted his thinking. "Hell, I like the old neighborhood. You
can wear what you want and speak your mind. Nobody cares what
you do for work—you're welcome at the barbecue because you're a
neighbor." While he still can feel out of place, Joe has felt more comfortable at his job ever since, no longer feeling less-than.

Most of my patients who, like Joe, have found freedom in this
area started by acknowledging their discomfort. "I've always hated
writing—I'm afraid that I'll use the wrong word." "I can't stand
it when people talk about some book or play I've never heard of."
They also often feel better when they become more open about their
background. "I never heard that word growing up." "Yeah, I don't
think my parents ever went to the theater."

Of course, feeling comfortable with our origins or identity is
harder when we're exposed to pejorative comments or microaggres-
sions. They can involve social class, race, ethnicity, gender, nationality, sexual orientation—the list is long, and it can be important
to call these out. "You know, I feel put down when you talk about
working-class people that way." "That remark makes me uncomfortable." It's not that we don't differ from one another—it's the
belief and signaling that one class or group is *better* than another that
makes us miserable. Connecting with others who share one or more
of our identities, and exploring together the messages we've received
about those identities, can help begin to free us from assumptions
about superiority or inferiority.

"May you be very busy"

Some years ago, an anthropologist from Thailand was writing to his American colleague. He ended his letter with the line "May you be very busy." Confused, the American called his colleague to ask what he meant. The Thai professor explained, "It's my impression that in your culture, busyness is a sign of social status. Patients wait for the doctor, lawyers wait for the judge, vice-presidents wait for the CEO. I was just being nice, wishing you high status."

This leads us to another crazy area of status signaling. In modern life, complaining of busyness has become the quintessential humble brag. "How are you doing?" "Pretty good, but between all the TV interviews and meetings with world leaders, I just don't have enough time for my family."

I fall into this trap regularly. Afraid to miss out on some opportunity, I schedule too many professional engagements. This works pretty well to ward off self-evaluation collapses—temporarily. When I'm stressed out trying to get through my to-do list and don't have time to take care of everyday chores, I get to feel important. But like all self-aggrandizement, the good feeling doesn't last for long. Sooner or later a disappointment comes along and I crash—and notice that all my busyness has indeed kept me from having enough time with family and friends.

Check this out in your own experience. Do you ever feel important because you're busy? Because other people need or are expecting things from you? Because you don't have enough time for ordinary chores and pastimes? Do you ever feel less significant, or less important, when you have idle time? Being mindful of these patterns can make it easier to occasionally say "no" to new commitments and allow opportunities for more open space—so we can cultivate gratitude for the little things, make richer connections, and open to new experiences.

Human feathers

Why do clothes go in and out of style so often? How is it that we can instantly date a movie based on what the actors are wearing? And why do we spend so much time and money looking for the right outfit for one occasion or another?

While we need clothes to stay warm and dry, our choices in apparel clearly go beyond this. They have a lot to do with how we wish to appear to one another. We attract sexual partners, impress potential clients, customers, or employers, and even try to avoid persecution (if we're members of a marginalized group) with our choice of garments.

Not keeping up with the latest fashions can also signal that we're not chill, with it, or part of the in-crowd. Have you ever felt bad about being out of date? Ever feel insecure in your fashion choices, concerned about how others will judge you? Worried about whether you're overdressed or underdressed for an occasion? Legions of fashion consultants work first to threaten, and then help us avoid, embarrassment.

And then there are the trend-setters. Take hipsters, for example. They like to live in run-down neighborhoods, eat weird foods, and wear clothes that others think are gross—which on the surface doesn't look like a pathway to higher social status. The psychologist Steven Pinker offers some insight:

> Trend-setters are members of upper classes who adopt the styles of lower classes to differentiate themselves from middle classes, who wouldn't be caught dead in lower-class styles because they're the ones in danger of being mistaken for them. The style trickles downward, sending the hip off in search of a new form of outrage.

The take-home point is that none of us is immune to these concerns. The clothes we wear, places we live, foods we eat—virtually everything we do has status-signaling aspects. I doubt that it's possible to transcend this entirely. While monks and nuns get some freedom by wearing standardized outfits, and some schools give kids a break (financially and psychologically) by requiring uniforms, opportunities for class signaling are everywhere. Where and when do you do it? Here's a practice that can help you see.

Exercise: Looking under one another's clothes

The next time you go out in public, try to be mindful of all the ways in which you react to other people's status signals. Notice when you have positive judgments based on someone's appearance ("they're safe," "they're like me," "they're respectable," "they're important") or negative ones ("they're dangerous," "they're one of 'them,'" "they're disgusting"). Be kind to yourself—as we've been seeing, these sorts of judgments are very human (and even avian).

As soon as you notice the judgment, take a moment to reflect that this other person is a son or daughter, has had hopes and dreams, successes and failures, joys and sorrows, just like you. This is an ordinary human being, vulnerable, doing the best they can.

You can remind yourself of our common humanity whenever you find yourself involved in judging yourself or others based on appearances. It's a great antidote to dressing for success or trying to find just the right thing to wear.

Another approach is to purposely risk being judged negatively around appearance to see if it really matters (this isn't a good idea before a job interview or an important date but can be illuminating when the stakes are low):

When Pete was in middle school, he developed a bad case of acne. Other kids called him "pizza face," and he became withdrawn and depressed. In his teenage years, Pete responded by wearing the latest clothes and being impeccably groomed. Now middle-aged, acne long gone, Pete was stressed, spending a lot of his precious free time shopping for clothes, caring for them, and standing in front of the mirror each morning trying to look his best. He'd then wolf down breakfast, barely saying hello to his wife and kids before rushing off to work. His teenage daughter complained that she actually had to wait for *him* to get ready before school events. Something was wrong with this picture.

So Pete tried an experiment. On his days off, he deliberately went out unshaven, hair uncombed, wearing old clothes. At first it made him anxious—what would everyone think? But after a little while, he found that it didn't really matter. They still let him into the supermarket and hardware store. The other people were all thinking about themselves, and it didn't much matter what he looked like. It helped him become less fastidious and have more time to connect with his family. Now he could complain about waiting for his daughter to get ready instead of the other way around.

The divide grows

In the late 1800s, the industrialist J. P. Morgan said he'd never invest in a company where directors were paid more than six times the average wage of employees. By 1982, the average CEO in the United States made 42 times the average worker's income; more recently the CEO of JPMorgan Chase earned *395 times* the salary of a typical worker at his company.

What does this have to do with our struggles with self-image, social comparison, conspicuous consumption, and status symbols? As it turns out, when income differences are bigger, social distances become larger and social stratification plays a bigger role in our lives. When there's more inequality, we also feel less connected to one another, have less feeling of common humanity, and have more need to signal where we are in the hierarchy. This makes status symbols that much more important.

Things may be different in less individualistic cultures. Some years ago I was in the Kyoto, Japan, train station. I was about to ride the escalator when a man showed up in a neatly pressed white uniform with a matching white tool kit. He took out various brushes, cloths, and cleaning products and set to work—cleaning the escalator handrail. I had never seen a professional escalator handrail cleaner before.

While it's impossible to know what others are thinking or feeling, particularly when they're from a different culture, he behaved as though he felt dignified in his job and was dedicated to doing it well. Somehow, doing his part to keep the train station clean mattered.

Could we learn something from his attitude (at least as it appeared to me)? This little exercise can help us see how shifting our thoughts (heads) can change our hearts:

Exercise: Working with dignity

The next time you're doing a job that's not particularly fancy, where you start to feel resentful because doing it makes you feel less than others, try this. Whether it's cleaning a bathroom, filing papers, filling out forms, or whatever brings up the feeling, begin by just being mindful. Bring your attention to the sensations of the task. If it's the dishes, notice the sensations of the soapy water. If it's picking up trash, bring your attention to the bodily sensations of bending and carrying.

Then pause to reflect on the purpose of this job, of how it, in its own small way, is contributing to the greater good. See if you can shift your focus from what the job says about your value or status to how your work and your role at the moment might be benefiting your family, community, or the wider world.

Dalia had mixed feelings volunteering for the PTA. She wanted to support her kids' school and liked feeling part of the community, but hated doing menial tasks: "I didn't go to grad school to stuff envelopes." "I shouldn't be spending my time cleaning baking pans." She found herself thinking that other moms who had important jobs out in the working world weren't stuck doing these things. But then she'd remember that this was her choice and she was lucky to have the resources to be there for her kids.

So Dalia tried engaging more fully with the tasks at hand. She noticed her self-image concerns coming up but then reminded herself of what mattered most to her and chose to be guided by her values. "I practiced bringing my attention to the pans and washing them wholeheartedly." She reminded herself, "Everything's not about me. The point is to support my kids and the rest of the community. It's OK to not look so special." This approach felt a lot better.

Pushing back

It's not a surprise that when economic inequality increases, so does our concern with material success. Haul videos, where people show off the results of their latest shopping trips, are a big hit on You-Tube and Instagram. In a survey of American 18- to 23-year-olds, 91% indicated that they had no or only minor problems with mass consumerism. In another study, 93% of teenage girls reported that shopping was their favorite activity. And it's not just the kids. In America, many affluent people buy McMansions and drive giant SUVs—ready to take on all challengers on the way to the mall.

If we want to be happier and healthier, we need to push back against these trends. Studies show that when we focus on material values, we have more conflict with others, engage more in social comparisons, and are less likely to be motivated by the intrinsic joy of our activities. We have less compassion for others, poorer physical health, and fewer positive emotions like joy, enthusiasm, gratitude, and peace of mind. We're more anxious and depressed, have headaches and stomach trouble, experience less vitality, drink more alcohol, smoke more cigarettes, and watch more TV.

You wouldn't be reading this book if you didn't know from personal experience that feeling less than others is painful. A fascinating study bears this out: People were asked to imagine being in a poorer society where they'd be less well off than they are today but where they'd be one of the richer individuals. Fifty percent of subjects said that they'd trade up to half of their income to be better off than others. And there's the Russian story about a man whose neighbor has a goat. He encounters a genie who offers him one wish. After thinking for a moment, he says, "Kill my neighbor's goat." We need help!

Darwin to the rescue

Some 6–7 million years ago our evolutionary tree split and led to two species of ape: chimpanzees and bonobos. We're close to both genetically. Chimp troops are headed by a dominant male, based on size, strength, and his ability to form alliances. Following the pattern discussed in Chapter 2, dominance confers access to scarce resources. According to the primatologists Frans de Waal and Frans Lanting:

> Chimpanzees go through elaborate rituals in which one individual communicates its status to the other. Particularly between adult males, one male will literally grovel in the dust, uttering panting grunts, while the other stands bipedally performing a mild intimidation display to make clear who ranks above whom.

Bonobos, however, are different. They have less conflict between neighboring groups, females are at least as important as males, and dominance hierarchies are much less pronounced.

Bonobos are also big on sex. They engage in a lot of sexual activity, including mutual masturbation, in every combination of ages and sexes. They use sex not just for reproduction but to relieve tensions in situations that might otherwise cause conflict. As de Waal put it, "Sex is the glue of bonobo society." They're particularly enthusiastic about sexual activity during feeding time, when it apparently helps them avoid conflicts. Not surprisingly, bonobos are much better at cooperative tasks than chimps.

As you might expect, scientists have been very interested in the genetic differences between chimps and bonobos. It turns out that a lot of their behavioral differences seem to be related to a particular section of DNA that's important in regulation of social, sexual, and parenting behavior.

The good news is that humans actually have the bonobo rather than the chimp pattern. If only we can cultivate our cooperative rather than status-seeking impulses—to feed our inner compassionate wolf—we can become less concerned with status signaling, get along better, and feel less stressed, exhausted, and unhappy. We might even help save our planet in the process, since status-seeking conspicuous consumption wastes precious resources and increases our carbon footprint.

How might we cultivate our bonobo nature? We've touched on a number of approaches in this chapter. Yet another way to relax our status judgments—including those signaled through conspicuous consumption—is based on an observation by Ram Dass, the

Harvard research psychologist who became a well-known spiritual teacher:

Exercise: We're like trees

When we walk in the woods, we see all sorts of trees. Some are tall, some short, some bent, others straight. Some are rotting on the ground, some are just beginning to grow. We understand that each tree is the way it is because of all sorts of factors—it didn't get enough light, it's old, the seed landed in a clearing. We appreciate the tree, and the forest, just the way it is, without a lot of comparative judgments.

But the minute we get near humans, we lose this perspective. We launch into "You're too this," "I'm too that," "You're better," "I'm better." We compare ourselves to others, judging both ourselves and others as good or bad, superior or inferior.

Begin by closing your eyes for a few moments and attend to your breath. Once the mind has settled a bit, recall a time when you took a walk in the forest. Remember the sights, sounds, and smells. Notice your acceptance of the diversity of plant and animal life. Feel your nonjudgmental equanimity.

Next take a moment to consider how we're all a lot like the trees. We were all brought here on the tide of evolution. The randomness of our birth, our genetics, cultural influences, our good and bad fortune in life, have shaped each of us to be who we are. From this perspective, the way we are, and what we do, isn't to anyone's credit or fault.

See if you can renew this attitude as you encounter other people throughout your day. When judgments arise in the mind, just ask yourself, "How might this person have come to be as they are?" "Would I judge a tree in the forest the same way?"

We can find freedom from the tyranny of social comparison and the struggle to measure up that goes with it by catching ourselves in the act of signaling status and judging others, and by deliberately shifting our focus to notice our commonalities. Since we all get hooked by different sorts of comparisons, being mindful of our judgments can help us see and address the ones that most activate us. And tapping our capacity for compassion, we can, like the happy bonobos, substitute connection for competition.

But letting go of our judgments can be hard, in part because it is so easy to get addicted to feeling good about ourselves—including by feeling superior to others. We naturally crave the ups because they're so much more pleasant than the downs. Fortunately, as we'll see in the next chapter, there are proven methods to overcome addictions that can help us break free from even this one.

EIGHT

treating our self-esteem addiction

Quitting smoking is easy; I've done
it hundreds of times.
—MARK TWAIN

HAVE YOU EVER SEEN a sea slug? Some are very pretty, in a
giant-snail-without-its-shell sort of way. But they're not very smart.
They only have about 20,000 nerve cells, compared to the 100 billion
or so in humans. Yet they're still smart enough to become addicts.

An organism's capacity for addiction is based on the most basic
of learning principles. It all starts with liking one experience more
than another. Even bacteria have this down—they'll move toward
a nutrient and away from a toxin. But to develop an addiction, we
need another faculty—memory. To create a habit, we need to be able
to recall, "The last time I did that it felt good [or bad]." Then, for
a habit to be an addiction rather than just any old learned behavior,
we need one more element: It has to feel good in the short run but
bad in the long run.

As we've seen in one arena after another, self-esteem boosts fit
the addictive pattern perfectly. Whether it's getting likes on social
media, buying that new car, having our team win, falling in love,
or thinking we're a saint, we feel great—briefly. But soon we either
habituate to our new status, slip down a rung, or become exhausted
trying to keep from slipping. What's the solution? It's finding another
boost, of course! Ad infinitum.

Fortunately, as with other addictions, there's a way out. You've been working on the first step—becoming aware of all the ways you might get caught up in trying to feel good, and avoid feeling bad, about yourself. Hopefully, the preceding chapters have also given you a glimmering of how it might feel to break free. The next step is to use what we know about addictions to further extricate ourselves from our self-judgment habit.

Learning to behave

A basic principle of animal learning has been known for well over 100 years: If a behavior is followed by a pleasant experience, an animal will tend to repeat it; if followed by an unpleasant experience, it will be avoided.

As cognitively sophisticated *Homo sapiens sapiens* ("who know that they know" or "wise humans"), you might think that this wouldn't be compelling to us—but you'd be wrong. We can be conditioned through animal learning to do almost anything, often unknowingly (turns out we're not so *sapiens* after all).

Getting hooked

Remember the exercise in Chapter 1 where I invited you to recall a self-evaluation high and then a collapse and notice how each felt in the body? The boost sure feels a lot better than the collapse. This situation, in which one feeling is so much better than another, is the perfect medium in which to grow an addiction.

Scientists have been working out how this operates neurobiologically for decades. As far back as the 1950s, James Olds and Peter Milner of McGill University planted electrodes in the septal regions deep within rats' brains. They crafted an experiment in which the rats could send a little electricity to this region by pressing a lever. The rats quickly learned to do this enthusiastically, as often as 2,000 times per hour, presumably because it felt so good. They craved this self-stimulation so much that they pressed the lever to the exclusion of eating and had to be disconnected from the device to prevent death from starvation.

Researchers later discovered that the neurotransmitter *dopamine* is released into a related reward center, the nucleus accumbens, in response to all sorts of addictive behavior—from romantic love to taking drugs like amphetamines, cocaine, and morphine. The area is also activated by positive reinforcements such as food, water, sex, and, of particular interest here, *self-esteem boosts.*

Wanting to be "in"

Anything we rely on to feel good about ourselves can become an addictive trap. But perhaps our most potent booster, and the one that arguably addicts us more than any other, is being liked, admired, or respected. Our wish for others to think highly of us is biologically based. We're social animals. It was a death sentence to be all alone in prehistoric times, and as young children we need to be cared for by adults to survive. Our powerful, universal desire to be loved stems from these basic needs. On top of this, more resources, as well as opportunities for reproductive success, generally flow to popular individuals. Our hunger to be seen positively by others, as well as to feel loved, runs deep and starts early.

Psychologists find that by age 4 children can reliably identify their most popular peers. By high school many of us sat in a cafeteria organized by popularity and barely spoke to, much less dated, anyone outside of our crowd. As one kid put it recently, "If you're popular, if everyone is talking about you, you can go out with whoever you want. You can be friends with anyone. It just, like, feels good."

According to social psychologists, there are two paths to popularity. One involves status: being well known, emulated, having power, and being well endowed in whatever dimension matters to the group. For younger kids, this might mean being physically strong, athletically talented, pretty, funny, gutsy, smart, or wealthy (having a backyard pool or motorbike can do wonders). For adolescents, these markers don't go away, but we add being sexy, daring, having sexual conquests, dating a high-status girl or boy, or occupying a leadership position (think captain of the football team).

The other way to be popular is by being *likable.* This involves being kind, trustworthy, and pleasant to be around. Likable kids (and adults) ask questions of others, have a sense of humor, behave fairly; are generally happy, polite, and patient; and are good at sharing. To add to our "adolescence can be hell" theme, likability matters much more for younger kids than it does for teens, when status becomes more important.

Yet researchers find that people who seek external rewards such as fame, power, wealth, and beauty in pursuit of popularity have more anxiety, depression, and discontent—long-term pain. Those who seek close, caring relationships, pursue personal growth, and enjoy helping others—intrinsic rewards and qualities associated with likability—tend to be happier and physically healthier. There's an important message here: There's a way to be "in" without being "above." It's called authentic connection, and it's one of the gifts of being ordinary.

Popularity on steroids

Being chosen for the school play or varsity team, hanging out with the cool kids, and having a hot boyfriend or girlfriend all feel great. Being rejected for the play or team and not being able to get a date all feel horrible. It's not a surprise that even a little social success or popularity can hook us.

And now, after centuries of addicting ourselves to popularity with conventional means, we humans have access to a superpowerful, concentrated, short-lasting, extremely addictive path to feeling popular—that reliably makes us miserable in the long run. We call it *social media*.

You may know the story: In the early 2000s a sophomore at Harvard wrote the software for a site called Facemash. Using photos of undergraduate students available through the university's computer system, he posted pairs of pictures and asked users to choose the "hotter" person. The site attracted 450 visitors and 22,000 photo views in its first 4 hours online. It took a few days for the Harvard administration to shut it down and compile charges to expel its creator, Mark Zuckerberg. Facebook was born.

While social media may indeed help connect us with one another, its most addictive attribute is its effect on our feelings about ourselves. Some 3.6 billion people spend hours liking other people's posts on Facebook, Instagram, and YouTube. Zuckerberg recognized early on that people will quickly become addicted to receiving likes and that this could be parlayed into a multibillion-dollar business.

Because it's so easy to replicate the experience of social media in the laboratory, there's been an explosion of research into the brain activity of users. For example, in 2016, psychologists at UCLA examined teen brains while they viewed a simulated Instagram feed. It consisted of pictures that the subjects had submitted along with pictures from "peers" that were actually provided by the researchers, with random numbers of likes attached.

How did adolescent brains respond to their photos being liked? With activation of the nucleus accumbens (the same reward center activated by cocaine or sex) as well as an area that lights up when we're thinking about ourselves in relation to others. As one kid said when asked why a successful social media presence is so important, "It's like being famous. . . . It's cool. Everyone knows you, and you are, like, the most important person in the school."

How does this, like other addictions, make us miserable in the long run? Spending time pursuing likes for Photoshopped depictions of our lives, from people we may never have met, indeed gives us a sugar high. But it can also leave us lonely, robbing us of opportunities for genuine connection to real people, of the chance to love and be loved.

Recovering from self-evaluation addiction

Successful addiction recovery programs typically begin with *recognizing the problem*. This often is not easy. Alcoholics who socialize with other alcoholics may not see their drinking as excessive, and political junkies (like me) may think spending evenings watching cable news is just staying well informed. Similarly, those of us who are addicted to self-evaluation boosts (that is, *pretty much everyone*) may not see the suffering it's causing. We're like fish in water. After all, everyone else is checking their phones all day long (96 times for the average American).

Every time we get notification of a post, text, or email we get a little activated. Will this be news that makes me feel good about myself and well-liked—or another disappointment? Social media just wouldn't be as engaging without the chance to amass likes, friends, and followers. The problem is that each time we get positive attention, we become that much more addicted to boosts. The dopamine "squirt" that activates our nucleus accumbens sets us up to crave more.

Recognizing our addiction

How might we see our addictions more clearly? The exercises in earlier chapters can help. *What Matters to Me?* and *Riding the Self-Evaluation Roller Coaster* in Chapter 1, along with the invitation to examine your own inner primate in Chapter 2, can help us see the particulars and pervasiveness of our self-evaluative concerns. Practicing mindfulness and directing it to our self-judgments, as in *Mindfully Riding the Self-Evaluation Roller Coaster* in Chapter 3, can refine our attention to them, while *Identifying Emotions in the Body* in Chapter 4 can help us tune in to the feelings associated with each high and low. If you haven't already tried these exercises, you might want to go back and see what you discover. Exploring the evanescence of success, the crazy messages we get from our culture, and the pull of conspicuous consumption (Chapters 5–7) can all help us see our particular addictions more clearly. We need to have clear heads and open hearts to develop helpful habits.

It also helps to understand how addictive habits develop. Repetition plays a role. There's a nice metaphor for this process that lines up well with modern neurobiology. It comes from a talk the Buddha gave 2,500 years ago:

> Imagine a chariot driver heading across a dusty plain. On the first trip, the chariot creates grooves in the dirt. This makes it a little more likely that the next time across, the chariot will follow the same path. If it does, the grooves will deepen and start to become a rut. It then becomes even more likely that the chariot will follow the same course on subsequent trips.

Habit formation works like the chariot metaphor, but with a few important twists, each of which predisposes us to get hooked on self-evaluation boosts. First, if a behavior is met with pleasure or relief from pain, the grooves deepen rapidly (and feeling positively about ourselves feels really good). Second, if we've inherited instincts that predispose us toward the behavior, the grooves will deepen with very little practice (and we're biologically inclined to want to raise our status or be liked). Finally, intermittent, unpredictable rewards, like slot-machine payouts, make the grooves particularly durable (and self-esteem boosts tend to be intermittent).

While it's therefore going to be challenging to let go of the boosts, the good news is that, like other addictions, it's possible to break free.

Working with triggers

Effective addiction treatments for everything from cigarette smoking to gambling use the same basic approaches. After acknowledging the problem, the next step is identifying the triggers that lead to the troublesome behavior and seeing if we might limit our exposure to them.

What might this look like for addiction to positive self-evaluations? It depends on our particular triggers. Sometimes we want a boost immediately after suffering a disappointment, feeling rejected or ashamed, or failing at something. There's no way to avoid these moments, but we don't have to deliberately expose ourselves to opportunities for self-judgment.

Exercise: Limiting exposure to self-evaluation triggers

We've seen how social media gets our comparing mind going, and how we often feel our self-esteem rising or falling each time we go online. When our neurons squirt dopamine, we feel really good—for the moment. To keep the addictive grooves from deepening, we might try to limit our Facebook, Instagram, or dating site checking to once a day and look for texts and email every hour rather than every few seconds. Have you sent out an Evite for a party? See if you can only check for responses when you actually need to know how many people are coming.

We can try the same for other traps. If your appraisal of yourself rises and falls every time you get on the scale, you might want to limit weight checks to once a week. Find yourself looking in the mirror to check your hair or outfit all day long? Try doing it only in the morning. If you've got a business, try to refrain from monitoring sales figures hourly.

As in other addictions, sometimes we decide to limit our checking but find ourselves doing it anyway. It's just too tempting. After all, self-esteem boosts can immediately erase, temporarily, the pain of crashes. I can't count the number of times I felt defeated or inadequate until some victory, affirmation, or sign of affection came along and wiped away my ache. Seeking self-esteem highs is such a perfect storm of hardwired instinct and learned behavior that we often need help to tolerate, rather than act on, our craving.

Alan Marlatt, an addictions specialist at the University of Washington in Seattle, invented a great practice for this called urge surfing. He noted that whenever we have an impulse toward some action, we feel it in the body as a set of sensations. The sensations of an urge are actually distinct from whatever triggers them. So, for instance, we might first feel hunger in the belly and then feel the urge to go to the fridge as a physical tension, perhaps in the chest, shoulders, or another area. We all feel urges in different ways, but they usually have a sensory, physical component.

Urge surfing involves mindfully focusing our attention on wherever in our body we feel an urge to do something. We discover that urges are like waves. They build, reach a crescendo, and then subside for a bit. The more consciously we can observe this, the more freedom we develop to choose whether or not to act on the urge.

You can experiment with urge surfing whenever you feel the impulse to check your phone yet again for texts or email, see if there are new developments on social media, monitor sales numbers, or do anything else in pursuit of a self-evaluation lift. It's a great little habit-shifting exercise:

Exercise: Urge surfing*

Close your eyes and connect with the breath. As you breathe, notice the sensations in the body—where there might be tension or discomfort and where there's comfort or ease.

Next recall a recent situation where you wanted to check your phone, tablet, or computer for something to make you feel better about yourself. Perhaps you were worried about missing out, maybe you were wondering how a project was going, wanted to see if your team was winning, or you felt that you needed to respond to a text or an email immediately to remain in someone's good graces.

Stay with that urge to check and pause right before the feeling peaks, right before you grab the device. Stay with that wave of desire. Feel it in your body. Try to stay balanced at that edge. Breathe and lovingly relax into the experience.

Be aware of the physical sensation. Put your hand over the area where you feel it. Do you notice tension, pressure, or another sensation? Does it include fear? How much space does the sensation occupy? Breathe along with the urge. Let your breath comfort you. If the urge starts to feel too intense, just bring your attention back to the breath for a few cycles.

Notice how if you stay with the urge to check your device, it may increase in intensity. See if you can stay with the wave rather than fighting it or acting on it. Just lovingly ride the wave of your experience.

Use your breath as a surfboard to keep yourself steady. Know that the waves will come and go, rise and fall. You can't control the waves, but you can learn to surf. See if you can ride your desire to check your device.

Finally, reflect for a moment on how you would like to spend your time instead of checking your phone, tablet, or computer to feel better about yourself.

See if you can use urge surfing throughout your day not only to limit addicting screen time but to feel less compelled to do things to feel good about yourself generally.

Megan was a 32-year-old graphic designer being driven crazy

---

*Adapted from *Reclaim Your Brain* by Susan Pollak. Audio available at *giftofbeingordinary.com* and *guilford.com/siegel4-materials*.

by Internet dating. She had broken up with her girlfriend 9 months earlier, felt ready to date again, but didn't like bars, worked mostly at home, and had no natural places to meet other women. She tried Match.com. What a roller coaster! Every time an interesting woman made contact, her mood soared. Full of confidence and optimism, she thought, "This is great. I'm fun. I'm attractive. I'm sure I'll be in a relationship again soon." But when things got quiet, or a date ghosted her, her spirits sank. "I'm over the hill. I'll never have a family of my own. I'm too fat." Her mood sometimes rose and fell several times a day, and she felt driven to keep checking. She was desperate for good news, but as with a slot machine, got payouts only intermittently.

It took time and effort, but Megan eventually used urge surfing to feel the regular urges to check Match, allowing most of them to come and go without acting on them. She decided to respond to messages only once a day, after work, before going to the gym. Working out helped put the good or bad feelings into perspective, and she could ground herself in the positive feeling of taking care of herself instead of being wholly dependent on boosts from social media.

While limiting exposure to triggers can help with any addiction, it has limitations. In the realm of self-evaluation, unless you're a hermit on a desert island, triggers are *everywhere*. Every time we come into contact with another person, or tackle some task, the mind starts making judgments. Luckily, there are other approaches to addiction treatment we can also use.

Befriending pain

Interrupting the addictive sequence anywhere in the chain from stimulus to reinforcement can help. Many of us notice that we're particularly driven to seek self-evaluation boosts when we've just suffered a disappointment: a friend seemed distant, our child messed up again, we felt guilty that we didn't return a call. If we can become adept at *being with* the discomfort of these disappointments—strengthening our heart's capacity to open to hurt—then we won't be so desperate for another boost to escape the painful feeling.

Remember the practice of directing our attention to an itch or an ache during mindfulness practice in Chapter 3? How turning attention to discomfort, being with it, and noticing that it changes over time makes it easier to tolerate? We can do the same with the bodily sensations when we feel bad about ourselves. I invite you to try this as a meditation practice—it can help fortify you to deal with your next crash. Try to give yourself around 15–20 minutes.

Exercise: Embracing a self-esteem injury*

Find an alert and dignified posture, with the spine more or less erect, and gently bring your attention to the sensations of the inbreath and the outbreath. Try to follow the sensations of breathing through complete cycles. Allow thoughts to arise and pass, gently and lovingly returning your attention to the breath whenever it strays.

Next allow yourself to recall a recent time when you felt bad about yourself—perhaps a moment of failure, shame, or rejection. It's best to start with something moderate and not too overwhelming. Notice how the disappointment feels in the body. Place your hand over the area of discomfort in a caring, loving way.

Now just breathe with, or into, the physical sensations. We're not trying to make them go away, but rather to increase our capacity to *simply feel* the sensations. Try to approach the sensations with kindness, with an attitude of "It's OK, sweetheart—we all fall down regularly."

If you notice aversion responses arising—"I hate this"; "When will this stop?"; "This is a dumb exercise"—just allow those thoughts to come and go, gently returning your attention to the bodily sensations of the injury or disappointment.

If the discomfort fades, try to ramp it back up a little. Perhaps you'll need to recall another injury, or perhaps just recall the first one in greater detail. The idea is to maintain the discomfort throughout the exercise so that you can develop confidence in your capacity to be with it while being kind to yourself.

---

*Audio available at *giftofbeingordinary.com* and *guilford.com/siegel4-materials*.

Many people find when they try this exercise that initially they have a strong aversion response to the emotional pain—after all, we're hardwired to want to come out ahead in social comparisons, be liked, and otherwise feel good about ourselves. You might have an impulse to seek a new boost to make the feeling go away. But if you practice this exercise regularly, you'll get to see that the pain of a collapse really is, like other emotions, a set of physical sensations accompanied by thoughts and/or images. Surprisingly, when we open to the sensations without resistance, they tend to transform and we might even need some effort to ramp them up again.

Isabella was in her first real job after college, leasing commercial real estate. She had passed her tests but was full of self-doubt whenever a deal fell through. "I shouldn't have pushed him so hard." "I should've known the owner wouldn't go for that build-out." But she was resilient, and a few minutes after getting the bad news she was back working on the next deal. All this kept her very stressed, however, feeling desperate for the next success.

So Isabella tried seeing if, before jumping back onto the horse, she could tolerate being with her feelings of failure for a little while. It was hard at first. "I was afraid I'd give up if I didn't get right back to work. And I really wanted to get the sinking feeling in my stomach to stop." But when she took a few minutes to just be with the sensations of hurt, be kind to herself, and remind herself that we all have plenty of failures and disappointments in life, she could relax a bit. In fact, she found that by taking a little time to mourn her loss, she actually returned to her work with a clearer head and a less desperate attitude. Reflecting on her pain also helped her to see which building blocks of self-esteem were hooking her. "I guess I really want to be the most successful kid in the class." "I want everyone to think I'm a great worker."

The more courageous we can be about feeling the pain of shame, failure, or rejection, and the kinder we can be toward ourselves in the process, the less compelled we become to engineer another boost to erase our pain. In the coming chapters we'll explore other exercises that can help with this, including different ways to be loving toward ourselves when we're suffering and ways to use today's wounds and disappointments to heal past hurts.

Nontoxic pleasures

Breaking free of our self-esteem addiction requires the full three-*H* effort: working with our heads, hearts, and habits. We've talked about reducing exposure to triggers, learning to tolerate injuries, and surfing our urges to act on cravings as ways to break free of addictive loops. Yet another useful approach is to dig new, more wholesome grooves in the dusty plain—to practice alternatives to our addictive behavior that have more positive consequences.

If you're in the habit of medicating the day's disappointments with alcohol, you might try taking a walk in the park, going to yoga, meditating, or visiting a friend. If your poison is cookies, you might try to develop a fruit habit. If you're struggling with cigarettes, you might try chewing gum. Should you feel compelled to check for likes on Facebook or Instagram, call a friend or hang out with your family. This is what Megan was doing when she went to the gym after checking Match—finding a more sustainable path to well-being than waiting for a new date to make her feel better.

Why don't we naturally turn to these sorts of pleasures in the first place? Why do we so often head for the addictive behavior instead? Here again, it's our biological predispositions at work.

There seem to be at least two types of happiness. One is the happiness of excitement—the rush of dopamine flooding the nucleus accumbens, adrenaline flowing through our veins. This is the happiness that comes from recreational drugs, alcohol, romantic love, wild adventures, sex, and self-evaluative boosts of all sorts. It can be great fun and may not have any downsides. It's pleasure based and is called *hedonia* by psychologists.

The other form of happiness, *eudaimonia,* involves a deeper satisfaction with life. It's a state of well-being, meaning, and gratification, rather than a feeling of immediate pleasure. We experience eudaimonia when we hold a sick friend's hand, appreciate a flower, or feel awe entering a church or temple—not an exciting high, but a deeply meaningful moment. It's the happiness that flows from embracing our ordinariness.

Many nontoxic alternatives to addictive behavior foster this latter form of happiness. They lead to contentment more than excitement and come from doing what matters most to us, guided by our values. Interestingly, the Buddha (apparently an early addictions treatment specialist) spoke about these two forms of happiness. He said, "What others call happiness, that the Noble [Awakened] Ones declare to be suffering. What others call suffering, that the Noble Ones have found to be happiness." He suggested, based on his personal experience with mindfulness and related practices, that the peace and contentment that come from being present, engaging fully in experiences here and now—whether pleasant or unpleasant—turn out to be more fulfilling in the long run than seeking pleasure.

Because hedonic happiness is relatively easy to come by (it's ever available in the fridge or on our devices) and is so readily addictive, it's very easy to get caught up in it. This isn't to say there's anything wrong with great sex, ice cream, having a drink, winning the lottery, or getting an A on our report card. There's no need to become an ascetic. It's just that if we're not attentive, pursuing hedonic happiness to the exclusion of other kinds can leave us less content in the long run. Just as we might, if they've become problematic, want to develop substitute habits for beer, cookies, or cigarettes, it can be helpful to do this for self-esteem boosts.

One particularly effective substitute is savoring the present moment. To the degree that we can use our mindfulness practice to step out of the thought stream and develop some higher-resolution consciousness, we'll tend to engage more fully in the here and now, feeling gratification and fulfillment without needing to think highly of ourselves. This can involve everything from enjoying the taste of an apple to communing with nature or God (being wary of the "look how spiritual I am" judgment that's just another dopamine squirt).

Then there's the transformative magic of human connection— perhaps our most powerful antidote to the addictive pursuit of self-esteem. Connected relationships reliably bring physical and mental well-being while dramatically lessening our concerns with social comparison and popularity. They're a rich, fulfilling, meaningful alternative to self-preoccupation, available to ordinary folks. And the great news is that they're not that hard to cultivate.

PART IV

Breaking Free

FINDING TRUSTWORTHY PATHS TO HAPPINESS

NINE

make a connection, not an impression

> You can make more friends in two months by becoming interested in other people than you can in two years by trying to get other people interested in you.
>
> —DALE CARNEGIE

WHEN WAS THE LAST time you really lost it, felt out of control? Got so upset that your thinking went off-line? Chances are it happened in a relationship, when someone said or did something that made you feel hurt, angry, or scared.

When was the last time you felt really safe, loved, warm, and fulfilled—not concerned with how you looked, whether you were a good person, or whether you were a success or failure, well liked or not? Chances are that *also* happened in a relationship, when you connected deeply with someone.

Relationships are where self-esteem injuries hurt the most and where our attempts to keep up our self-image get the nuttiest. But they can also save us from the self-evaluation roller coaster and be our path to a meaningful life. It all depends on the types of relationships we pursue.

Wired for love

Our need for connection runs deep. Fundamentally, we all want to feel loved and safe. It was downright dangerous to be thrown out of the tribe on the African savanna, and as babies, if we're not connected to caregivers who respond to our needs, we're toast. While psychologists used to focus on how to foster autonomy and independence, the science now points clearly to safe social connection as far more important for lifelong well-being. It's the central ingredient in successful parenting, as well as the secret sauce in therapy, predicting good outcomes much more robustly than anything else. It's so central to our well-being that our nervous system evolved pathways by which safe social connection can quiet our stress response.

Life is often hard, but as the Turkish proverb says, "No road is long with good company." How might we develop the sorts of connected relationships that help us feel warm and content, give life meaning, and make our journey easier? How might we transform the relationships that make us insane? Let's start by looking at what fuels the crazy ones.

Romance: Rocket fuel for self-esteem

Do you remember your first taste of passionate, romantic love? Remember that first touch or kiss? Remember feeling like you couldn't wait for the next phone call, text, or date?

What fueled the magic? How it is that despite otherwise living in a nuanced and complicated world, where we like and dislike all sorts of things about most other people, when it comes to romance another person can suddenly be perfect? How does everything about that person—hair, hands, feet, laugh, smile, and personality— become so wonderful?

While romantic enthusiasm undoubtedly helped our ancestors mate, which was important for the survival of our species, a powerful element in intense romantic love is its effect on our self-appraisal. Here's how this works: If I see you as valuable and desirable (you're attractive, cool, smart, sexy, rich, trustworthy, kind, funny, or in some other way special), and you want *me*, then *I* must be pretty great myself. All of my emotional injuries and insecurities from childhood onward are suddenly wiped out. I'm no longer a dorky kid being picked last for the team in gym, sitting alone in the cafeteria, or stuck home alone on a Saturday night. If you're great, and you think I'm great, my self-evaluation woes are over.

This worked like a charm for Joey. He had a pretty good childhood, was successful at school, and had loving parents. But around puberty it became clear that something was wrong. All the other kids were having a growth spurt, and he wasn't. Before long he became the shortest kid in his class. His parents took him to doctors who told them, "Some kids are just short."

Joey's feelings about himself plummeted. He hid out in his room. When he was around other kids, he felt like a runt. He was interested in a number of girls but always thought, "No way she'd ever like me."

When he grew up, Joey bought expensive cars and clothes, drank fine wines, traveled the world, and eventually spoke several languages fluently. But he always felt short—until he met Melanie. She was gorgeous, funny, and outgoing. Unbelievably, despite being taller, she fell in love with him. What a change. "It's the first time since I was a kid that I actually felt cool and confident."

Newton was right

Why don't these sorts of romantic solutions to our self-evaluation struggles last? Why do we have so many ups and downs? Trouble usually starts the moment something interrupts one of our idealizations. Maybe you hurt my feelings by not texting enough, planning something nice for my birthday, or laughing at my jokes. Perhaps you squeeze the toothpaste tube from the middle or don't put down the toilet seat. I begin to wonder, "Maybe you're not really so great after all?"

As soon as I start to think you're not actually so great, your desiring me no longer solves all of my problems. If a mere mortal (or worse) likes me, well, that's no longer much of a support to my self-image.

It's even worse if I keep you idealized, but you don't like me anymore. I'll shift from "I'm great because I'm with a fantastic partner" to "I'm a reject."

There are countless other brittle self-esteem-related romantic patterns we can also fall into, such as putting ourselves down to build up our partner in an attempt to hold on to them, or being domineering and controlling to try to keep our partner from abandoning us.

Have you ever noticed how a 5-minute interaction with your beloved can ruin your whole day? It doesn't take much for most of us, even in more stable romantic relationships, to shift from "You're wonderful, and being with you makes me feel great" to "You're no good, and being with you makes me miserable." To the extent that our relationships are based on propping up our feelings about *ourselves,* we don't see our partners clearly. Rather, we relate to projections, images of our mate that can shift in a flash.

That's what happened to Joey and Melanie. After they had dated for about a year, he started to think that, even though she was attractive, funny, and outgoing, "She's just not smart enough." He had grown up in a family that labeled everyone as either intelligent or not, and he began to worry that she was in the latter camp. After all, she watched reality TV. As doubts about Melanie took hold, back came Joey's insecurities. He started to feel short again and sickened at the thought of reentering the dating world.

Addicted to the highs

As we've seen, anything that quickly and powerfully moves us from pain to pleasure is a candidate for addiction. It's therefore no surprise that people everywhere become obsessed with their beloved, thinking about them constantly. We get super-excited before seeing each other and go into withdrawal when we're separated. We regularly do foolish, reckless things to try to hold on to relationships. And we're subject to relapse: years after ending a crazy relationship we can find ourselves seeking out our old love on Facebook, screwing up our life in the process.

When lovers' brains were scanned while they looked at pictures of their beloved, a dopamine-producing reward region connected to the nucleus accumbens (the center activated by likes on social media and drugs like cocaine) had increased activation. The more attractive the partner, the more activation occurred.

So we're biologically predisposed to get addicted to romance. This makes perfect sense, since it powerfully taps two basic needs: to feel good about ourselves (raising our status in the primate troop) and to feel wanted (so we won't be cast out into the wilderness). But as with other addictions, there's a way out. We can develop a different, more stable kind of love that's actually a powerful antidote to the very self-evaluation concerns and comparative judgments that addict us to romance.

Moving beyond Cupid

After breaking up with Melanie, Joey went through a series of tumultuous, painful relationships. They followed a predictable pattern. He'd feel lonely and inadequate despite dating a number of women, each of whom had some romance-killing flaw. "She's not sophisticated enough." "The chemistry isn't right." "I'm just not that excited by her sexually." Then he'd meet someone who seemed really great, and his feelings about himself would soar and crash depending on whether she seemed to like him. He'd become despondent waiting for a text, feel on top of the world after finally receiving it, only to sink again the next day if she went dark.

After several years of these ups and downs he met Kim. She wasn't particularly stunning or brilliant, which at first put him off. But there was something alluring about her. She was unusually honest and introspective, and demanded the same from him. He began to open up in ways that he never had before and felt a connection that wasn't based on thinking that he, or she, was so special. "It's weird—she actually likes me more when I admit that I'm sad or anxious." "We spend hours staring into each other's eyes, just being honest." And the biggest surprise of all: "We have a great sex life, but there's something different about it. It's like we merge into one another and I stop thinking about me. We play, experiment, and cuddle a lot."

The many forms of love

Joey wasn't the first person to discover this different sort of love. The ancient Greeks called passionate, addictive love—the kind that lights up our reward centers, feels like a roller coaster, and is so closely entwined with our self-esteem—*eros*. They had a god by the same name, the son of Aphrodite, the goddess of sexual love and beauty. Eros (or Cupid, as the Romans called him) was quite mischievous, and then, as now, he caused all sorts of problems for gods and mortals alike, unpredictably shooting his arrows into unsuspecting hearts.

It turns out that when people are engaged in passionate romantic love relationships, they show more activation in a brain region associated with self-evaluative thinking called the *posterior cingulate cortex* (PCC). So *eros* is pretty self-focused, which makes sense given that it's so connected to our self-appraisals. We think a lot about our romantic partner, but as with other addictions, there's an often unspoken, even unseen subtext: *What can you do for me?*

The other types of love described by the Greeks are all pathways to safe connection. They include the affection between parents and children, the love of friendship, and *agape,* selfless love extended to all people—which in Christian traditions became both love for God and God's love for us. It's these sorts of love that get activated, to different degrees, in relationships that aren't so tied to our self-esteem.

Studies have shown that both mothers caring for their children and nonobsessed lovers have less PCC activation when thinking about their kids or partners. And when people practice loving-kindness meditation, in which they generate loving feelings by wishing others well, the reward pathways activated by passionate romantic love are quieted. It seems that we, like Joey, can learn to love in ways that are less addictive, less focused on ourselves, more fulfilling, and likely to cause less crazy behavior.

None of this is to say that romance or sex shouldn't or can't be fun or exciting. It's just that if we can temper our self-evaluation concerns, it will feel more sustainable and connected. What role have self-esteem concerns played in your intimate relationships? Have you found paths to deeper, more secure connections instead?

Exercise: Separating love from self-evaluation

Take a few moments first to close your eyes, mindfully attend to your breath, and bring your attention to the present moment.

EARLY PASSION

Now think back to one of your earliest, most passionate love relationships (yes, *that one* will work). Recall how your feelings about yourself shifted when your beloved showed interest in you. What were the building blocks of your self-esteem at the time? What were your greatest insecurities? What happened to those insecurities when your partner showed affection?

Next recall what it was like when your beloved was angry, rejecting, or indifferent toward you. What happened to your feelings about yourself? What happened to your insecurities?

OTHER LOVE

Now see if you can recall an intimate love relationship in which self-evaluative concerns played a smaller role. Remember how you felt toward, and with, that person. What drew you to the relationship? What pulled you away? How did you feel about yourself while in the relationship? How did you feel about yourself when that partner was angry, rejecting, or indifferent toward you? What made this relationship different?

LOVE TODAY

Are you involved in a love relationship now? Do your self-evaluative concerns play a role? Does the thought of being together make you feel like hot stuff? Does thinking that your partner's not so great or disappointing make you feel like you're "settling"?

Nurturing intimate connections

I'm sorry to break the news, but if self-esteem concerns are playing a central role in your current relationship, everyone's going to be disappointed.

But that doesn't necessarily mean you're with the wrong person. We're not going to kill off our self-evaluation worries—they're biologically based. And we wouldn't want to live a life with a partner who didn't generally value and respect us. But it can be very freeing to deliberately nurture those aspects of our relationship that create safe connection rather than building our egos.

While every couple's path to connection is different, there are some reliable ways to work with our heads, hearts, and habits that make us more likely to connect in lasting and satisfying ways.

Risk honesty and vulnerability

In safely connected, loving relationships, we feel seen, heard, and known by our partners. Keeping up appearances, hiding our shame, trying to look strong—these all get in the way. Joey was shocked that Kim actually *liked* hearing about his fears and longings, and she felt loved and cared for when Joey listened to hers.

Set aside time to talk. Risk telling your partner the truth about your day—particularly what touched your heart—and invite your partner to do the same. "It hurt my feelings that my boss didn't like my idea." "I'm worried about my sister." "The sunset was beautiful driving home." Notice when your impulse is to constrict, tense up, pull back, and keep thoughts and feelings to yourself, and see if you might open up and risk honesty instead. Notice what fears might be holding you back from sharing.

Surrender

Whether making love or just holding hands, deep connection involves surrendering to the moment and to one another. We can facilitate surrender by bringing our attention to the present moment (mindfulness practice helps) and reminding ourselves to let go. This was new, and particularly powerful for Joey. "I always used to keep my guard up, keep a part of me separate, hold back. Not with Kim. Feeling so close, I sometimes get scared that I'm losing control or going to disappear, but when I give in, it's great."

What does my partner need?

A powerful alternative to worrying about what our relationship says about us is to focus on helping our partner meet their needs. If you're in an intimate relationship, take a moment right now to think of three things you do that reliably alienate your partner from you (probably won't take long to come up with the list). For me with my wife, my reliably alienating moves include (1) sounding arrogant, (2) not making eye contact when she's telling me something important, and (3) criticizing a member of her family. Next think of three things you do that bring you closer. Possibilities for me are (1) taking the time to really listen, (2) making the bed, and (3) starting dinner before she finishes work. Just deciding to lay off the former and do more of the latter can go a long way toward fostering connection.

It's useful here to remember that sometimes what our partner needs isn't what we need. So, our partner may need some space when feeling hurt, while we might want to reconnect immediately. One person may turn to sex to connect, while another may need to feel connected in order to have sex. Part of safely connecting is asking our partner what helps *them* to feel close and responding accordingly—which itself will make your partner feel known, heard, and loved. And if your partner isn't good at asking you what you want or need, risk telling them anyway.

Make connection the goal

I shudder to think of the number of times that I've been worried about something, spoken to my wife in an agitated voice, and ruptured our connection. "Did you cancel the newspaper?" "What did the doctor say?" "Do you have the receipt?" In each instance, I was focused on some external goal and was oblivious to the tone of my voice. Often there was a self-evaluative threat fueling my anxiety. I didn't want to feel stupid, sloppy, or foolish by not being on top of one thing or another.

Fortunately, my wife has been a good teacher. She has pointed out that it is far less efficient to speak rudely and then have to process her hurt feelings, than it would have been to just speak nicely in the first place.

Try to notice, when focused on accomplishing some task, what's happening in your relationship. Is your tone bringing the two of you together as a team, or are you alienating your partner in your pursuit of the goal? Is a self-esteem bruise making you grumpy? Sharing your pain can bring you closer. Just reminding ourselves that we've got at least two objectives—accomplishing the task and staying connected—can go a long way toward building connection.

Practice relational mindfulness

One technique for staying relationally attuned is to practice relational, or interpersonal, mindfulness. It helps to establish a regular individual mindfulness practice as a foundation first, so you can notice carefully what's happening in you and your partner when you interact.

Exercise: Three objects of awareness

Remind yourself that your intention is to connect as best you can with your partner. During your interaction, try to be conscious of three realms. You'll probably find it difficult to attend to all three simultaneously, so just rotate your attention among them:

1. Notice the thoughts, feelings, and sensations occurring in your own body and mind. Use your body as a source of information— observing when you feel tension or constriction and when you feel relaxed and open. When tension arises, deliberately breathe into the tense areas, letting them open up.
2. Look at your partner carefully, taking in their facial expression, body posture, and gestures. See if you can sense what they are

feeling each moment. Notice how your own body reacts to shifts in your partner's body language, words, and posture.

3. Notice how connected you feel to one another, and how this continually changes. This is the sense that I *feel felt* by you and you *feel felt* by me. It can be hard to describe, but there are times when we feel more like a "we," and moments when we feel more like "me" separate from "you." When we're connected, we usually feel warm, safe, and close rather than wary, defensive, or distant.

As you try to be mindful during your interactions, notice what makes you feel closer or more distant. You'll probably find that when your mind shifts into evaluation mode—judging yourself or your partner—you feel more disconnected. But when you're just trying to be honestly and humbly present, to understand and be understood by one another, you feel closer.

Nurturing connection in the wider world

Every interaction we have with others can be an opportunity either to activate our self-evaluative concerns or to connect. Consider relationships at work, for example. How often does competition over who had the better idea, who did more work on a project, or who the boss likes best get in the way of everyone pulling together in the same direction? As a colleague of mine quipped one day in frustration: "The meeting went on for almost 2 hours. Everything that needed to be said was said in the first 20 minutes, but not everyone had said it."

While much of the world's population struggles to keep themselves and their families alive, the rest of us regularly feel deprived based on status comparisons with peers, despite living better than the aristocrats and monarchs of old. Imagine what a king or queen would have given 200 years ago for central heat, air conditioning, or antibiotics. And the variety of foods in a modern supermarket—even off season—would've blown their minds. But none of this stops us from feeling deprived when a coworker gets a bigger raise or our boss seems oblivious to our contributions.

Similar concerns screw up friendships and family relationships. "You were always Dad's favorite." "He always got what he wanted." "I'm just an afterthought." Sometimes we're able to feel part of a "we" that allows us to celebrate others' accomplishments. But a lot of times their success makes us feel diminished. Whether at work or home, these concerns reliably get in the way of feeling connected.

How might we shift from relating competitively to connecting instead?

Exercise: Connecting instead of competing

Start with a few moments of mindfulness practice to tune in to your inner experience. Then recall a time that you felt competitive in a familial, friendship, or work relationship. Who was your rival? What is it about them that got your competitive juices flowing?

Next recall a situation in which you were losing the competition with that person. What do you feel in your body? Does the feeling remind you of other moments in your life? Was there an earlier time when you struggled with the same emotion? Just stay with the feeling for a little while.

Take a moment to reflect on what quality, skill, or attribute of yours is invalidated by losing to this person. How important is it to you to be equal or ahead in this area? Who would you be if you weren't so great in this way? Might it be OK for your rival to be better or ahead?

Assuming that you could survive without coming out on top, consider how you might join with the other person in a common goal. What matters to you both? Is there a way to be on the same team?

Kitty was a fourth-grade teacher being driven crazy by Aiysha, who taught the class across the hall. Aiysha was always staying late at school, developing new projects for the kids, and redecorating the bulletin board outside her classroom. Even though Kitty was a perfectly good teacher, well liked by parents, students, and administrators, Aiysha's over-the-top dedication made her feel inadequate. Being with Aiysha made her feel like she did as a kid hanging out with her older sister and her friends—less-than in every way.

What was the self-evaluation issue Aiysha activated? No secret here. Kitty wanted to feel like she was a good teacher, but Aiysha's exploits made her feel that she wasn't good enough. Did she want to stay late every day to keep up? Nope. Might there be a way to connect with Aiysha instead, to simultaneously get out of the self-evaluation trap and enjoy the support of a connected relationship? Bingo.

Aiysha clearly had her hands full with all her projects, and since they both taught fourth grade, Kitty offered to work with her on some of them. They planned a field trip to a tech company and then set up a fourth-grade website together. It involved some extra work but was well worth it. Feeling connected to her as a friend and partner made it easier to accept Aiysha's never-ending accomplishments and to feel OK about her own.

Some of the supports for connection that work in intimate relationships also help with friends, family members, and coworkers. Risking honesty and vulnerability, if we feel that the other person basically has goodwill, can be particularly powerful. Once Kitty and Aiysha had worked together, Kitty told Aiysha how inadequate she had been feeling. Aiysha shared her own feelings about having a sister who was a high-powered attorney. They actually had a lot in common.

Addressing the other's needs can go a long way too. If your boss seems to be getting critical or uptight, instead of perseverating on what you might have done wrong or whether you're succeeding or failing, try to figure out what pressures your boss is facing and see if you might be able to address them, or be supportive with gentle humor or kindness. Recognizing when it's not about us can change everything.

Staying conscious of relationship, not just the task at hand, is also helpful. The *Three Objects of Awareness* exercise on pages 138–139 can work anywhere. Try to be conscious of what's happening inside you and inside the other person, and particularly try to sense what's happening to your sense of connection, what seems to bring you together more or push you further apart.

Shifting our focus in this way is especially helpful when feeling anxious before high-stakes encounters like a job interview, first date, or meeting with potential in-laws. Instead of marshaling your energies to make a good impression, focus on making a connection. As the poet Maya Angelou put it, "People will forget what you said, people will forget what you did, but people will never forget how you made them feel."

Overcoming obstacles to connection

Because feeling inadequate or one-down can be so painful, most of us have automatic protective reactions that get in the way of connecting safely to others. Let's look at a few of these and how we might overcome them.

Pushing people away with anger

> Before you embark on a journey of revenge, dig two graves.
>
> —Confucius

Other animals get angry for good reason. They respond with aggression when they, their children, or their relatives are physically attacked; when competing for food or a mate; or when another animal encroaches on their turf. We, on the other hand, mostly get angry when our self-image is threatened—when we feel criticized, shamed, unlikable, unattractive, or incompetent. We defend our mental image of ourselves with the same vigor we'd use for physical safety, if not more.

Tom was raised by an ambitious father who ran the biggest company in town. He was always whipping Tom into shape. "Hold the bat higher." "Use your wrist more when you throw." Supportive remarks were few and far between.

At age 15 Tom's family moved, and he fell victim to a group of tough guys in his new school. They shot spitballs when the teacher wasn't looking and knocked his books out of his hands in the hallway. By the time he left for college Tom was determined never to be belittled again—no matter the cost.

Unfortunately, years later, his determination backfired. Scanning for injustice at work, he lost more than one position because he *had* to stand up for himself. "If you won't respect me, screw you, I'm out of here." Each job loss left Tom feeling more like a failure.

Why do many of us get aggressive despite the obviously problematic consequences? One reason is that responding to slights with anger can feel pretty good. In a moment of righteous indignation, everything is so clear: I'm great, you're terrible, and all is well with the world. In Buddhist traditions, anger is described as being seductive, having *a honeyed tip and poisoned root*. Sooner or later we find that holding on to resentment is like setting ourselves on fire and expecting the other person to be disturbed by the smoke. We pay a much higher price than our enemy. And one of the greatest costs is rupturing relationships.

In coming chapters we'll look at ways to release our anger and cultivate forgiveness. They all involve recognizing the hurt or fear beneath our anger and considering what made the other person act as they did. For Tom, it took losing several positions and feeling stuck in his career to find another strategy.

His next job was at a business run by its founder, now in his 60s. One day his boss, who was generally a nice guy, lit into him for making a mistake on an order. When Tom's anger rose up, not wanting to lose yet another job, he paused and asked himself, "Why is it getting to me?" "What does this remind me of?" It was high school again. Then he stepped back and wondered, "Why is he coming down on me so hard?" It didn't take long to realize that sales had been slipping, they were losing out to online competition, and his boss didn't want to go out in failure. The insight helped. Tom saw his boss as the decent, though frightened, guy that he was. "I'm sorry—I understand why you don't want any screw-ups right now" was all it took to reconnect with him. When we can see that other people's behavior isn't about us, we don't have to respond out of our accumulated pain.

Distancing with criticism

Another defensive maneuver that reliably prevents safe connection is being judgmental. I once had a patient, Suzanna, who was studying biblical scripture. One day she had a realization. " 'Do unto others as you would have them do unto you' isn't just a biblical injunction—it's a law of nature." Suzanna noticed that the more she was judgmental of others, the more harshly judgmental she would be toward herself. "After getting annoyed at everyone for their sloppy reports, I get paranoid about making mistakes in my own writing." Even if she could muster a momentary boost by thinking of herself as superior, before long the judgmental attitude came around and bit her. Suzanna noted that the Bible itself points to this danger: "Judge not that ye be not judged" (including by yourself!). Just being more aware of this process helped. When her critical voice got going, she started to think, "There I go again" and not take it so seriously. Seeing us all as imperfect, ordinary, struggling beings made it much easier to be nice to herself and connect with her coworkers.

It's lonely at the top

There's a famous story from the Tang Dynasty:

> A powerful Chinese prime minister asked a meditation master for the Buddhist perspective on egotism. The master glared and said, "What kind of stupid question is that?" The minister, suddenly angry and defensive, snapped back, "How dare you speak to me like that!" "That, your excellency, is egotism," replied the master.

Why is egotism such a turnoff? When we're with people who think they're better than us, we usually start to feel inadequate or competitive or sense that the relationship won't be gratifying. In fact, one way to identify egotistical individuals is to notice whether they engender competitive feelings in those around them, making everyone feel disconnected. It's also difficult to negotiate with conceited people. They tend to demand that they get their way, because yielding tarnishes their image. Research studies suggest that people with elevated self-esteem (who rate themselves highly) are actually *more* likely to become aggressive when symbolically threatened than are people with average or low self-esteem. And we know how anger does wonders for connection.

Another way conceit can screw up connection involves putting others down to build ourselves up. *Mansplaining* is an all too prevalent gendered example. Have you ever seen a discussion between a man and woman where the guy "explains" something to the woman in a way that communicates, "You dummy, I can't believe you don't know how this works!" It's a surefire connection killer.

At age 29, Maggie was on a roll. She had scored $2 million in venture capital for her green startup and hired a staff of talented people to get it off the ground. Almost everyone who heard her pitch was impressed—she was smart, charismatic, and exuded confidence.

The trouble started when the engineers told her that the company's process didn't work as well in the field as in the lab. She told them not to let the results leak and pushed them to try harder. "Just get it to work, or I'll find someone else who can."

It wasn't until the company went belly up that she saw how her hubris had made things worse. Flipping from being a superstar to a failure was excruciating. When she went out for a beer with the CFO—one of the few people at work she hadn't completely alienated—she heard the truth: "Sorry, Maggie, you really became an asshole near the end. Nobody wanted to be near you, and it killed everyone's motivation."

This was another hard pill to swallow. But when she eventually got back on her feet and joined another company, her attitude was different. She became a team player instead of trying to be the top dog. Not only did she get along better with everyone, but her self-image wasn't on the line as much. "No matter what happens, we're all going to win or lose together."

It's lonely at the bottom

While egotism is a recipe for relational disaster, its opposite, feeling inadequate, isn't great either. It, too, can cut us off from others. If we have a low opinion of ourselves, we tend to expect rejection, which reliably gets in the way of making connections. We may act awkward, try too hard to be likable or interesting, or hesitate to reach out. "She'd never be interested in me." "I'd be embarrassed to call—it's been so long since we spoke." "I sounded so stupid." "We were never really friends." I can't count the number of opportunities for connection I've missed because I was afraid that the other person wouldn't be interested and I'd feel rejected.

Feeling inadequate can also lead to poor relationship choices. Have you ever continued to date or hang out with a person you didn't really like because you were afraid you wouldn't find someone else? Ever hired someone less skilled because the more qualified candidate might have shown you up on the job?

How about group affiliations? Sometimes we want to be part of a club, or even gang, to feel better about ourselves—even if we don't really like the other members. And bigotry, along with the injustice that flows from it, often involves compensating for inadequacy feelings with the fantasy of being superior to an entire race, gender, age group, nationality, or economic class.

Thinking of ourselves as either better or worse than others robs us of the safe social connection that's one of our best antidotes to concerns about superiority or inferiority. Good to remember when we find ourselves believing in either judgment.

I have a little shadow

In Chapter 4 we visited the idea that we all have shadows or exiled parts—aspects of our personalities that we don't like to acknowledge, try to hide, and wish would go away. Rather than disappearing just because we don't like them, however, our shadows reliably show up in our views of others—particularly individuals or groups we look down upon—reliably getting in the way of connection.

For example, a lot of us are uncomfortable with, or even unaware of, our sexuality, greed, aggression, and other less noble impulses. It's common for us to project these qualities onto others, portraying out-groups as thieving, violent, lascivious animals who want to attack "our" women or seduce "our" men. We see this in Nazi portrayals of Jews, white supremacist portrayals of African Americans, and nativist portrayals of immigrants, to name just a few of countless examples.

Many of us do the same in more personal arenas. We might judge overweight people, or those with obvious addictions, as "gluttonous" or undisciplined—since most of us have difficulty accepting our own struggles with self-control and might enjoy feeling self-righteously superior. These projections not only cut us off from countless opportunities to connect, but they perpetuate social injustice. We can begin to interrupt them by being honest about our shadow.

Exercise: Owning our shadow

Start by bringing to mind a group or type of person you look down on (don't worry, you won't have to admit this to anyone). List below a few of their attributes or behaviors that you particularly disparage (if you need extra space, go to *giftofbeingordinary.com* or *guilford.com/siegel4-materials*). Then see if you can identify times when you've displayed those qualities yourself or otherwise behaved like them:

Quality or behavior	When I was like them

The other day I was talking with Steve, a former neighbor who grew up in New England and recently moved to the South for a new job. He started on a rant about how selfish and ignorant his new neighbors were, oblivious about protecting the environment. He was particularly pissed off at the duck hunters for being cruel, exploitative, and not respecting nature.

Since Steve was usually a decent guy, and I sensed that his anger was getting in the way of adjusting to his move, I took a chance and asked him, "Do your neighbors down south remind you of anyone you know, or maybe even a part of yourself?" He snapped back, "Thanks a lot" and suggested that I keep my psychological theories to myself. But a few minutes later he cooled off and said it was true—he hated his own obliviousness. In fact, he often thought, "The world's a mess and I'm not doing enough to help." As soon as he connected with his self-centered side, he admitted that his new neighbors were actually more friendly than folks up north and that he felt ashamed about his own big carbon footprint, since he regularly flew back and forth. Seeing the role of his shadow helped him shift from feeling alienated to feeling connected.

When we realize that we're not actually better or worse than anyone else, we can enjoy being part of an ordinary "we" instead of worrying about being above or below others.

Identity recategorization

Another way to see what we have in common and feel more connected involves reevaluating our identity. My daughter is a political scientist who has studied how this might reduce Sunni–Shia tensions in the Middle East. When people think of themselves as primarily Sunni or Shia, rather than as Muslim, hostility increases. But when religious and civic leaders convey the message that, more importantly, "we're all Muslim," tensions diminish.

Something similar happened after the 9/11 attacks in the United States. Sharing the fear and pain of having been attacked, Americans from many walks of life began to shift their identities from being members of smaller subgroups to being "American." Social psychologists tell us that it worked (temporarily, at least) to lessen racial and other intergroup tensions. They call the process *identity recategorization*.

As it turns out, in almost every situation, we can find a next level of "we-ness" that can help us move beyond the disconnected folly of superiority and inferiority. Sunnis and Shias can notice that they're both Muslims; Jews, Christians, and Muslims can see themselves as sons and daughters of Abraham; people worldwide can notice that we were all born to mothers and we're all human beings struggling to feel safe, healthy, loved, and happy. We can even, at times, transcend our preoccupation with our own species to see that we're all part of nature.

The next time you find yourself in a judgmental frame of mind, denigrating others, or thinking how great you or your group are, you can experiment with the question "What do I share with them?" See how you feel noticing your commonalities; how it feels to identify with others on the next higher level. We can add *identity recategorization* to our toolkit for enhancing connection throughout our day.

A word of caution: As we work to loosen the judgments and identifications that alienate us from one another, we still have to be attentive to our differences. Privileged groups have oppressed out-groups for millennia, causing enormous suffering. We therefore need to try to understand others' experience, honoring that it may be quite different from our own. Papering over pain in an effort to come together doesn't work—we still need to address past injuries and ongoing injustices in order to genuinely connect.

There are many other ways we can work with our heads, hearts, and habits to cultivate connection. Practicing gratitude and doing something for the benefit of the wider world, which we'll explore shortly, both help. It's not an accident that all of the world's religious traditions see gratitude and service to others as paths to spiritual growth, and modern science is confirming that they are reliable paths to well-being.

But perhaps our most valuable resource for cultivating safe connections with others involves an often-neglected, biologically based instinct that is much more developed in humans than in other species but can nonetheless easily go off-line—to our peril.

TEN

the power of compassion

> If you want others to be happy, practice
> compassion. If you want to be happy,
> practice compassion.
> —Dalai Lama XIV

HAVE YOU THOUGHT LATELY about the differences between reptiles, fish, birds, amphibians, and mammals? As it turns out, all these creatures share the concerns about dominance, social rank, and sex appeal that, as we've seen, cause us all a lot of distress. But they differ in one important regard—and this difference can help save us from our competitive concerns and self-evaluation woes while connecting us more deeply to one another.

Our tend-and-befriend system

Mammals nurse their young. In fact, some mammals look after their young for quite a while after they're weaned (sometimes for decades—kids living in their parents' basement after college come to mind). To motivate us to do this, our brains evolved powerful circuitry called the *tend-and-befriend system*. It fuels our dedication to our children, as well as our wish to care for others close to us. It's the force behind the fact discussed earlier that we, along with other mammals, will sacrifice for close relatives (one child, two brothers, eight cousins) and sometimes even nonrelatives.

While all mammals share this altruistic impulse to some degree, primates, and particularly *homo sapiens,* take it to the next level. Paleontologists believe that our caring capacity took a giant leap forward around 50,000 years ago during the cultural big bang. It's when we find the first skeletons of ancestors who had suffered injuries or diseases that would not have allowed them to survive on their own, but who nonetheless lived to an advanced age. Around the same time that we became artists and sophisticated toolmakers, and began thinking about ourselves, we started taking care of disabled friends and relatives. Our heart-centered tend-and-befriend system became more central in our lives.

How can this system help move us toward greater connection and less self-preoccupation? One way is by taking over from the other motivational systems that trap us in competitive concerns.

All animals have some version of the threat-response system. It's one of our most basic instincts—to be on guard for danger and either flee, freeze, or fight to protect ourselves. We all know the feeling of adrenaline coursing through our veins when we're threatened, and we've all had the urge to run away, hold still (the deer-in-the-headlights response), or fight back. When we feel *safe,* this system is quiet.

All animals also have some version of a second, goal-seeking system. It's the motivational force behind our addictions—that good feeling we get finding food when we're hungry, warmth when we're cold, sex when we're turned on, or a like on Facebook or Instagram. In mammals, this system primarily involves the neurotransmitter dopamine—and as discussed in Chapter 8, dopamine squirts in our brain's reward center are very addicting. When we feel *satisfied,* this system is quiet.

A challenge that we face as humans is that these three major motivational systems—tend-and-befriend, threat response, and goal seeking—aren't of equal power. If we sense danger—we've just come face to face with a lion or we're in the path of a bus—our fear-based system readily trumps the other two. In these moments, we don't care about other goals, and we can lose sight of others' needs.

When we don't sense any immediate danger, we feel safe enough to turn our attention to pursuits like food, sex, getting respect, or building up our retirement savings. "What should I have for dinner?" "I wonder if she might want to make love?" "How can I make more money?"

It's usually only when we don't feel threatened *and* our basic needs are met that we open our hearts and turn our attention to others in need.

Of course, there are exceptions. The obvious ones involve our children and close friends or relatives. Even when we feel threatened or our basic needs aren't met, we try to come through for them. And sometimes the needs of a stranger are so compelling that even though we feel vulnerable ourselves, we help. But often, when our desires for safety and satisfaction aren't met, our generosity doesn't extend very far and strangers are out of luck.

Why should we care which motivational system is running the show? One reason is that caring for others supports safe social connection, which helps calm the other two systems (hugs can do wonders when we feel threatened or deprived). And in the moments that we're caring for someone else, we're not so focused on social comparison or self-evaluation—we're focused on the other's needs. Finally, loving connection feels good and gives life meaning. After all, where would you rather live—in a dog-eat-dog world or in one where people look after one another?

Feeding the compassionate wolf

Remember the story in Chapter 2 about the Cherokee grandfather advising his grandson about character development and the story about the chariot making ruts in the dusty plain in Chapter 8? Our behavior rewires our brain, reinforcing whichever motivational system we use most frequently. If we operate repeatedly in fight-freeze-flight mode or pursue immediate desires, we beef up those brain circuits, becoming ever more inclined toward our fears and addictions. But if we deliberately exercise our tend-and-befriend system, we can strengthen it instead.

There are many ways to fortify our caring side. Cultivating connected relationships naturally helps. Another approach, which itself supports connection, is to deliberately cultivate *compassion*.

The English word *compassion* comes from Latin and Greek roots meaning to "suffer with." It begins with empathy. To be compassionate we need first to be able to sense another's feelings. Researchers suspect that we do this in part by activating *mirror neurons* that allow us to experience in our own bodies the feelings that we imagine are occurring in someone else's (if you've ever attended an erotic or horror film, you've felt mirror neurons in action).

Compassion involves a particular sort of empathy—empathy for painful experiences or losses. It also involves an altruistic wish, a desire for the other person to feel better or be well. When a friend is hurting, we feel their pain *and* we wish in our heart for our friend to feel better.

There are many different exercises that can help us cultivate compassion. I invite you to try various ones in this chapter to see which are most effective for you.

Practicing loving-kindness

A well-researched practice for developing compassion for both ourselves and others is *loving-kindness meditation*. There are many variations of this technique, and they all involve cultivating goodwill toward ourselves and others. These practices develop the habit of opening our hearts, strengthening the altruistic or well-wishing aspect of compassion.

Many people find it helpful to do some mindfulness practice before loving-kindness meditation to attune to emotional responses. You might therefore start by following the breath for a little while, or perhaps doing some slow walking or listening meditation, and then try the following exercise. The exact phrases used to cultivate loving-kindness in this exercise are not critical—it's best to experiment with different words or images to find what works best for you:

Exercise: Loving-kindness practice*

Start by bringing to mind the image of a naturally loving, kind being. This might be a friend, family member, or mentor; an inspirational figure from the past such as Mother Teresa, Nelson Mandela, or Martin Luther King; a living teacher such as the pope or the Dalai Lama; or a religious figure like Jesus, the Buddha, Moses, or Muhammad. It can even be a special animal or a place in nature that brings you feelings of loving-kindness.

Read the rest of these instructions first and then close your eyes, imagine this being is with you, and feel their presence. Notice what feelings arise in your heart. Then begin wishing this naturally loving being well. It often helps to place one hand over your heart and the other hand on top of the first—feeling the warmth and gentle pressure of your hands on your chest as you do this.

Try silently repeating words that convey a wish for the other to be well. Use a soothing, caring, loving tone. Some traditional phrases are:

May you be safe,
May you be happy,
May you be healthy,
May you live with ease.

Feel free to use whatever phrases resonate for you—you're just trying to gently generate a feeling of love and kindness. If the mind wanders, just gently bring it back to your chosen image.

Once you're able to feel a bit of loving-kindness toward your naturally kind and loving being, try directing the feeling toward yourself. You might find effective words by asking, "What does my heart desire?" "What do I long to hear from others?" and wishing this for yourself. It might be love, kindness, understanding, safety, or something else: "May I feel loved just as I am," "May I feel free," "May I feel good enough," "May I not matter so much!" Or you can always try the traditional phrases:

---

*Audio available at *giftofbeingordinary.com* and *guilford.com/siegel4-materials*.

May I be safe,
May I be happy,
May I be healthy,
May I live with ease.

Simply repeat whatever phrases most speak to you in a kind, loving, soothing voice, wishing yourself well. Try keeping your hands gently on your heart as you do this.

If you find that your mind seems particularly stuck in a problematic pattern or attitude that's getting in the way of being kind and loving toward yourself, experiment with phrases to address this directly. For example, you might try "May I learn to let go," "May I be peaceful," "May I accept whatever comes," "May I have the courage to face my fears," or "May I learn to forgive." Here again, play around to see what feels most alive for you.

Once you've directed loving-kindness wishes to yourself for a little while, try shifting your attention to someone else who is important to you. One by one, call to mind (and heart) people who matter. Eventually you can expand your focus to include small groups, such as immediate family members or close friends. Holding them in your heart, continue to repeat whatever phrases resonate for you, directing loving, kind wishes toward them. Expanding the circle further still, you might move on to your coworkers, clients, neighbors, or any other group of which you are a part. Eventually, try sending warm wishes to wider and wider communities, until you're including your town, country, and eventually everyone on the planet.

The exercise can even be expanded to include all living things. In a classic version, we eventually direct loving-kindness very broadly:

May all beings be safe,
May all beings be happy,
May all beings be peaceful,
May all beings live with ease.

THE INNER DARTH VADER

Sometimes loving-kindness practice flows freely, and we readily feel love and caring toward others. But sometimes we find ourselves disconnected—not feeling much at all. Personally, I find that this happens more when I'm obsessively anxious—worrying about my to-do list or planning and strategizing how to solve problems. I try to generate loving-kindness but just get caught up in thinking. In these moments, I find it most helpful to either get some physical exercise, do some yoga, or practice mindfulness to step out of the thought stream and get into my body before trying loving-kindness practice again.

In other moods, negative feelings can arise, such as cynicism, criticism, or anger. Or we find that we can expand the circle of compassion to encompass some people but not others, based on our conditioning or beliefs. Some years ago, I taught this exercise in a workshop, and one participant reported, "I can feel loving-kindness toward all sentient beings except [leader of the *other* political party]." Whatever might arise in our hearts and minds, it's usually best to try to open to whatever is happening.

Otherwise, we run into the problem that *what we resist persists*. Our attempt to push away negative feelings becomes like trying not to think of a flying elephant—the mind suddenly fills with winged pachyderms. While loving-kindness practice can connect us with our warmth and compassion, it can also help us see where we keep our guard up because of our hurt or fear. It's best to respect our limitations and be patient with ourselves.

Jolene, a paralegal, was in a lot of pain after being passed over for a promotion. She was alternately hurt and angry that her boss didn't recognize her contributions. "I've done a really good job." "I stay later than almost everyone else." "What's wrong with her—why won't she give me any credit?" Full of anger and sadness, she thought that some loving-kindness practice might be soothing.

At first it was comforting—the practice reminded her of the feeling she had in her mother's arms as a little girl. She felt like she was still lovable, even if her boss didn't recognize her efforts. But when she tried to extend loving-kindness to others, the image of her boss kept coming up, and it was hard to include her. "She doesn't deserve it. Screw her." Rather than try to force it, Jolene was able to see that she wasn't ready to forgive her boss; the hurt and anger were too raw. But she could still use the practice to comfort herself.

BACKDRAFT

Another challenging reaction to loving-kindness and other compassion exercises is what psychologist Chris Germer calls *backdraft*. It comes from the observation that firefighters feel a door in a burning building before opening it, since if there are smoldering embers on the other side, opening the door will let in oxygen and cause the flames to flare.

In a similar way, if our tend-and-befriend system has been shut down—perhaps because we haven't felt much love (in the past or lately)—generating love can bring our emotional pain to the surface. We become like a young child who skins their knee and sits frozen on the ground until a loving adult comes to help. As soon as the adult picks the child up, WHAAA!!—all the feelings of distress flow out.

With backdraft, too, it's important to respect where we are at the moment. If loving-kindness practice brings up too much vulnerable feeling, you don't need to pursue it right now. You can look for ways to feel safer first—perhaps by reaching out to connect with friends, spending time in nature, pursuing spiritual interests, or otherwise connecting to the wider world—before working with heart-opening practices.

Transcending blame

Sometimes what blocks our tend-and-befriend system and disconnects us from others is our impulse to blame. Most of us carry resentment toward people whom we feel treated us unfairly and might see ourselves as better than them. To free up our capacity for compassionate connection, it helps to look closely at exactly how blame works and how we might use our heads to soften our hearts.

If a 6-month-old baby keeps us up at night crying or fussing, we don't usually blame them. We think about the causes and conditions for the distress—perhaps a wet diaper, hunger, digestive distress, or overtiredness—and try to address these. If a 6-year-old starts to misbehave, we might start to think, "Spoiled, willful child," but more likely we'll wonder about difficulties at school, lack of a nap, feeling neglected, or sibling rivalry. When a 16-year-old sassy teenager acts up, it doesn't take us long to think, "What a rotten kid."

When exactly in the developmental trajectory did the child's behavior become their fault? When did we decide that the child's behavior was a product of *free will* rather than causes and conditions?

When we blame someone, we're implicitly saying that under the same circumstances *we* wouldn't do what they did. Examining this more closely, we're saying that if we had the exact same genetic makeup and learning history as the other person, we would've behaved differently. This, of course, is absurd, since if we had the same genetic makeup and learning history, we would *be* the other person, and naturally would behave exactly as they did.

Reflecting on this can sometimes help when blame gets in the way of compassionate connection. Our challenge involves timing: If we leap over our anger and blame to try to get to a compassionate perspective prematurely, we may just bury our real feelings and they'll eventually come back to haunt us (this trick is sometimes called a *spiritual bypass*). But once we've allowed ourselves to acknowledge and feel our anger and judgment, we can also reflect on what may have caused the other person to do what they did. This can help us relax our blaming judgments and see the other person as a fellow ordinary struggling human being, no better or worse than us.

Developing a compassionate perspective doesn't mean condoning injustice or hurtful behavior. There are many circumstances where it's necessary to constrain others, voice outrage, or right wrongs. But acting against injustice while understanding what motivated the other person is different from blaming the other for being bad. The former allows us to feel compassion and connection, while blaming doesn't. Our challenge is to open to angry feelings and use them to bring about change, while also trying to see the factors and forces that motivated the other's behavior. This allows us not only to experience compassion for the offender, but maximizes the possibility that we may be able to communicate with them in useful ways.

Several weeks after not getting promoted, Jolene learned more about her boss's predicament. It turned out that she was under pressure from *her* boss to promote someone else, and that's why Jolene lost out, even though her boss actually really appreciated Jolene's contributions. "It helped to put myself in her shoes. I guess she was in a bind—it wasn't really about me."

The Dalai Lama has written extensively about developing compassion, particularly toward those who hurt us. People sometimes ask him whether he feels anger toward the Chinese government, which views him as a terrorist and forced him and his followers to flee Tibet. He usually says, "Of course I feel anger toward *my friends the enemy!*" Interesting phrase—recognizing their competing interests, but somehow not blaming the other. He also tells a story about a senior Tibetan monk who was released after years of incarceration in a Chinese concentration camp. The monk told the Dalai Lama that at times he fell into despair, lost all hope. The Dalai Lama asked him, "You mean you were afraid that you'd never be released from prison?" "No" said the monk. "I was afraid that I'd lose my compassion for my Chinese captors."

While I doubt that I'd be very good at letting go of blame while imprisoned in a concentration camp, the monk's lifelong compassion practice apparently allowed him to do it.

It's not personal

Often when we don't understand the factors and forces that make others behave as they do, it's because we're taking their behavior personally. I once heard psychologist Rick Hanson suggest an exercise that goes something like this: Imagine you're canoeing down a river, planning to enjoy a picnic. Suddenly there's a bang, your canoe goes over, and you and your lunch are soaking wet, floating downstream. You realize that some obnoxious teenager has turned your canoe over as a prank. What do you feel?

Now imagine the same scenario with a twist: This time when you come up for air, you realize that a big log had drifted downstream and bumped into your canoe. What do you feel?

In both situations, you're cold and wet and lunch is ruined. But when we feel personally attacked, blame arises, and we feel much worse—we're full of anger. And if our self-image is challenged— "Who do you think you are, doing that to me?"—we feel worse still.

When we're able to see the causes and conditions that make

others behave as they do, we respond a bit differently. If my friend treats me poorly, or my colleague ignores me, perhaps it's not really a commentary on my worth. Perhaps my friend or colleague is tired, worried about something, trying to bolster their own sinking self-esteem, or reacting out of some childhood injury. This is both humbling and liberating. We're not that important. We're only playing a bit part in the other person's drama.

Cultivating compassion for ourselves

As challenging as it can be to develop loving-kindness or compassion toward others, and to see their behavior as the natural unfolding of causes and conditions, it can be even harder to see ourselves through this lens. When you make a mistake, how do you usually speak to yourself? Most of us wouldn't have many friends if we spoke to others the way we talk to ourselves: "You idiot!" "Why weren't you more careful?" "What were you thinking?" "How could you be such a jerk!"

There are many reasons we speak to ourselves harshly when we feel we've failed. We may have internalized the voices of parents or teachers who criticized us in the past. We may have absorbed devaluing cultural messages about our personal characteristics or identity, especially if we're part of a marginalized group. We may want to beat others to the punch—criticize ourselves before they can do it. We may imagine that by criticizing ourselves we'll be motivated to improve, and without punishment we'll be lazy and fail again. We may even criticize ourselves to avoid competition with others—after all, the submissive primate who kowtows before the leader gets some scraps and avoids getting beaten up.

Psychologist Kristin Neff, who pioneered research into self-compassion, teamed up with Chris Germer to develop the popular 8-week mindful self-compassion (MSC) program that teaches how to develop compassion for ourselves instead (see *centerformsc.org*). They point out that when things go wrong, we fail, or we make a mistake, most of us fall into "an unholy trinity" of *self-criticism, self-isolation,* and *self-absorption.* First, we beat ourselves up, criticizing ourselves more harshly than we ever would another person. Then, because we feel bad about ourselves, we withdraw—we feel ashamed and don't want to be seen or touched. We're then left self-absorbed, cut off from others, obsessively thinking about how bad we are.

We can cultivate self-compassion as an antidote. Instead of self-criticism, we can develop *self-kindness*; instead of self-isolation, we can cultivate an appreciation for our *common humanity*; and instead of reacting to our painful experience with self-absorption, we can practice *mindfulness*—being with, allowing, and accepting our pain. Self-compassion requires shifts in our heads, hearts, and habits.

There are many techniques available for making these shifts. Drs. Neff and Germer have found that it's usually helpful for developing self-compassion to address all three components.

Self-kindness

There are many different ways to be kind to yourself when you screw up or fail. You can engage in self-care, by eating well, exercising, meditating, doing yoga, and practicing soothing activities. You can seek out supportive relationships and connect with caring friends and family. You can spend time in nature or pursue spiritually uplifting experiences. You can deliberately reframe your mistake, or failure, in more understanding language: "Yes, it wasn't great to eat the whole container of ice cream, but you were feeling really stressed and were hungry." "It's true, you got carried away in the argument, but he really hurt your feelings." You can try talking to yourself with kind words and tone, perhaps as the naturally loving being in the loving-kindness meditation above might. You can even find ways to talk to your critical voices to put them in perspective (you'll learn ways to do this in the next chapter). And perhaps the simplest, most powerful way to be kind to yourself is to get a hug.

Of all the things I learned in Psychology 101, one of the most memorable was the story of Harry Harlow and his cloth and wire monkeys. While these days we see his experiments as examples of animal cruelty (they spurred the animal liberation movement), his studies illustrated something very important about infant development.

It was the 1950s, and researchers were investigating the effects on children of being raised in sterile orphanages without love and affection—which had happened a lot during and after World War II. Harlow decided to explore primates' needs for affection by creating inanimate surrogate mothers for baby monkeys out of wire or cloth. In one study, the wire mother held a bottle with food, while the cloth mother had no bottle. Overwhelmingly, the baby monkeys preferred spending their time clinging to the cloth mother, visiting the wire monkey only briefly to feed.

This experiment confirmed the idea (which seems obvious today) that "contact comfort" was essential to the psychological development and health of infant monkeys—and inspired shifting the care of human orphans from institutions to foster families.

What does this have to do with developing compassion for ourselves? Hundreds of studies have shown that we, too—no matter our age—thrive on touch. This isn't surprising. Cats purr when we pet them, dogs love being patted, and even baby rats thrive if they're licked affectionately by their mothers. In humans, specialized nerves in our skin are actually programmed to respond to stroking at the rhythm that most of us instinctively use when we're being affectionate. And the nerves respond only to a hand at body temperature—not to one warmer or colder.

We can harness our hardwiring for affectionate touch to activate our tend-and-befriend system and help us with our self-esteem collapses. If a caring friend is handy, we can ask for a hug. But even if one isn't, we can hug and stroke ourselves. While this might feel silly or awkward at first, your body is programmed to get the message, and you may find that it works surprisingly well:

Exercise: Affectionate hugging and stroking*

The next time you're suffering emotionally, if nobody is watching, give yourself a hug or gently stroke your arms, your face—whatever helps you feel most loved and cared about. Perhaps recall what felt soothing to you as a child. A hand on your cheek, rubbing your tummy, rocking.

*Adapted from *Teaching the Mindful Self-Compassion Program* by Christopher Germer and Kristin Neff.

Sense what pace and pressure feels best. Notice what feelings arise as you tenderly stroke yourself. Do you feel soothed and comforted? Do other feelings arise? Does it arouse longings for more?

If you've been starved for touch, this exercise may be difficult—you may experience the backdraft discussed earlier. It may initially intensify your hurt feelings. If the exercise feels very uncomfortable, please feel free not to pursue it—this practice is not for everybody. But if it's not too intense, you may find that over time the practice allows you to integrate difficult emotions and settle into feeling held.

Take your time and experiment with different types of touch, on different parts of your body. See which help you feel loved.

Once you've practiced this privately a few times, you may find that you can conjure up the same feelings in public with a simple (less obvious) gesture. Try just holding or stroking your hand, or perhaps your arm or leg, in a way that's not too conspicuous. You might even find that, with some practice, just imagining a hug or caress can generate a similar feeling.

A related way to soothe ourselves when we're agitated or self-critical is with affectionate breathing:

Exercise: Affectionate breathing*

Sit in a comfortable, relaxed, alert posture. Take a few deeper-than-normal breaths and let them out slowly, through pursed lips. Then breathe normally, gently bringing your attention to the sensations of breathing. Focus on the rhythm of the breath. Notice how the breath is nurturing, supporting your life. Just be with the rhythm for a while.

Now allow the breath to soothe you—as though you're being lovingly caressed or rocked with each inhalation and exhalation. Imagine that with each inbreath you're breathing in whatever you might need at the moment—love, care, nurturing, support. As you breathe out, let yourself experience a sense of ease or relaxation. Continue rocking and soothing yourself from the inside in this way for as long as you like.

---

*Adapted from *Teaching the Mindful Self-Compassion Program* by Christopher Germer and Kristin Neff.

Noah's attempt at do-it-yourself home renovation was once again not going well. He couldn't get the new toilet to stop leaking. Predictably, he started beating himself up. "What could be so hard about installing a toilet?" "It's not rocket science." "I should be able to get this." His wife, hearing his self-critical rant from the next room, suggested he might try being nicer to himself. "What would your dad say?" she asked. "He'd probably tell me that these things don't always go right the first time." While Noah was resistant to her kindness at first, he eventually let his wife give him a hug. Letting in the understanding voice of his father and the affection of his wife helped him bounce back—and fix the leak.

Common humanity

To counter self-isolation, in addition to getting a hug, it can be helpful to remind ourselves of our common humanity. There are many pathways to this. Among my favorites is simply viewing our own actions through the eyes of a caring friend:

Exercise: Self-compassion letter*

Recall something that made you feel bad about yourself—whether a mistake, a moral lapse, a weakness, or a failure. If there was a particular painful incident, recall exactly what happened, how you felt at the time, and how you feel now. Allow yourself to mindfully be with the difficult feeling for a few moments.

Next bring to mind a wise, kind, compassionate companion. This can be a mentor, a family member, or a friend. They don't have to be 100% wise, kind, and compassionate—just generally so.

Imagine telling your tale to your companion as they listen closely. Notice what it feels like to share your story with someone who cares.

Now put yourself in your companion's shoes and write a letter to yourself from their perspective. Convey in the letter your companion's compassion, pointing out how you're only human and how your shortcomings connect you to the rest of humanity.

After you've written the letter, put it aside for a while and reread it later.

*Adapted from a workshop presentation by Kristin Neff.

I've had the opportunity to do this exercise with many groups. Certain themes emerge repeatedly. Our wise and compassionate companions say things like "I love you anyway," "We all make mistakes," "I remember feeling the same way when . . . ," or "We all win some and lose some." It's amazing that almost all of us have a wise, compassionate part that recognizes our common humanity—the problem is that this part goes off-line when we're beating ourselves up for our shortcomings.

Another way to appreciate our common humanity is to be a wise and compassionate friend to someone else. Just take a moment to think about someone who has experienced failure, rejection, shame, or feelings of inadequacy lately. Imagine how this person is feeling, what thoughts are going through their mind. Now imagine letting this person know that you've been there too. Share with them some of your failures or disappointments and the feelings and thoughts that you experienced with each one. If you can do it face to face, better still!

Mindfulness

The third skill we need for self-compassion is mindfulness, to enable us to be with, accept, and open to our painful feelings as moment-to-moment sensory experiences rather than getting self-absorbed in our thoughts about how bad or inadequate we are. We'll explore how to use mindfulness in this way in the next chapter.

Compassion for others

Cultivating compassion for ourselves is an important foundation for being compassionate toward others. This is because our emotional injuries make us circle the wagons and get stuck in our threat or drive-and-achievement systems, losing touch with our capacity to connect with and care about other people. When we have ways to take care of our own hurts, we're better able to care for others.

Practices designed to cultivate compassion for others build on this foundation, activating and reinforcing our tend-and-befriend

system. One that has received a lot of attention among Western scientists and mental health professionals comes from Tibetan Buddhist
tradition. It's called *Tonglen* ("taking and sending") and involves
using the breath as a vehicle for cultivating compassion. The exercise
involves visualization, which can powerfully activate our emotions.
In its classic form, we practice bringing to mind someone who is suffering, breathing in and feeling the person's pain, and then breathing
out compassion for this person and for all others who are similarly
suffering. Since this can sometimes feel overwhelming, an alternative, used in the mindful self-compassion (MSC) program, includes
breathing in compassion for both ourselves and the other person—
providing a bit more comfort and soothing for ourselves in the process. Here is an adaptation of the MSC exercise.

Exercise: Sweetened Tonglen*

Begin with a few minutes of *Affectionate Breathing* (page 163). Once
the mind and body have settled a bit and you feel some safety and
comfort, bring to mind someone you care about who is suffering. Let
yourself feel this person's pain, noticing how it feels in the body. Each
time you inhale, bring some love, care, and comfort to yourself. Each
time you exhale, send some compassion toward them. Imagine that
your outbreath bathes them in warmth, care, or whatever they might
need.

Continue breathing in love, nurturing, and care and sending it
out to the person who is in pain. If you like, try expanding the circle to
include others who may also be suffering, connecting to a sense of
common humanity.

Compassion for the competition

We've seen that activating our tend-and-befriend system is hardest
when we're feeling threatened or deprived. It can be challenging to
be compassionate when we've just lost a competition, fallen behind,

---

*Adapted from *Teaching the Mindful Self-Compassion Program* by Christopher Germer
and Kristin Neff.

felt left out or rejected, or been criticized. We often launch into fight-or-flight or achievement-seeking mode in these moments to try to make the bad feeling go away.

An alternative is to try to be kind to ourselves, give ourselves a hug, send ourselves some loving-kindness, and examine our situation from the perspective of a loving friend. We can follow that with trying to cultivate some compassion for the competition— generating warm feelings toward whoever might be threatening our self-esteem in the moment.

Exercise: Compassion for the competition

Start with some *Loving-Kindness Practice* (pages 154–155). Generate loving feelings toward a naturally loving and kind being, then focus these feelings on yourself. You might add in some soothing, allowing your breath to caress and nurture you from the inside as in the *Affectionate Breathing* practice (page 163).

Once you're feeling some loving-kindness, comfort, and safety, bring to mind someone whose accomplishments or qualities trigger envy or self-evaluation challenges for you. Perhaps it's someone who has abilities, accomplishments, or relationships that you long for, who is more popular or skilled than you, who never seems to notice or value you, or who otherwise triggers feelings of inadequacy.

Notice the feelings that arise. Breathe into these feelings, bringing loving-kindness to whatever pain emerges.

Next—and this can be challenging—try wishing this person who triggers you well. Wish them continued success; give them your blessing. Imagine that this person is your son or daughter and you'd like them to be prosperous and happy.

Notice whatever feelings arise—including the inner Darth Vader— and be kind to yourself in the process. Practice loving-kindness for both yourself, struggling with your hurt, and the person whom you are wishing well.

This last exercise is a tough one, but worthwhile. It can be a powerful antidote to our usual feeling, which is "If he's great, I'm not. If she doesn't notice me, I'm worthless." This takes a million forms: "If she's gorgeous, I'm ugly," "If she's smart, I'm dumb," "If he's successful, I'm a failure," on and on with whatever building blocks we use to try to feel good about ourselves. To the extent that we can wish the person who gets us going well, we can free ourselves from our self-preoccupation and relax more into being an ordinary human being. As the Dalai Lama suggests, "Be kind whenever possible. It is always possible." Not a bad habit to develop.

Now that we have an understanding of the myriad ways we can get caught in social comparison and self-evaluation concerns, and have learned techniques for activating our tend-and-befriend system to generate compassion for ourselves and others, we can use these tools to revisit past emotional injuries—to heal the buried trauma from all the times that our hearts were broken, our feelings were hurt, and we wound up feeling bad about ourselves. While this can seem daunting, the fruits are totally worth it. Working with our injuries can further help us break free from self-evaluation worries while connecting more deeply and lovingly to everyone in our lives.

ELEVEN

you have to feel it
to heal it

When you bury feelings, you bury them alive.
—A PATIENT

KATHY LOVE ORMSBY HAD it all. She had been valedictorian in her high school, was premed in college, and was a star athlete. She had broken the women's record for the 10,000-meter race. Now, running in the national championships, she fell to fourth position. Rather than face the shame of not being number one, she turned off the track, ran out of the stadium, crossed a field, and jumped off a bridge. Tragically, she wound up paralyzed from the waist down.

While most of us don't literally jump off a bridge in response to our feelings of failure, we can sure feel tempted. The pain of not living up to expectations or losing competitions, both literal ones and those we imagine in our minds, can feel like too much to bear. We do all sorts of things to try to get rid of the pain. We drink, visit the fridge, binge-watch TV, work, surf the web, text, and play video games to escape it. We seek out new victories, projects, or accomplishments—new self-esteem enhancers—to wipe it out. While considerably less harmful than the bridge, all of these strategies leave us scarred, because, as one of my patients put it eloquently, "When we bury feelings, we bury them alive." And when these feelings begin to rise up from the grave, we feel inexplicably anxious, depressed, or agitated, flooded by emotions that seem out of proportion to our current circumstance.

It turns out that the buried pain of our earlier injuries is a major source of present-day shame and related feelings of inadequacy. Emotions and memories of past defeats and humiliations get triggered by our current failure or disappointment, making our present situation feel that much worse.

This sort of triggering happens to me all the time. For example, I was recently at a professional meeting with well-known people in my field. During the speakers' cocktail hour, several of them were more interested in talking with each other than with me. Feeling left out, I asked myself, "Does it really matter?" The answer was "no." I'm fortunate to have friends and professional opportunities. Hell, I'm even at an age when many people retire. But I still got upset.

So next I asked myself, "Why does it bother me so much to feel like I'm out of the in-crowd?" "What might this remind me of?" While we all wish to feel loved and accepted, it didn't take long for specific memories of seventh grade to rise from the grave. I came from a different school than most of the other kids, wasn't great at sports, and was out of it when it came to teen fashion and popular music. I was definitely not "in" with the cool kids, and it hurt. I remember anxiously looking for a lunch table in the school cafeteria, acutely aware of my many shortcomings—being skinny, having pimples, feeling nervous, and not understanding critical elements of adolescent culture—to name just a few. Since I didn't have the emotional resources to fully feel the pain at the time, nor the emotional maturity to recognize that we all want to feel loved and accepted, I distracted myself with building things and doing science experiments, in addition to less wholesome pursuits like breaking windows with the tough kids in the hopes of joining a not-completely-uncool crowd. But the feelings didn't disappear; they just got buried, forming a reservoir of pain ready to be rekindled at the conference.

Very few of us escape some sort of developmental injury. As a result, most of us are regularly activated or triggered by perceived current threats that remind us of past ones. We tend to react in one of two ways: Either we overreact to our present situation, feeling more pain from a self-esteem challenge than we otherwise would (my experience at the conference), or we shut down, numbing or distracting ourselves, blocking out our current pain the best we can, accumulating more unresolved injury in the process. This latter maneuver then leaves us even more vulnerable to being triggered by the next threat to our self-image, while cutting us off from potentially nurturing relationships.

Identifying the link to seventh grade, along with recognizing my universal human desire for connection, allowed me to open to my feelings at the conference while making my reactions easier to manage. You can do the same, recognizing and feeling the emotions associated with past collapses, seeing their universal nature, and becoming less reactive to present ones. Here, too, it helps to work with our heads, hearts, and habits.

Opening to pain

I first heard the phrase *you have to feel it to heal it* from psychiatrist Dan Siegel (no relation, and incidentally, he always makes me and others feel included at conferences). It's become a touchstone for many psychotherapists. As we're able to accept, feel, and thereby integrate our past injuries, they lose their power to derail our current life.

There are lots of ways to develop the emotional resources we need to do this work. Physical self-care helps. When we have enough sleep, get regular exercise, eat a healthy diet, and take time to de-stress, we're much better able to handle painful emotions. Safe social connection also helps. When we can share our experiences openly and honestly with friends, family, or perhaps a therapist or clergy member, we feel connected and supported by them, which naturally reduces self-evaluation concerns. Mindfulness practice, in which we allow thoughts, feelings, and sensations to arise and pass, and gradually build our capacity to *be with* rather than *distract from* pain, is another valuable resource. And both compassion and self-compassion practices can help us to self-soothe when we're hurting.

Supported by these resources, we may be ready to try revisiting past failures, rejections, and humiliations and integrating the emotions associated with them. Timing and pacing are important here, however. If this isn't a time when you feel you have the strength and support to explore past hurts, just mindfully focusing on safe present sensory experiences—the sensations of walking, the taste of food, the feeling of a breeze, or nature's beauty—may be more sensible. But if you feel up for the challenge, working with past injuries can go a long way toward freeing you from current and future social comparison and self-evaluation concerns, while supporting your capacity for loving connections.

"NAME IT TO TAME IT"

This is another useful aphorism psychotherapists use these days. When dealing with pain in our heart, it helps to use our head to identify it. One way to zero in on the pain of past rejection, failure, or shame, as well as to put it in perspective, is by writing a self-esteem autobiography. It doesn't matter if you're not much of a writer. You can do this just with notes or bullet points. You can even dictate it. The idea is to visit our self-evaluation highs and lows in enough detail to be able to heal the hurt surrounding them. This exercise can be done all at once (which will take a while) or in bits and pieces whenever you have the time and inclination to revisit it.

Exercise: A self-esteem autobiography

Begin with the earliest memory you have of feeling successful or proud of yourself. Take a moment to see what comes to mind. Then make a note of the experience. Now close your eyes, recall the incident in as much detail as you can, and notice the thoughts, feelings, and bodily sensations that arise. Just be with them for a little while. Savor the experience.

Next try to recall your earliest memory of a self-esteem collapse—a moment of failure or rejection in which you felt dejected or ashamed. Again, just make a little note. Close your eyes, recall the incident in as much detail as you can, and notice the thoughts, feelings, and bodily sensations that arise. Just be with them for a little while. If they're very painful, place your hands over your heart and practice a little loving-kindness for yourself (see Chapter 10).

The self-esteem autobiography proceeds this way, boost and collapse after boost and collapse, in each developmental stage.

After your earliest memories you might explore positive and negative self-evaluative moments in preschool, elementary school, and high school, continuing period by period, decade by decade, until you get to the present. Recognize how natural your reactions were, how almost everyone would've felt as you did.

You'll probably notice that various issues were more relevant during some times than others. When, for example, did concerns about being intelligent, strong, athletically skilled, sexually attractive, or creative kick in? Have any concerns lost their power? When? Everybody's criteria for feeling good or bad about ourselves are different, as are our developmental trajectories. The idea is to connect with your particular memories and the feelings associated with them.

As you construct your autobiography, notice which periods were most fraught with self-evaluation challenges. What were the feelings associated with the more difficult episodes? Be kind to yourself as you recall them. Give yourself a hug, put your hand on your heart, or even hold or stroke your own hand—whatever feels most loving and soothing. Imagine how many other people have had similar experiences.

I've introduced this exercise to many people. It seems that we've all had countless joys and sorrows, starting quite young. Early joys include "winning the dance contest," "being picked for the school play," "having my grandma smile at my song," "painting a really beautiful Easter egg." The earliest boost I can recall is a memory of my father being impressed that I had used big words at a young age. I knew from his smile that this was somehow a good thing.

These moments are balanced by a huge range of early sorrows: "being teased and sent away by my older brother," "having to stand in front of the classroom after peeing my pants," "being told that I throw like a girl." For me, it's a memory of bringing a long string of lollipops to nursery school to celebrate my birthday and being told by the teacher, "This is a healthy school—we don't eat candy here." It's these injuries, however big or small, that need our attention.

You may notice once you've begun your self-esteem autobiography that each new day provides fresh material. See if you can notice all the moments that your feelings about yourself go up and down, even if only slightly, and how each little boost and collapse feels in your body. Congratulate yourself on noticing! The more conscious we become of these ups and downs, the easier it will be to let go of the highs and heal the hurts of the lows.

Being with feelings

Accepting the pleasant feelings associated with thinking highly of ourselves is relatively easy for most of us. But as you identify the more painful emotions connected to collapses, you may wonder how to work with them. How might you integrate difficult memories so that they aren't triggered so strongly by current events? Mindfulness practice can help. You may want to try the following exercise first with a mild injury, building up to hurts that are more painful, including feelings of shame, failure, or rejection that still haunt you today. This practice was originally developed by the meditation teacher Michelle McDonald and later popularized by psychologist Tara Brach to work with difficult feelings generally. I've adapted it here to work with the wounds of self-esteem crashes.

Exercise: RAIN for self-esteem injuries*

Begin with a period of focused attention practice to develop some stability and refinement of attention. You can follow your breath, listen to sounds, or attend to another sensory object.

Recognize: Once the mind has settled a bit, call to mind a painful episode from your self-esteem autobiography. Try to recall the incident in as much detail as possible—who was present, what the environment looked like, how old you were, what your body looked and felt like, and what thoughts and feelings arose. Allow yourself to feel the difficult feeling and notice how it manifests in the body.

Allow: We usually feel aversion to the pain of a self-esteem collapse—we want to escape it, to get it to go away. Instead, in this exercise we practice just allowing it to be, observing any aversion responses that arise, repeatedly bringing our attention back to the feelings associated with the collapse.

---

*Audio available at *giftofbeingordinary.com* and *guilford.com/siegel4-materials*.

Investigate: In this step we simply explore in as much detail as possible the sensations associated with our emotion. "Investigate" it in the sense that you might investigate a flower, appreciating its complexity and noticing all of its component parts, as well as noticing your reactions to it.

Natural awareness: This final step involves lovingly accepting the feeling as a natural human experience, a part of the changing kaleidoscope of consciousness, an expression of common humanity, that you need neither to cling to nor to push away. Don't try to "fix" the problem, but rather just stay with the experience for as long as it remains vivid to you. Putting your hands over your heart, giving yourself a hug, doing some loving-kindness practice, or using your breath to gently rock and soothe yourself from the inside as in *Affectionate Breathing* (see Chapter 10) can make this easier.

You can apply the RAIN approach to any feeling that arises as you review your self-esteem autobiography, using it as a tool to integrate collapse-related emotions that you may have buried alive. You can also use it to better understand and accept your feelings around boosts to connect with their pleasurable, as well as addictive, nature.

Chen, a 45-year-old nurse, was struggling with feelings of failure at work—again. A well-known surgeon had spoken to him harshly. "I know that I did a good job. Why do I let her get to me?" Tuning in to the feeling, he felt his head and shoulders slump and sensed a familiar pain in his belly. He then had a powerful association—this feeling was almost identical to the way he felt as a young man when girlfriends broke up with him.

Chen decided to revisit the breakups mindfully, practicing RAIN. At first it was hard—the impulse to get away from the feeling of rejection was powerful. But as he talked himself through the steps, he saw that he could stay with the pain, feeling it in his body. "Then it hit me. I've been running from this pain for my whole life." This insight felt like a relief—if he could muster the courage to turn toward this feeling, get to know it, and allow it to be, he could stop running. He'd even be able to tolerate the surgeon, since really the only danger was that she'd rekindle an old feeling.

Identifying the origins of our feelings of inadequacy and

learning to bear the emotions associated with them can go a long way toward freeing us from our self-evaluation concerns. The key is to connect, as Chen did, with the memories that shed light on our current sensitivities. Sometimes they go back pretty far.

George was a 32-year-old successful financial planner. He was married with a wife and kids but repeatedly found himself envious of his neighbor who made more money, pissed off whenever he had to wait for anything, and generally agitated. He had had gratifying romantic relationships when he was younger and had become an outstanding singer, but his mind always was full of negative thoughts: "She doesn't really love me"; "I sucked at that song." Years later he was anxious that his wife would leave him, even though she never showed signs of infidelity or suggested separating.

While George was exploring his history of self-esteem collapses in therapy, he came across a deeply disturbing photograph. He was 8 years old. His older brother had apparently forcibly put a bra on him, while his other brother laughed and his father snapped the "funny" picture.

As he looked at the photo and tried to open to the feelings it aroused, he realized that this was just one of a long series of childhood humiliations. It didn't help that his father had his own self-regard issues, so he needed his son both to be a star and to never eclipse him.

"No wonder I always need to prove myself. No wonder I feel so competitive with other guys!" The more he could connect with his memories of childhood injuries, and the more he developed the courage to feel the pain of them, the less compelling his self-image concerns became. He even came to develop a refreshingly different attitude toward new waves of hurt and anger: "Oh well, here we go again. Guess I've got more work to do."

This sort of psychological effort isn't easy, but the consequences of avoiding it are worse. As Proust put it, "One is cured of suffering only by experiencing it to the full." Nonetheless, as mentioned before, timing is important. Sometimes our hearts aren't ready; the emotions feel too intense to bear. We may need to put aside the difficult feeling for the moment and focus more on developing a sense of safety. Again, exercise, eat well, get enough sleep, connect with friends, spend time in nature, bring your attention to the present moment—set aside time to do whatever you find nurturing and refreshing. If we can get in the habit of taking care of ourselves in this way, we'll feel more equipped to explore painful feelings when they arise.

Shame

As we explore our self-esteem collapses, most of us discover one particularly painful emotion. It's a feeling that we go to great lengths to avoid and one that plays an important role in most emotional injuries. The emotion is known by virtually all of the world's cultures and can even drive us to jump off a bridge. We call it *shame*.

Psychologists like to distinguish between shame and guilt. We feel *guilty* about our behavior—things we've done that we think are bad. We feel *ashamed* when we think that *we* are bad. Shame is directly connected to self-judgment and our longing for love and acceptance.

The capacity to feel guilt is useful for getting along with others. People who lie, cheat, and steal without guilt cause everyone around them a lot of grief. Shame, however, is usually not so useful. While it can help socialize us, more often than not, feeling that we are bad people just causes unnecessary pain. It drives us to withdraw and hide, robbing us of opportunities for loving connection.

Shame takes many forms. We can feel shame around moral failings—like being dishonest or selfish—but also about being inadequate, unwanted, weak, unintelligent, insecure, vulnerable, or needy. The list is typically a mirror image of the qualities or abilities we rely on to feel good about ourselves. Sometimes we just feel some mild embarrassment, but other times we're downright mortified.

It's hardwired

Psychological experiences that show up across cultures and history are usually built into the wiring of our nervous system. As mentioned before, because it was so dangerous to be alone on the African savanna, and because we desperately need adults' love and care when we're young, we humans evolved an intense aversion to the threat of being cast out—which we experience today as shame.

Virtually all cultures rely on it to socialize their members. We learn not to leave the bathroom door open, take things that belong to others, talk too loudly, or take the last piece of cake without asking—all to avoid feeling ashamed. Just think of all the temptations we pass up because they're not worth the pain of shame. Sometimes this socialization is so effective that we're not even aware of thoughts, feelings, and impulses that would cause shame were we to acknowledge or (God forbid) act on them.

Shame is physical. The parasympathetic branch of our autonomic nervous system takes over and we collapse. We hang our head low, lower our eyes, and hunch our shoulders. We shut down, sink, and want to hide. If we had a tail, we'd lower it between our legs. Shame overlaps with a basic mammalian response to extreme stress— the mouse-in-the-jaw-of-the-cat reaction. In a life-threatening situation, the mouse goes limp to preserve resources and hopefully make the cat lose interest. Here, rather than reacting to the threat of being eaten, we shut down in response to the threat of being cast out of the group.

Shame and self-esteem crashes go hand-in-hand. You can't rank much lower than being ejected from the primate troop. Our bodies react similarly to both, and in both cases we want to hide, if not disappear entirely. But if we can learn to accept the things we're ashamed of, and especially if we can acknowledge them to others, our shame tends to melt away, softening our negative self-judgments.

My daughters' high school had a great custom for helping with the pain of rejection during college application season: *the wall of shame.* The school put up bulletin boards and invited seniors to post their college rejection letters. The combination of making the letters public and seeing everyone else's helped all the kids feel less ashamed and kept their self-esteem from plummeting.

Sometimes, of course, our shame has deeper roots. Here, too, embracing rather than hiding the truth is helpful: Mary Ann, now in her mid-70s, was deeply ashamed during her last family visit. While she tried to be polite talking with her kid brother, inside she was screaming, "Why don't you just *shut up!*" Her brother had always been slow intellectually and a bit crude, and now, nearing 70, he was really embarrassing—loudly displaying his bigotry. He reminded her of their unhappy origins living with a bigoted, alcoholic father. She kept thinking, "My brother's behavior shouldn't bother me," but it did.

One of the ways that Mary Ann had dealt with her childhood pain was by priding herself on never being cruel like their angry father, so she now hated herself for feeling angry at her brother, whose behavior wasn't really his fault, since he really didn't know any better. It was a double whammy—she felt bad about herself both for coming from the family she did and for getting mad.

Talking all this out, Mary Ann eventually realized, "I guess I'm still ashamed of where I came from. But it's true—I didn't choose to be born there." Harder still was accepting that even though she was a generally good person, she still got angry and judgmental. "I guess I'm also only human."

A particularly poignant moment of shame and negative self-judgment can occur when our good feeling about ourselves is based on a wish rather than reality. Have you ever been at a party or event and walked toward an acquaintance who began to smile? You start to smile back and say hi, only to discover that the other person was actually looking at someone else and hadn't noticed you at all. Painful.

Embarrassing as this is, it's even worse in the romantic arena. Have you ever thought someone you're attracted to was signaling similar interest in you, but it turned out they were just being friendly? Being caught with our self-esteem soaring based on the misperception that someone likes us is especially mortifying. Not only were we unworthy of the other's affection, we were also deluded about our worth, and now they know. This humiliation is compounded if we come from a background that tells us pride is sinful. As they warn in Japan, "The tallest reed of bamboo is the first to be cut."

A social emotion

The ancient Greeks had shaming down to a science. Each year the citizens of Athens were asked whether they wished to hold an ostracism—the democratic process of throwing someone out of the city. While most of us don't fear being formally ejected from our community anymore, we certainly worry about informal versions. Just imagining public rejection is acutely painful.

Because shame is a social emotion connected to fantasies of being shunned, the most powerful antidote to it is air, light, and safe social connection—finding ways to let other people know about our shame. This experiment requires courage.

Take Stu's experience. For years, he was conflicted about sex. He enjoyed sex with women and in fact had never been with a man sexually, but when fantasizing, he often thought about guys. "What will my friends think if they learn I've secretly been gay all these years?" It made him feel like a double failure—he saw being gay as somehow "weak," and being gay but not coming out as even weaker.

Stu kept this secret until he had the good fortune of meeting Maddie, an adventurous soul who enjoyed playing out sexual dramas. Being with her gave Stu the courage to reveal his homosexual fantasies—and as it turned out she not only had similar thoughts about women, but had been with several sexually in the past. Knowing that he wasn't alone in having homosexual feelings went a long way toward lessening his shame and helping him let go of self-judgments around sexual desires. Better still, freed of these worries, he had more fun in bed with Maddie than with anyone ever before.

Sometimes being open about the source of our shame is easy, while other times it requires a lot of sacrifice. That's because some shame fits the facts—we really will be rejected if people find out what we've done—while other times our feeling of shame is out of proportion to the likely outcome of being honest. But even when the consequences are rough, it's often worth it to come out of hiding and risk reconnecting with others.

As a psychologist, I regularly see how sharing shameful thoughts, feelings, or behavior in therapy can liberate people from painful self-judgments: the grandmother who was afraid to handle knives and felt like a terrible person because she once had an impulse to stab her grandson; the feminist women's studies professor who wanted to try ballroom dancing but was afraid it would make her look like a sellout; the teenager who thought that he was perverted because he masturbated "all the time." As they each gave voice to their experience, they came to realize that these are simply human thoughts, feelings, and behaviors shared by many others. Their shame faded, and they no longer thought that they were awful or inadequate. It freed the grandmother to cook with her grandson, the professor to get an evening gown and sign up for dance lessons, and the teenager to enjoy himself in private. I once heard it said that being "embarrassed" is just being caught being who we are. If it's OK to be who we are, our problem is solved.

SHAME FROM ABUSE OR NEGLECT

Many of us feel shame stemming from our parents' shortcomings. When we're young and are neglected or criticized, we can have two possible interpretations. Either there's something wrong with our caretakers or there's something wrong with us. The first hypothesis is just too dangerous to entertain—since without adults to provide for us, we wouldn't survive. So, when criticized or neglected, almost all kids go for the second interpretation: I must be bad or defective. This is a good opportunity to work with our heads.

Often our caretakers were overwhelmed with their own needs, had difficulty managing their own lives, were distracted, or were just a bad fit for our temperament. As a child, there's no way for us to understand this, so we assume "I'm bad," "I'm disgusting," "I'm stupid," "I'm damaged goods," or "I'm not good enough"—all in response to the painful feeling of not getting the love and care we long for. These can become core beliefs that color our whole lives. Does any of your negative self-judgment or shame come from being neglected or criticized by your parents or other caregivers? Might it help to consider what actually made them act as they did?

SHAME FROM GROUP IDENTITY

Oftentimes our shame is a social emotion shared by a larger group to which we belong—especially if that group has been oppressed, marginalized, or abused by the wider society. Here liberation movements can be very helpful. Gay pride, Black pride, women's liberation, trans pride, and similar movements have helped countless people move from feeling ashamed of who they are to celebrating it. Working for social justice with like-minded friends can begin to heal the psychological injuries caused by racism, sexism, classism, and other cruelties.

I've also seen patients who felt ashamed about all sorts of other characteristics—like being heavy, feeling anxious, getting depressed, struggling with substance use, or having a special-needs kid—transform their shame into a sense of connection and common humanity by sharing their experience with others going through the same thing. Do you feel shame about belonging to a group some people look down on? Have you been injured by their aggression, large or small? Might you join with others to push back?

LONGING TO RECONNECT

Recognizing that shame is a social emotion can help us notice that beneath our impulse to hide is usually a deep longing to connect safely. We hide because we fear that others will reject us and we'll feel even more alone. But seeing that the intensity of our shame reflects how deeply we care about connecting, how deeply we long to love and be loved, can bring us out of isolation and into relationship. There's a wonderful poem by Daniel Ladinsky, based on the writing of the 14th-century Persian poet Hafez, that can encourage us:

With That Moon Language

Admit something:

Everyone you see, you say to them,
"Love me."

Of course you do not do this out loud;
otherwise, someone would call the cops.

Still though, think about this,
this great pull in us
to connect.

Why not become the one
who lives with a full moon in each eye
that is always saying,
with that sweet moon language,
what every other eye in this world
is dying to hear?

If you could always be aware that everyone else also wished to be loved, how might that change your life? For most of us, when we recognize the universal human longing for connection that underlies all of our shame, we're more likely to actively reach out to others, let them know what we're going through, and reconnect. The problem is, of course, that reaching out when we want to hide, even when we notice our desire to reconnect, isn't easy.

One way to support reconnection is by separating guilt from shame—separating bad feelings about what we've done from the belief that we are fundamentally flawed. All of us behave badly at times, but this doesn't necessarily make us bad, unlovable, or deserving of shunning. If we feel guilty that we've behaved poorly, we can ask ourselves, with as clear a head as possible, "Who did I wrong? Can I move toward this person, admit what I've done, and sincerely apologize? Might I make reparations through kindness or some other gesture?" Separating shame associated with a self-esteem collapse from guilt about our misbehavior can help us rejoin the human family.

There's also a curious relationship between guilt, shame, and self-compassion that can help us. When we treat ourselves harshly for our missteps, we feel ashamed. We want to hide what we've done from the world and to distance ourselves from the pain of our shame—sometimes by becoming defensive or blaming others. If instead we can be kind to ourselves when we err, then we have less need to deny our mistakes and we're more likely to feel remorse about our behavior rather than ashamed of who we are. This eases negative self-judgments and makes it easier to apologize or make reparations. One particularly effective way to be self-compassionate during moments of failure or rejection is to lovingly explore our different parts.

Working with our parts

We saw in Chapter 4 that when we practice mindfulness, we don't exactly find a coherent "self" but rather a collection of parts. As mentioned there, Dr. Richard Schwartz developed internal family systems (IFS) therapy to help people befriend these diverse parts of themselves. Since shame involves rejecting parts of ourselves, this approach can be particularly helpful in working with it. The technique can feel hokey at first, but with a little experimentation, most people find that it's a great way to work with shame and other emotional wounds. Like the other reflective exercises, this one is most effective if you prepare by doing a little mindfulness practice first.

Exercise: Befriending our inner critic

Recall the last time you either actually screwed up or just felt you had and became self-critical. How did you speak to yourself? What words did you use? What was your tone of voice? Did the voice sound like anyone you know (perhaps a critical parent, teacher, or sibling)? How did you feel toward the critical voice? Did you hate it? Fear it? What do you imagine made your inner critic be so harsh?

Next take a moment to speak to your critic. You might find it helpful to give it a name. (Mine is just "Critical Ron.") Let it know that you want to understand its concerns and appreciate its efforts to take care of you. Ask your inner critic, "What are you afraid would happen if you weren't doing such a good job criticizing me?" Usually the answer is something like "I'm afraid that you'd screw up again and get into worse trouble." Often our critic is trying to save us from additional rejection, embarrassment, shame, or failure by whipping us into shape.

If you find that your critic actually means well, you might try offering it a little kindness and then ask if it might consider relaxing a bit, stepping aside, allowing you to try to handle things on your own. Ask your inner critic if its efforts have paid off. Are its admonishments truly motivating? Are they truly necessary to keep you safe or ensure your success?

We can also use this approach to accept, and be kind to, the young, vulnerable parts of ourselves that we hide out of shame. As mentioned earlier, in IFS therapy these parts are called *exiles*, since we usually try to banish them.

Exercise: Caring for our wounded parts

Close your eyes and recall a time that a young part of you felt ashamed or inadequate, was rejected or criticized. Next ask the injured part, "What might you need right now?" This may feel awkward, but usually the part will answer. Sometimes it needs love; sometimes it wants to be understood; it might want a hug or a teddy bear. If possible, in your imagination, offer the part what it wants. Be soft, gentle, and supportive.

As you're communicating with this vulnerable part, see if you can find a name for it—this might be what you were called when you were younger or another name (for me, Ronny). Picture this part of you in your mind's eye—how tall it is, what its life is like, what the circumstances were when it got hurt. How did this part feel during the moment of failure or rejection? What did you do in response? If the inner critic became active at the time of the injury, ask the part, "Did you believe the critic? Did the criticism hurt?"

Giving the young, wounded, exiled part of ourselves an opportunity to talk and be understood can go a long way toward integrating painful emotions that were too much to bear when we were little.

There may be other parts of ourselves that are important to address here too. Sometimes when we experience rejection, shame, or failure there's a part of us that tries to save us from pain through distraction. It may drive us to drink, become aggressive, take crazy risks, eat too much junk food, or engage in unwise sexual behavior—all to try to keep vulnerable feelings at bay. This part, too, may need attention. Ask it, "What are you afraid would happen if you didn't create a distraction?"

Many people find different critics, and different exiled parts, associated with different emotional injuries and painful self-judgments. You can use your self-esteem autobiography to identify them and then work to welcome, accept, and get to know them all.

Joy was 40 years old, had a great husband, and was outwardly successful in her work at a small nonprofit serving foster kids—but she still struggled with feeling discouraged, thinking that she wasn't really doing a good job at work or life. Her inner critic was relentless: "You should've been more assertive in the meeting." "You should've prepared more." "You shouldn't take rejection so hard." "Your work–life balance is out of whack." No matter how hard she tried, she couldn't win, or relax.

Pained by this inner commentary, Joy tried talking with her critical part. It had been with her since childhood. The critic, who sounded very much like her father and was always pushing her to succeed, said that he needed to goad her to protect her from disappointment. She told it that while she understood it was well-meaning, the net result was actually to keep her from doing her best, since she was always fearing failure, and the fear got in her way. She asked if it might hang back a bit and see if she could do OK without the constant criticism.

Joy then turned her attention to another part—the vulnerable little girl inside. All she ever wanted was to make her daddy proud, to think that she was a good girl. Joy became tearful connecting to her longing, and then felt a sense of strength as she realized that this really wasn't so much to ask—after all, she *was* a good little girl; she deserved to be loved as she was.

By inviting our different parts to speak like Joy did, recognizing what they need and fear, we can open to and learn to accept the complicated web of thoughts, feelings, and memories involved in moments of shame or self-esteem collapse. We can gradually heal unintegrated wounds—moments when our pain was too intense to fully allow into awareness. The more we can open to these experiences, the less power current disappointments have to tank our feelings about ourselves, and the freer we become to live our lives fully in the present.

Gaining perspective

As we work with our different parts and explore our injuries, we often find that it's easy to lose perspective—our hearts can readily overwhelm our heads. We blow our present-day missteps out of proportion because they resonate with past mistakes that we never fully acknowledged and accepted. We then condemn ourselves harshly for minor failings, causing a lot of unnecessary suffering.

While some healthy remorse can certainly be useful, a little bit can go a long way toward motivating us to improve or keeping us in line. Because so much of our shame and so many of our negative self-judgments first occurred when we were young, we tend to see them through a child's eyes. We confuse misdemeanors and felonies and don't objectively ask ourselves, "How terrible really was what I did?" Asking this question can help us engage adult parts of ourselves in the healing process.

Sometimes we feel shame or inadequacy, or feel that we're unlovable but can't clearly link these feelings to a particular difficult experience. "I just feel I'm bad." "I don't know, I've always felt that I'm not good enough." These core beliefs may have developed out of many painful moments. We can try to look at these through adult eyes. We can ask ourselves, "What's the evidence that I'm a failure?" "Who wrote the rules?" "Where did I get the idea that I'm inadequate?" "Who chose the comparison group?" "Where did my inner standard come from?" Sometimes we assume there *must* be something wrong with us simply because we feel so bad about ourselves—which is pretty circular reasoning.

The more carefully and lovingly we're able to look at our shame and feelings of failure, the more we can put them in perspective. We can come to see that our mistakes are like single broken tiles in a complex mosaic, surrounded by lots of intact ones. As we increasingly see ourselves as good but also imperfect people, we become less gripped by shame and feelings of inadequacy.

This work of healing past shame and moments of feeling inadequate requires addressing all three *H*'s: our heads, hearts, and habits. We need to think clearly, feel it to heal it, and instead of hiding the things we're ashamed of, seek opportunities to share them with others. It can also help to try things we avoid for fear of failure or rejection, like the time I took tango lessons in Argentina despite being the slowest student they ever encountered (it was rough, but my teacher and I survived). For someone else it could be participating in a community road race where you may well come in last, or preparing just a "good enough" dinner for guests.

The process can take time. It's important that we pace ourselves—we can't heal all of our past injuries at once without becoming overwhelmed. Also, many of us develop narratives early on about who we are and what's wrong with us, which we use to guide and interpret all of our subsequent experiences. It can be challenging to unseat these, to view ourselves through loving adult eyes, to think clearly about what we've done and who we are. While initially it can be unnerving to discover that we're not who we once thought we were, the freedom is totally worth it.

TWELVE

separating the doer from the deed

> Why are you unhappy? Because 99.9% of everything you think, and everything you do, is for yourself. And there isn't one.
>
> —WEI WU WEI

HAVE YOU HEARD the story about the mother who gave her grown son two new shirts for his birthday? He went to his bedroom and came out wearing one of them. Looking at him, her heart sank. "What's the matter? Didn't you like the other one?"

Sometimes we just can't win. We strive to do everything right—accomplish great things, befriend the right people, behave righteously—but we still slip up somewhere, miss the mark, and wind up feeling terrible about ourselves. If you've gotten this far in the book, you already know that the answer isn't to become more perfect. It's instead to make a connection rather than an impression, to be kind to yourself for your inevitable human failings, to open to the pain of past and present self-esteem collapses, and to counter our hardwired tendency toward shame.

Useful self-evaluation

While I've been pointing out the myriad costs of self-evaluation, it isn't entirely useless. Clearly, it's a good idea to assess our physical fitness before attempting to climb Everest, a bad idea to perform brain surgery if our understanding of anatomy is limited to carving a Thanksgiving turkey. Knowing the limits of our abilities, having the wisdom to ask for help when we need it, and understanding how to develop the aptitudes we need to reach our goals are all important life skills.

But ironically, the more common (and troublesome) kind of self-evaluation we've been discussing—judging ourselves as worthy or not—usually gets in the way of these more useful appraisals. Differentiating useful self-evaluation from the troublesome sort is another way we can free ourselves from our struggles to feel good about ourselves.

Albert Ellis was a pioneering cognitive psychologist who was fond of pointing out the errors in our thinking that cause unnecessary suffering. His insights and methods for becoming more clearheaded can be surprisingly useful in liberating us from feelings of shame, inadequacy, and failure.

Ellis called the troublesome, addictive kind of self-appraisal we've been discussing throughout this book *conditional self-esteem.* Ellis points out that it involves a *global* rating of our worth, based on whether we've been good or successful in terms of whatever criteria we use to define our value. It goes up and down regularly and is based on a fundamental assumption that we don't usually examine very closely:

A good act = a good (valuable, lovable) person

A bad act = a bad (worthless, unlovable) person

We're so accustomed to making these judgments, and experiencing self-esteem boosts and collapses based on them, that we don't notice the faulty premises they rest on.

We regularly confuse being with doing, and our conclusions are startling: "I'm good because I lost weight." "I'm bad because I gained weight." "I'm good because I earn a lot of money." "I'm bad because I don't earn enough." When we state these assumptions out loud, they sound absurd. Yet we often live as though they're true.

We also live as though there's some weird mathematical equation that determines whether we're good enough or not, successes or failures, righteous or sinners. But we rarely examine the math. How many positive self-evaluations are enough to be OK? How many negative ones are necessary for us to be failures or rejects? Which grades count? Do recent evaluations count more than earlier ones, or is it our cumulative average that matters? Who invented the measurement scale? Our parents? Our teachers? Our siblings? Our bosses? Our friends? God? What's the ultimate consequence—will we wind up in heaven or hell based on our overall score, or is it just the last grading period that counts?

Karim, a lovely, talented, aspiring musician with three great kids, had been discussing his grading system in therapy for several weeks. One day, I asked him to share his grade du jour. "Uh, about a negative five." And yesterday? "Maybe negative two—it was a better day." I asked him what his best day had been over the last week, and he said, "Oh, wow, Saturday was pretty good—my credit card debt was down from last month and I had lost 3 pounds!" Grade? "Zero." Karim realized he only included in his grading system areas of difficulty. His global assessment was based on his financial success and his weight—being a good father and husband, a loyal friend, and a skilled musician didn't figure into the equation. A zero was therefore the best he could do. Faced with a rigged system, Karim decided to try stepping out of the game by noting every time a global assessment arose. He was embarrassed by how often this happened, but it helped him not take the judgments so seriously.

Many of us find that our evaluative system is disproportionately influenced by recent events. Rather than being like a cumulative, lifelong GPA that changes gradually, our global assessment of ourselves can swing wildly with each success or failure. As my colleague Paul Fulton remarked, "I'm only as good as my last session. If it went well, I'm the world's most talented psychologist. If it went poorly, I need to find another line of work."

The more carefully we look at our system of self-evaluation, the less solid and sensible it seems. This is because no math actually works for global ratings—they're too arbitrary and too mercurial, and many of us are ridiculously hard graders. But most of the time we don't examine our assumptions. Instead we assume, as Ellis put it back in 1957, "A person should be thoroughly competent, adequate, talented, and intelligent in all possible respects; the main goal and purpose of life is achievement and success; incompetence in anything whatsoever is an indication that a person is inadequate or valueless." (Not much has changed since 1957 in this arena.)

Its many costs

There are considerable costs to living as though we can arrive at a global rating of our value. When we're just looking objectively at our skills and talents, we can be problem centered: What abilities do I need to accomplish my goal? What do I need to do to develop those skills? But when our worth is on the line, we get mired in one-upmanship, one-downmanship, and self-consciousness—and get derailed by anxiety or depression when we imagine that we've come up short. We posture to appear competent but secretly feel like imposters. In all of this striving for success, we not only become less effective in the world, but fail to notice what really matters, missing out on opportunities for meaning and connection.

Luckily, we can instead learn to realistically appraise our talents and weaknesses, successes and failures. It's very freeing to clear our heads in this way. Therapists since Ellis have developed all sorts of exercises that can help.

Realistic self-appraisal

I came across many parent guidance books during 25 years working in a child and family clinic. Almost all encouraged parents to communicate a simple but remarkably elusive idea to their kids when they misbehaved: "You're not bad—your behavior is inappropriate." While very true, this reality is hard for both kids and adults to embrace.

There are many different ways to awaken to the truth that our worth isn't based on some mathematical summation of our good and bad deeds. We can turn to religious values—we're all God's children, Jesus loves us, or we're all endowed with what Buddhist traditions call *basic goodness*. We can base it on relationship—someone loves (or once loved) us no matter what we say or do. Or we might use logic to see that nobody is actually good or bad—these are culturally conditioned ideas that we mistake for absolute reality. However we get there, we want to arrive at what Ellis called *unconditional self-acceptance* instead of *conditional self-esteem*.

This notion is shared by many seminal thinkers in the mental health field. The pioneering psychologist Carl Rogers identified self-acceptance as a central ingredient in psychotherapy: "By acceptance . . . I mean a warm regard for [the client] as a person of unconditional self-worth—of value no matter what his condition, his behavior, or his feelings." We can work to develop this feeling of acceptance whether or not we behave intelligently, correctly, or competently and whether or not others respect, love, or approve of our behavior—separating our evaluation of our abilities and behavior from this sense of meaning or worth. We can live as though we, and everyone else, are neither "good" nor "bad"—but rather just all ordinary human beings. And we can use this awareness to connect, realizing that in this regard we're all very much in this together.

Unconditional self-acceptance is a little different from the self-compassion we explored in Chapter 10. Self-compassion involves holding ourselves in a loving embrace as we experience pain—it's heart centered and relational. Self-acceptance is a bit more head-centered. It involves recognizing the absurdity of our changing valuations of ourselves, accepting ourselves whether or not we perform well or gain approval from others.

Cultivating unconditional self-acceptance

Since self-acceptance involves clear thinking, an important step in cultivating it is to examine the origins of our assumptions about our value or worth. Many of our beliefs are so deeply rooted that we don't see them as beliefs at all, but rather as immutable realities.

It can be helpful to reflect on your most basic assumptions or core beliefs. What are the characteristics of a good, valuable, worthy person? What were the earliest messages you can recall that informed your ideas about this? Were there particular people (such as parents, siblings, teachers, or clergy) who delivered those messages?

As you think about your own worth, and the worth of others, who do you imagine gets to judge success? Is it the people who first taught you your value system? Do you carry images of them inside you? Or are there other, more recent people in your life who define good and bad, success and failure? Do cultural values or religious teaching play a role in your evaluations?

As you make judgments about your goodness or badness, your value and your worth, which deeds or attributes determine your global assessment? (You might consult your self-esteem autobiography from Chapter 11 for ideas about this.) Is it defined by your skills? Your relationships? Your ethics? Your accomplishments?

Finally, what timeline do you use for your global assessment? Is it based on your most recent performance or an average of all your positive and negative self-evaluations throughout life?

Sometimes just reflecting on the assumptions we use to judge our value as Karim did, and noticing how our grading system works, brings perspective to our self-evaluations. We're not trying to stop honestly assessing ourselves, we just want to see how we leap from noticing specific talents and weaknesses, successes and failures, to generalizing these into global assessments of our worth.

Another way to work on developing self-acceptance is to follow the advice of the parent guidance books using an approach analogous to the self-compassion letter in Chapter 10:

Exercise: Educating the inner child

Recall a recent time you made a global rating of your worth, feeling like a success or failure, good or bad, lovable or not. Then imagine that you're a child coming to this conclusion.

Next bring to mind a naturally wise, kind, loving being (perhaps a caring parent or mentor, or the loving being you used in *Loving-*

Kindness Practice in Chapter 10). Imagine that this being is talking to the childhood you. What would they say about your self-assessment and your global ratings of yourself?

The aim of this little exercise is to access the voice inside that is naturally wise and gets how harsh and unrealistic (though universally human) our global assessments can be. We actually have the capacity to offer parental guidance to ourselves—we just have to tap into it.

After reflecting on his global self-ratings, Karim brought to mind his grandmother, who had been the most loving and level-headed member of his family when he was growing up. In his imagination, he spoke with her about his financial difficulties, his weight, and how bad these made him feel about himself. She smiled. "For years I felt like I was a failure since I never went to college or had a career like my brother Omar. I felt uncomfortable whenever I was with him." But what she liked most about getting older was seeing how we're actually all in this together. "Helping him through his divorce, and then his cancer, changed all that. I felt close to him again. I got it that we all have our struggles, nobody is better or worse than anyone else, and we're all fragile creatures." She then gave Karim a big hug.

Questioning our crazy, cruel philosophies

Another way to free ourselves from our global assessments of worth is by challenging them in our minds and our behaviors—working with our heads and habits. For example, many of us struggle with perfectionism, feeling that any mistake makes us failures.

Navajo weavers, who are famous for their rugs, routinely include at least one incorrect knot in every carpet to temper the egotism of perfectionism. They're on to something important. Deliberately screwing up can be an excellent way to loosen our preoccupation with self-evaluation.

There are countless ways to do this, some easy, others more challenging:

Exercise: Deliberate imperfection

The goal of this exercise is to challenge our perfectionism by deliberately making mistakes or doing things poorly, investigating our emotional response, and through this process learning to accept our imperfection. You can start with easy screw-ups and, if you're up for the challenge, build to the ones that are more difficult to tolerate. As you're doing each activity, be mindful of the thoughts and feelings that arise and be kind to yourself. We all make mistakes—regularly.

The following suggestions are just possibilities, ranked roughly in order of difficulty. Feel free to decide how "imperfect" you're willing to be or to invent and try out your own mistakes:

- Next time you're driving somewhere and have extra time, deliberately pass your exit.
- Shop for an item online and buy it from an overpriced vendor.
- Send someone (not your boss) an email containing spelling errors.
- Go about your day wearing only one earring.
- Put on socks that don't match.
- Go out with your hair uncombed, wearing torn or dirty clothes.
- Sing off-key or dance awkwardly in public.

You might even try one of these if you're feeling especially courageous:

- Stand on a street corner and tell passersby that you've recently been abducted by aliens (stop if any of them say it has happened to you also).
- Call out the stops for fellow passengers on a subway or train (don't try this in a quiet car).

As you make your mistakes or embarrass yourself, notice the thoughts, emotions, and bodily sensations that arise. See if you can simply *be with* the discomfort. Try giving yourself a hug, a kind word, or another form of self-compassion for comfort.

Once you've spent a little while being with the inner experience of imperfection, ask yourself: Did I really become a bad or inadequate person? Did my global assessment of my worth change?

Experimenting with being imperfect and investigating our reactions can help us see more clearly the silliness of global self-evaluations.

An alternative approach to seeing through our perfectionism is to *try to be perfect*. Here's the assignment: Take a perfect shower. Or write a perfect poem. Or fry an egg perfectly. See what happens to your belief in perfection.

The ball is in our court

Exploring the absurdity and unreliability of our global judgments and the promise of unconditional self-acceptance makes it clear that we are actually the ones who define our worth, value, or adequacy, based on how we choose to interpret our successes and failures, virtues or vices, competencies or weaknesses. While we develop our evaluative habits naturally from messages we receive from others over a lifetime, we don't have to be slaves to them.

We can come to see that we're all just ordinary human beings who are smart but also dumb, conscientious but also lazy, skilled but also inept, adored and rejected, and all of this is in constant flux. Our assessments change with our good and bad fortune, positive and negative feedback, as well as with our shifting scales and methods of measurement. And we're all in this together!

Carla, now 50, had spent much of her life stuck in all-or-nothing thinking—first about her grades, her looks, and her popularity; later about her career and her parenting. As a teenager, if she didn't get an A, if friends got together without inviting her, if she got a zit, her mood plummeted. As an adult the same thing happened if she didn't get a great performance review at work or if her kids were unhappy.

But recently something shifted. She went on a weekend hiking trip with a childhood friend. They decided at the last minute to splurge on an expensive restaurant, even though they hadn't brought appropriate clothes. The food was great, but Carla kept thinking, "I wonder what they're thinking about us; we're so underdressed." Turns out that her friend had similar thoughts, and neither of them wanted to be worrying about it.

So right there, on the spot, they formed the Fuck It, I'm Fifty club. They decided that every time they found themselves worrying about what everyone else thought, or judging themselves for not living up to some standard or another, they'd respond with "Fuck it, I'm fifty." Want to join? You can sign up at *fuckitimfifty.club* (really).

Seeing who you really are

If you're feeling adventuresome, you can try getting even freer of these global evaluations by looking more deeply into who you are. This approach was developed in ancient wisdom traditions and reprised by modern cognitive science. It can be disconcerting—but it has the potential to be very liberating. We'll begin by taking a close look into what's happening right now.

Close your eyes for a few moments and pay attention to your breath to sharpen your concentration. Now, as you read these words, try to identify where the "you" is that's reading them. Is it the hands holding the book? The eyes looking at the page? The body on the chair? Where exactly do you "hear" the words as you read them? It's not with your ears. They form in something you call your mind, right? Where exactly is this mind?

Next close your eyes and count slowly to five, then open them again. Where did you "hear" the numbers or "see" the figures? Where is this consciousness, this "you," that registered the experiences? Where is the "you" that did the counting?

Please close your eyes again and conjure up an image of your mother for a few moments, whether or not she's still alive. Where exactly did the image appear? Who was looking at her? You may sense where the image was, but where or what is the "me" that was looking at it? Where or what is the "me" that conjured the image?

Cognitive scientists tell us that most of us locate our awareness or consciousness somewhere in the head, behind the eyes. In fact, many of us act as though this were somehow "me"—the core of who I am—and that our bodies are vehicles for carrying around this important mental entity. We imagine that we could lose our possessions, our social role, even our arms or legs, but if we lost this awareness *we* would somehow be gone. We surmise that this is what goes away when we die, and indeed this node of awareness, somewhere in the head, is what many of us fear losing when we fear death.

The more carefully we examine our sense of "self," the stranger it gets. If I do something foolish and afterwards say, "I wasn't myself," who was I? Or as psychologist Steven Pinker asks:

> What or where is the unified center of sentience that comes into and goes out of existence, that changes over time but remains the same entity, and that has a supreme moral worth? . . . Say I let someone scan a blueprint of my brain into a computer, destroy my body, and reconstitute me in every detail, memories and all. Would I have taken a nap, or committed suicide? If two I's were reconstituted, would I have double the pleasure? . . . When does a zygote acquire a self? How much of my brain tissue has to die before I die?

These questions are definitely weird. We usually don't ask them. Rather, we spend most of our time talking to ourselves about ourselves. From mundane decisions ("I think I'll get the salmon with wilted spinach tonight—that'll be healthy") to existential fears ("What'll I do if the lump is malignant?"), self-referential chatter fills our waking hours. Listening to it all day long, we naturally come to believe that the hero of this drama must exist—and must be *very important*. As I heard a comedian comment the other day, "I can't die; I'm the main character in my story."

We don't often examine how we construct our sense of self. When we do, it can feel upsetting, since our conventional assumptions start to come apart. But noticing how insubstantial our sense of self actually is can help free us from worrying so much about ourselves and can put into perspective our constant judgments about our worth and how we compare to others.

Mindfulness practice can be a powerful tool to support this sort of examination. When we practice more intensively, the nature of consciousness becomes easier to see. We never find a stable, separate "self" inside. Rather, we observe a continuous flow of changing experience, constantly interacting with our environment. You can see this for yourself with a longer meditation:

Exercise: No one home

Begin if you can with 20 minutes or longer of mindfulness practice, spine erect, eyes gently closed, attending to the breath. Allow thoughts to arise and pass, like clouds in a vast sky.

Once the mind has settled a bit, and you've had a chance to observe your thoughts coming and going, see if you can find the observer of your experience. Where is the "me" or "I"? Can you actually observe a "me" or an "I," or do you just notice a changing kaleidoscope of contents, moving from a thought, to the breath, to a sound, to an itch, and so on?

Allow yourself to keep practicing for a while, seeing if you can find a stable self inside.

The more we do this practice, the more elusive the "I" tends to become. We begin to glimpse the insight suggested in the title of psychiatrist Mark Epstein's book *Thoughts Without a Thinker*—the thoughts come and go, but there's no stable "me" thinking them.

If these exercises feel too weird, you can try another approach to loosening the conventional sense of self that comes from yogic traditions. It's sometimes described as developing *witness consciousness*.

Exercise: Witness consciousness

Begin with a few minutes of mindfulness practice, spine erect, eyes gently closed, attending to the breath. Allow thoughts to arise and pass.

Once the mind has settled a bit and you've had a chance to observe your thoughts coming and going, notice that while the thoughts keep changing, the experience of observing the thoughts remains. This awareness is like the sky—sometimes filled with clouds, sometimes sunshine, sometimes stars—but the sky remains.

Notice that this experience of awareness, of consciousness, has been here your whole life. This awareness remains as long as we're awake and alive, regardless of our changing circumstances and whether pleasant or unpleasant thoughts, feelings, and sensations are arising.

Keep attending to the breath for a little while, allowing all the contents of the mind to come and go, noticing how the experience of awareness is always there.

It doesn't matter very much whether we come to the conclusion that there's no one home or that "we" are actually awareness itself (different meditative traditions see this differently). In either case, we come to see that all of the judgments about "me" and how I'm doing are actually thoughts and images that come and go and constantly change—and we don't need to identify with or believe in them.

Marta was 40 years old and recently divorced. While her marriage hadn't been great, the final straw was discovering that her husband had been having an affair with their neighbor. Understandably, her self-evaluations were pretty rough. She went back and forth between thinking "I'm a failure as a wife" and "My ex is such a &%★$."

Having practiced mindfulness on and off for a few years, Marta decided to attend a silent retreat. During her meditation, she noticed the thoughts about herself shifting, sometimes hour by hour, sometimes minute by minute. "I'm over the hill." "I'm ugly." "He's such a jerk—he'll regret losing me." "I'm really a great person." She also was able to see that these thoughts really were just words and images, each one accompanied by an emotion, arising and passing against the backdrop of awareness itself. As the retreat went on, she increasingly came to experience her mind and heart as a vast open space that could hold and allow countless changing thoughts, feelings, and sensations.

When she returned home, the thoughts about her and her ex kept coming, but she didn't get as stuck in angry or self-critical moods. When she had to negotiate with him about child support or scheduling for the kids, she was less likely to lie awake at 3:00 A.M., fuming. She felt lighter, freer, and more relaxed, as though her self-worth was no longer on the line.

Dropping the hot coal

Experiences like Marta's are a wonderful fruit of more intensive mindfulness practice, but they can also be challenging. We want to think we know who we are, that our thoughts about ourselves are somehow true, and that we exist in some stable, substantive way. It is indeed disconcerting to no longer feel very solid and to realize that the only relatively stable element in our awareness is awareness itself.

But these experiences can also be a great relief—like dropping a hot coal we've been clinging to unnecessarily. We might also say it's like jumping out of an airplane without a parachute, with a twist. At first it's terrifying, but eventually we find that there's no ground—we never actually go splat. Rather, we just move from one moment of changing experience to the next. And the more we see that there isn't really any stable "me" to be found—there are just thoughts about me and how I compare with you arising and passing against a backdrop of changing sensations and images—the less we tend to believe in our global ratings, the less we believe that we're good or bad, winners or losers, saints or sinners, lovable or not. Each moment of our life then becomes an opportunity to be more present, and more richly and lovingly connected to other people, to our work, to nature, to whatever is happening here and now.

CELEBRATING INTERBEING

Another helpful insight that can emerge with continued mindfulness practice involves seeing our interdependence more clearly. This too can help free us from the pain of self-evaluation, as we see that the very idea of "me" as a separate individual is illusory—built from linguistic conventions. Admittedly this too is a very weird idea. Let's try a little thought experiment together to illustrate it.

Imagine there's a little girl eating an apple. She takes a bite and sees half a worm in the remaining fruit. Being a bright child, she deduces what has happened and goes to spit out the stuff in her mouth. Here's a question to begin our thought experiment: If you had to choose, how would you characterize the material remaining in her mouth? Is it essentially apple + worm? Or has it already become the little girl? (Most people at this point say it's essentially apple + worm.)

Now imagine that there was no worm, so she continued chewing and swallowed the bite of the apple—but if she were having a bad morning it could come back up. How would you characterize the material now in her stomach? Is it still essentially the apple + gastric juices, or has it become the little girl? (People are often more mixed at this point.)

Next imagine that she's having a good morning, so the apple proceeded through her duodenum and into her intestines and the fructose from the apple has been broken down to glucose, and molecules of this glucose are now in her bloodstream—they're now her blood sugar. How would you characterize those glucose molecules? Are they still the apple, or have they now become the little girl? (Most people vote for the little girl.)

Finally, let's consider another part of the apple, known as cellulose or fiber. Imagine it's proceeding down her alimentary canal getting ready to be deposited into a familiar white porcelain receptacle. How would you characterize this material? Because I'm a nice guy, I'm going to offer you three choices: (1) It's still the apple. (2) It has become the little girl. (3) It's something else. (Most people choose "something else.") Does it strike you as odd that we don't like to think of our feces as being either our food or us, but think of it instead as "something else?" After all, what could it really be except for our food or us?

I trust that you see the problem. Where exactly is the point where an apple turns into a little girl? Or for that matter, when during your last breath did the thousands of molecules of oxygen that used to be the atmosphere of the room you're in turn into *you,* and the thousands of molecules of CO_2 that used to be *you* turn into the room's atmosphere? Have we just proven that you actually *are* the room's atmosphere?

This isn't just a fun intellectual game. The reality is that we are completely interdependent with the world around us, and the boundary between "me" and the rest of the world is created by my thoughts. The more we practice stepping out of our thought stream, the more we experience ourselves and the world as a biologist or physicist would describe it—a constantly changing, swirling system of matter and energy in constant interchange, of which this body and mind is a tiny part. This insight has enormous implications for our sense of ourselves, and also for getting along with others, because our notions of "us" and "them" that cause so much trouble stem from not noticing our interdependence.

As we get comfortable with the realization that we're all part of a much larger organism, it becomes easier to share, love, and connect, to have moments of intimacy where we're not holding back, protecting ourselves. We become less self-preoccupied and less concerned with our self-esteem and social comparisons. The Vietnamese Zen teacher Thich Nhat Hanh calls this *experiencing interbeing.* Here's an excerpt from one of his essays on the topic:

The Cloud in the Sheet of Paper

If you are a poet, you will see clearly that there is a cloud floating in this sheet of paper. Without a cloud, there will be no rain; without rain, the trees cannot grow; and without trees, we cannot make paper. The cloud is essential for the paper to exist. . . . If we look into this sheet of paper even more deeply, we can see the sunshine in it. If the sunshine is not there, the forest cannot grow. . . .

And if we continue to look we can see the logger who cut the tree and brought it to the mill to be transformed into paper. And we see the wheat. We know that the logger cannot exist without his daily bread, and therefore the wheat that became his bread is also in this sheet of paper. And the logger's father and mother are in it too. When we look in this way we see that without all of these things, this sheet of paper cannot exist.

If we're really just part of a seamless, interdependent universe, our struggles to be good enough, succeed, or be liked and respected really are pretty silly. While we have values and aspirations, our evaluations of our worth are truly ridiculous. Appreciating our interbeing, we can find instead the deep satisfaction that comes from being quite ordinary, interconnected with other people and the wider world. In fact, embracing our ordinariness can be a delightful way to further drop the hot coal of self-evaluation and lovingly connect ever more deeply with everyone else.

THIRTEEN

you're not that special—
and other good news

> When the game is over, the pawns, rooks, knights, bishops, kings, and queens all go back into the same box.
>
> —ITALIAN PROVERB

DO YOU KNOW WHO the king of England was in 1387? Back then, a lot of people knew, and he was a really big deal. Now not so much. Despite all the efforts we put into succeeding in life, our prognosis is poor and our legacy is short.

It gets worse. By many estimates, in only 50,000 years the earth will enter another ice age. In 600 million years, as the sun gets hotter, CO_2 will disappear from the atmosphere, and all the plants will die. In a billion years, the oceans will evaporate, and all remaining life on earth will be annihilated. It would seem that our successes and failures, our concerns about what other people think, and our worries about being good enough may not matter that much in the long run. Isn't it strange that despite the obvious fact that we're all in this together, and face a similar fate, so many of us persist in wanting to be both special and important?

The curse of specialness

When we look at a field of daisies, most of us don't think, "They're really pretty flowers, but the most special one, the really valuable daisy, is 236 rows from the front, 89 in from the left." We're fine with daisies being beautiful in their ordinariness, without one being more special than the other.

But when it comes to humans, we're uncomfortable with ordinariness. Who aspires to be "plain," "average," "regular," or "normal"? We've evolved a culture that increasingly denies the fact that we're all, in the end, very much alike.

Evidence for our growing attachment to specialness is everywhere. Take baby naming, for instance. In America in 1950, one out of three boys was given one of the 10 most common names, as was one in four baby girls. Being "normal" was prized. By 2012, fewer than one out of 10 boys, and one out of 11 girls, received a common name. The boys' names that have increased most in popularity in more recent years include Major, King, and Messiah—*extraordinary* is the new normal. As the pioneering researcher of human happiness Martin Seligman quipped, "It's as if some idiot raised the ante on what it takes to be a normal human being." These days, to be ordinary is to be a loser.

We order our personalized coffee at Starbucks, want to live in a unique house, and have a wedding like no other, all to establish our personal brand. Even churches have climbed on the bandwagon. Joel Osteen, pastor of America's largest evangelical church, says, "God didn't create any of us to be average." Incredibly, there's now a whole movement called Prosperity Christianity exemplified by the bestselling book whose title reveals how crazy this has become: *God Wants You to Be Rich.*

Personally, I became addicted to specialness at a very young age. I was praised for being bright and verbal and quickly seized on this to float my boat. While I was lucky also to get love from my parents, their seeing me as especially talented created a real problem. I became a hothouse plant, expecting to be successful at whatever I did. So a little later on, when I got chosen last for teams in gym, couldn't carry a tune or draw a picture, or was picked on by the tough kids, the blow was worse because I thought I was supposed to be special. I withdrew from arenas in which I was average or below, and even in areas where I had some talent, I felt I needed to excel more and more just to feel OK about myself.

This personal experience, along with all the patients I've seen who have struggled to be special, has made me a big fan of embracing ordinariness. It can also be a refuge for people who grew up being told that they were somehow below average, since being ordinary allows us all to join the human family.

This is not a new idea, of course. Almost all of the world's religious and wisdom traditions suggest that humility—the natural consequence of embracing our ordinariness—is central to well-being. "Blessed are the meek: for they shall inherit the earth" (Christianity). "The Lord will destroy the house of the proud" (Judaism). "Humility, modesty . . . absence of ego; this is said to be knowledge" (Hinduism).

Those of us hooked on specialness fear that if we're just ordinary we'll wind up lonely—we imagine that others like us only because we're special in one way or another. And while that's sometimes the case (as in addictive romantic love, for example), most of us are much more drawn to people who understand our common humanity and don't see themselves as above or below others. We feel safe, loved, and connected in their presence. In fact, some such ordinary people have, paradoxically, developed vast followings as spiritual teachers—precisely because they don't see themselves as great teachers or want vast followings. It really is an extraordinary gift.

I once attended a fundraiser for a wonderful 80-year-old Spanish priest who had spent his adult life in Africa setting up orphanages. Hundreds of rich, powerful, successful people competed to get their photos taken with him. He was totally unfazed by the hoopla and responded in every encounter like he was just a regular guy doing his work. He sure seemed well loved, happy, and content—while quite unconcerned with being special.

Embracing ordinariness, the priest had no need to pose or posture, nothing to hide, and was valued for his authenticity. Mike Robbins, who teaches leaders how to be more authentic, invites us to complete this sentence: "If you really knew me, you'd know that _____." (Try filling in the blank right now.) Would you actually wind up lonely if everyone saw the truth about you, saw you as the ordinary, imperfect person you are?

Freedom: nothing left to lose

There are a lot of other benefits to actually getting that we're ordinary human beings. Defending our specialness, or trying to prove we're not inferior, can be exhausting. If we're ordinary, we can use praise as encouragement to stay the course and criticism to effect changes—since ordinary people regularly make mistakes. Wise people have long known this. The father of American psychology, William James, reflected in 1882 on how freeing it can be: "Strangely, one feels extremely lighthearted once one has accepted in good faith one's incompetence in a particular field." More recently, psychiatrist Michael Miller suggested a corollary: "I know many people who have been ruined by success, but few by failure." In fact, failure can make it easier to connect with other mere mortals.

Bill had enjoyed good fortune in his career. He had worked his way up at his company, going from engineer to supervisor, manager, and then VP. He made good money and had a lot of influence. But he suffered from a disorder psychologist Paul Fulton once dubbed *late-onset, tertiary-stage, occupational narcissism*. He had become full of himself and not very nice to subordinates.

Then his company's stock price fell, there was a reorganization, and a new CEO took over. His new boss brought in new people, and Bill's status sank. Struggling with the pain of no longer being a big shot, he sought therapy.

We started by exploring how Bill felt before the reorganization. "I guess I got off on being the guy everybody listened to. I was tight with the boss, and they all wanted to be on my good side." Then we turned to his current situation. "Nobody really wants to talk to me now. Most of them probably think I'm a jerk." Bill felt too defeated to try lifting his spirits by attempting to claw his way back to the top. Instead, with my encouragement, he talked to family, friends, and even a few coworkers about his earlier hubris and his newly discovered humility and vulnerability. "It's embarrassing, but I guess I wasn't so special after all—I was just lucky. Not being on top anymore is still hard, but it's a lot less lonely." He even started going to church again. "Everyone there tries to support each other. Being a blowhard wouldn't go over too well. I think it's good for me."

Humility and embracing ordinariness also help us to forgive. Research studies suggest that when we think we're superior, we become self-righteous and judge others more harshly for their faults, seeing them as less forgivable. In fact, one clever experiment that made subjects feel superior to peers demonstrated that this diminished their ability to even identify, much less care about, others' feelings.

Our sense of specialness can also be toxic in another way—we feel shame when we think we're especially bad, unfit to be loved. Here seeing our ordinariness can be our salvation, since the painful experiences that make us feel especially terrible about ourselves are often universal. I still recall my relief when the leader of a therapy group told us in high school, "There are two types of boys: those who masturbate and those who lie about it." Whew.

A wonderful new application of big data is to alleviate shame by showing us how ordinary we all are. One program tracked Internet searches and used the results to reassure gay men living in areas where homophobia is rife that they weren't alone, even in their own neighborhoods. Another project helped adolescent girls worried about vaginal odor to feel normal by showing them how common Internet searches are for this concern. As it turns out, our shame makes us extraordinarily ordinary—since we're all ashamed of similar things. Being ordinary connects us to our common humanity. And acknowledging our ordinariness means that we don't have to posture and pose, feeling like imposters.

Like other ways of freeing ourselves from painful self-evaluation, embracing our ordinariness involves our heads, hearts, and habits. If we've been hooked on being better than others, it means seeing the folly of our attachment to specialness, feeling the disappointment of giving it up, and endeavoring to live as ordinary people. If we've been convinced that we're somehow less than others, it means examining the roots of that assumption and risking behaving as if we were OK just as we are. Every step we take brings us more peace, freedom, joy, and connection.

Diana loved going back home during breaks at grad school. "When I'm with my family, I don't feel like I have to prove anything." Chris loved camping alone. "It's great to have nobody around for miles and not worry about being seen or judged by anyone." And Anna cherished seeing her old friends from high school. "I just feel totally part of the gang. It doesn't matter what I do." That's the peace, freedom, and connection that celebrating ordinariness can offer.

Being who we are

I'm fond of a story I heard from Barry Magid, a psychiatrist and Zen priest in New York. Many affluent New Yorkers are concerned that their children get accepted to high-status, competitive preschools. The idea is that if your child gets into an elite preschool, it will enhance the kid's chances of getting into an elite elementary school. And if your child goes to an elite elementary school, chances are improved for the child's entering an elite secondary school. And of course, if your child goes to an elite secondary school, chances of getting into Harvard soar. And we all know that getting into Harvard is a guaranteed path to happiness.

It was in this context that Dr. Magid's wife was reviewing preschool applications for their son. She showed him one that had a full page for parents to describe how their child is extraordinary. Dr. Magid said to his wife, "Just write 'He's not special—he's an ordinary kid.'" That was the last his wife let him see of the application.

How might we celebrate being an "ordinary kid"? One way is to work with our hearts by playing with our feelings of inadequacy.

I once worked with Joseph, a bright, dedicated high school teacher whose grandfather had been a wealthy industrialist. As a result, his mother inherited a lot of money. She was now incapacitated with dementia, and he and his sister, her only heirs, were in charge of her finances. Since his mother had more than enough resources to receive good care for the rest of her life, my patient and his sister distributed some of her assets to themselves. He used his share to buy a house in an upscale part of town.

The problem was, whenever he went to neighborhood gatherings, Joseph felt inadequate. Almost all of his neighbors were movers and shakers, chiefs of hospitals and universities, politicians, or entrepreneurs. He felt that they had *earned* their wealth, while he had gotten his arbitrarily, through an accident of birth.

As Joseph struggled with his feelings of inadequacy, we hatched a plan. The next time he was at a gathering and felt inferior to his neighbors, he would silently repeat an affirmation. He would say to himself, "Yes, you may be very impressive and successful, *but I get my money from Mommy!*"

There was something about playfully embracing his ordinariness that really helped highlight the absurdity of social comparison, allowing him to connect more comfortably with his neighbors.

You might try this yourself with a little experiment. Right now, think of something you've done, or a personal quality, you're ashamed of (shouldn't take long to come up with one). The next time you're in a social situation where you're feeling uncomfortable about it, triumphantly (but silently) make a declaration, as though you were proud of your foible or limitation. "I'm fatter than you!" "You think *you're* selfish!" "I'm the most anxious guy here!" See if, like Joseph, it helps you feel less ashamed of, and more comfortable with, being ordinary.

Another way to embrace ordinariness is to work with our heads—developing a realistic appraisal of our strengths and weaknesses and then reflecting on how we came to have them.

Exercise: How I became me

Start with a review of your qualities and abilities. Using the blanks in the two columns below if you like, list several of your most important strengths and weaknesses—the qualities that make you feel good about yourself or special, and the ones that make you feel inadequate or inferior. (If you need extra space, go to *giftofbeingordinary.com* or *guilford.com/siegel4-materials.*)

Strength	Weakness

As you look at the list, note what feelings arise in connection with each strength and each weakness. Let yourself feel those emotions.

Next take a few moments to reflect on how each strength or weakness came about. Was it through the luck of genetics—you were just born good (or bad) at it, or with (or without) that particular talent or quality? Did it come about because of good or bad life circumstances—you had parents or others who introduced you (or didn't) to the ability, helped (or didn't help) you develop the skill or quality? Did it happen because of hard work (or avoidance)? Did that hard work (or avoidance) come about because of genetic or environmental influences?

Most of us find when we look at our lists that the origins of our strengths and weakness are all *impersonal*. Our desirable and undesirable qualities came about from factors and forces that aren't really about our worth, and even if we were actors in the process, there were impersonal forces and factors that predisposed us to behave in the ways we did. We are indeed all quite similar, and ordinary, in this regard too.

We're definitely in this together

I have a distinct memory of being 5 years old and seeing a woman who was older than even my grandparents. She had so many wrinkles that I felt startled—as though she were some sort of alien. Years later, at age 24, I was with a high school friend watching middle-school kids going around a skating rink. He pointed out that we were now twice their age. Startled again.

It seems that at every developmental stage I'm surprised that *I* have arrived here. Somehow I imagined that aging happens only to *other* people.

Sooner or later, aging threatens almost everyone's self-image. We may grow taller or more competent for a while, but eventually we peak and begin to decline. Whether it's physical strength, attractiveness, intellectual ability, or social status, we eventually all lose our edge to younger people. (There are exceptions. If we've staked our self-worth on being kind or generous, we may be able to keep this going until the end.)

If we actually got that nobody's specialness is going to last, we might be a little less attached to it. Realizing this can be freeing if we've thought of ourselves as especially inadequate as well—being one-down is also not forever. This is a challenging path to embracing ordinariness, but a very powerful one. Here's a little exercise that can help you connect with the impermanence of it all. It's hard, so don't try it if you're feeling shaky today. But if you're up for an adventure that can go a long way toward loosening our concerns with self-evaluation, read on.

Exercise: It all changes*

Begin with a few minutes of mindfulness practice. Spend 5 or 10 minutes just observing the inbreath and outbreath or another object of attention such as sound, or contact with the chair, gently returning your attention to these sensations should your mind drift into thought.

Once you've developed a bit of concentration, recall how you felt when you were a child. Imagine yourself sitting in your current posture with your child body. What might you have been wearing? How did you feel in your body? How did you appear in the mirror? In what ways did you feel special? How did you feel ordinary? Less than others? Be the child you once were for a few moments.

Next recall yourself sitting as a young adult (if you are currently a young adult, try recalling how you were a few years ago). How do you feel sitting in your younger body? How did you look from the outside? In what ways did you feel special? Ordinary? Less than? Be the young adult you once were for a few minutes.

Continue this exercise by envisioning yourself at your current age, first from the inside, sitting, and then looking at yourself in the mirror. Again, how do you feel special? Ordinary? Inferior?

Then move into the future. Imagine how you will look and feel at milestones such as middle age, retirement, or old age. In each circumstance, take some time to imagine how you would feel sitting in your current posture, how you would look in the mirror, and in what ways you'd feel special, ordinary, or less than others. Notice which ages are easier to imagine and accept and which are more challenging.

If you discover that one age is particularly difficult, you might try directing loving-kindness toward yourself at that age. For example, if it's difficult to be with the image of being quite old, hold that image in mind, place your hand over your heart, and suggest, "May I be safe, may I be happy, may I be healthy, may I live with ease" or similar intentions.

---

*Audio available at *giftofbeingordinary.com* and *guilford.com/siegel4-materials*.

The great leveler

Consider the king of England and the fate of our planet. An even more challenging but potentially even more effective way to see our ordinariness is by trying to face death head on. Most of us live in varying degrees of denial about death. Facing mortality is difficult but has the potential to dissolve our preoccupations with self-evaluation and to connect us more deeply to one another.

Psychiatrist Bob Waldinger directs the Harvard Longitudinal Study, the longest running study of human well-being (it began in 1938). He told me that when the researchers asked subjects near the end of their lives if they had any regrets, the most common were "I wish I hadn't spent so much time and energy worrying about what other people think of me" and "I wish I had paid more attention to the important relationships in my life."

The bumper sticker that says "Whoever has the most toys when he dies wins" also highlights the futility of our struggles to be special as well as the absurdity of feeling less than others. And while we might initially feel hopeless when we contemplate death, seeing the reality of impermanence can actually help us engage more fully and freely in each moment of our life and connect with everyone else who is in the same predicament.

Some 30 years ago I was traveling in Krabi, Thailand, and came across a fascinating Buddhist monastery. It was like a death theme park. Real human skeletons and skulls were on display everywhere, and the monks used them as objects of meditation. When people in the neighboring towns died, their relatives offered the bodies to the monks to perform spiritual autopsies—not to discover the cause of death or advance medical knowledge, but to help the monks get it that we're made of meat and sooner or later we all become dead flesh.

Upsetting as this sounds, the monks I met were not a gloomy lot. They went about their lives with a lightness, an appreciation of the present moment, based on an understanding of the impermanence of all things. It's not hard to see how keeping this in mind, and embracing it with our hearts, might free us from self-evaluative concerns. Notwithstanding tombstones of different sizes, in death we really are all very much the same.

Most wisdom traditions likewise encourage us to embrace mortality to find psychological and spiritual freedom. "For dust you are, and to dust you shall return" (Genesis). We "all go to one place" (Ecclesiastes). And there's the great Italian saying at the start of this chapter: "When the game is over, the pawns, rooks, knights, bishops, kings, and queens all go back into the same box."

Often the reality of our impermanence is suddenly forced on us. Gitu, a social worker in her mid-50s, lost her husband last year after a long and painful illness. It was a traumatic experience, and though she's relieved that he's no longer suffering, she misses him very much. But she also feels that she learned something important. "You know, I wouldn't wish this on anyone, but being with him during all those months of slowly dying had a silver lining. I get it more now that life is short and we all die."

Working through her grief, she's been using this awareness to change her life. Each day she pauses to ask herself, "What really matters?" Guess what? Being special, looking good, winning at the social comparison game, and racking up achievements aren't high on the list. Those preoccupations have lost their pull. It's caring for others, appreciating the present moment, and trying to make the world a better place that come to mind instead. "It's hard to explain, but even with all my pain, life feels more meaningful—and weirdly better—now that I'm focusing on what's most important."

Facing the reality of death is a tall order, of course, and may not be the best practice to adopt when we're feeling emotionally unsteady. But when we're not too overwhelmed, it can really help us let go of our concerns about being special or good enough, since how we compare to others is so obviously irrelevant once we're dead.

There are several ways to do this. During the American Civil War, when death was ever present, it became customary to remind oneself of mortality every day so as to better appreciate being alive. Buddhist monks do this by spending the night meditating at charnel grounds, watching bodies decompose or be eaten by animals. Less gruesomely, we can take a walk in a cemetery, noting birth and death dates, appreciating that we really don't know when our time will come. We can also create simple reminders for ourselves. To temper his performance anxiety, my colleague Paul Fulton would sometimes write on top of his presentation notes, "Dead Soon."

Another way to embrace impermanence and develop perspective on our worries about how we're doing is to contemplate the future of our social self. Most of us construct our sense of self from the reflections we see in the faces of others, from all the ways that people accept or reject, praise or blame us. In fact, many of us are more worried about being respected, wanted, or loved than we are about our health or longevity. This next exercise can therefore be difficult, but also very freeing. Try it when you're in a relatively stable place and up for challenge:

Exercise: The future of our social self*

Start with a few minutes of mindfulness practice to cultivate attention and open the heart and mind.

Then imagine that after all your worries about your health, all your concerns about diet and exercise, and all that brushing and flossing, it's finally happened. You've died. Life is going on without you. People who love you are sad. They're remembering everything that they loved about you. And they're remembering the things that they didn't like so much too. Notice how you feel imagining them thinking of you.

Next imagine that a year has passed. Your loved ones are increasingly getting on with their lives. Of course, they still think about you a lot, remembering the good times and sometimes the difficult ones. But they're getting more used to you being gone. It's becoming the new normal. They're still grieving, but they're also more engaged in other things, no longer continuously aware that you're not there. Notice how you feel imagining them a year after your death.

Now imagine that 5 years have passed. Your loved ones are fully engaged with their new lives. Of course, they think about you, but not as often. And while they still miss you, they're no longer grieving regularly—just at poignant moments that remind them of your time together. Notice how you feel imagining them 5 years after your death.

---

*Audio available at *giftofbeingordinary.com* and *guilford.com/siegel4-materials*.

Now imagine that 10 years have passed. Your loved ones are having trouble believing that it's been 10 years already. Their lives and the wider world have changed so much. So many things have happened. From time to time they imagine what it would've been like had you been able to be part of it all. Occasionally they wonder what you would've thought, how you might've reacted to the way the world has unfolded. Notice how you feel imagining them 10 years after your death.

Finally, imagine that 100 years have passed. Everyone you knew has also died. Any children they may have had are alive, but these people never knew you. The world is a strikingly different place. Life goes on, and there are few reminders that you were ever here. Notice how you feel imagining the world 100 years after your death.

For most of us, the reality of death can be hard to even imagine. We're so attached to our fantasies of having a future and to being the star of our little show, that glimpsing our fate is deeply unnerving. If we do manage to picture our death, we may at first become nihilistic—why bother doing anything if it's all going to end, if I'm just a speck of dust in a vast and meaningless universe? But even though it's painful and difficult to begin to let go of our illusions, once we get over our initial shock, it can be immensely freeing.

The more vividly we can see how impermanent everything is, including ourselves and everyone else, the easier it is to let go of our self-evaluations. Then rather than feeling like meaningless specks in an uncaring universe, facing our transience and ordinariness can actually allow us to connect lovingly to other people and the whole of creation, providing a deep sense of meaning. Because the less preoccupied we are with trying to feel good about ourselves, the easier it is to feel part of the wider world.

The joys of insignificance

Closely related to accepting our ordinariness and impermanence—and equally challenging—is embracing our insignificance. This is tricky, since it involves a paradox. Most of us are naturally very invested in mattering. And from one perspective we matter a lot.

We matter to our family, friends, and coworkers. We touch count-less people, and this adds up—we make all sorts of contributions to the world over our lifetimes. Our efforts benefit others in small and large ways, and each act of kindness and compassion really does help the world become a better place.

But from a broader perspective, we don't actually matter that much in an enduring way (think again of the king and the future of our planet). And our attempts to matter, to be important, get in the way of both our usefulness and our well-being.

My colleague consulted with me about Julio, a patient who lost his position in human resources at a community hospital when it was absorbed by a larger chain. He had been a valued, dedicated manager and had received an award for his work shortly before the takeover. While he got a decent severance package and enjoyed taking some time off, when he reentered the job market, the health care mar-ketplace was changing, and Julio felt depressed having to settle for a lower-level position. Exploring his feelings in therapy, he realized how attached he'd become to feeling that he was important. "In my old job, everyone consulted with me when they had problems." His new job recruiting providers was interesting, and he got to meet a lot of people, but "I'm definitely no longer center stage."

My colleague, personally interested in letting go of preoccupa-tions with specialness, started talking with Julio about the possibility of embracing his insignificance. At first he was put off. It seemed like a disturbing and emasculating prospect that ran counter to the way he'd lived all his life. But she pointed out that insignificance might not be so bad—if he didn't need to be important, he might enjoy the ordinary moments of life more. Perhaps he could feel less stressed, engage more with his friends and family, and find satisfac-tion in activities like playing the piano and gardening that he didn't have time for before? Maybe he could enjoy getting to know new prospects at work without needing to feel indispensable? Perhaps he could create a new habit—using each ordinary moment as a chance to be more aware, more connected, more fully engaged, yet relaxed?

While scary, since it meant giving up feeling important, this idea made sense to him. Julio remembered that at his former job he was forever trying to attend every meeting and be included in all the big decisions. "It wasn't really conscious, but I think I imagined that if everyone saw how important I was, I'd always be needed and have job security." Losing his job brought home the reality that ultimately none of us is really so important—whatever our role, we really can and will eventually be replaced (or "made redundant" as they say so poignantly in Britain).

As Julio tried to keep in mind the impermanence of all things and deliberately embrace his insignificance, he found he actually *did* enjoy the present moment more and felt more love and connection with the people who matter to him. While he works hard in his current position, he no longer harbors the fantasy that he's irreplaceable—which actually makes work less stressful and more fun. He actually is able to spend time in his garden, play the piano, and even enjoy just *being* at the beach with his family or spending quiet moments alone.

As counterintuitive as it may seem, our best shot at living well—and mattering in meaningful ways to those around us—may come from embracing exactly the realities that we most resist: our mortality, our ordinariness, and our ultimate insignificance. Like other approaches to overcoming our preoccupation with self-evaluation and status, embracing ordinariness helps open the door to our most reliable sources of well-being: safely connecting to one another and being more fully present to whatever we're doing at the moment. It even has the potential to transform us from feeling like a separate "me" struggling to be good enough or stay on top, to experiencing the peace, joy, and love that naturally arise as we discover ourselves to be cells in the vast web of life—what is sometimes described as spiritual awakening.

Sound good? Just turn the page. It's where your efforts to free yourself from the tyranny of self-evaluation have been heading.

FOURTEEN

beyond I, me, mine

All you need is love.
—JOHN LENNON

BACK IN 1895 Sigmund Freud wrote that the most we could expect of psychoanalysis was to transform "hysterical misery into common unhappiness"—not exactly the loftiest aspiration. About 100 years later, after decades of studying how to help people move from −10 to 0 on a scale of well-being, psychologists began to systematically ask the questions, "Can we do any better?" "Is happiness actually possible?"

It's about other people

This gave birth to the field of positive psychology, which explores the factors that lead to well-being and those that get in the way. A few decades later, the jury is now in. I've alluded to its verdict many times. As the psychologist Chris Peterson, one of the founders of the positive psychology field, put it near the end of his life: "Other people matter!"

Feeling safely connected to others turns out to be the central ingredient in human flourishing, while being disconnected is a risk factor for all sorts of ills. It's not the rich, privileged, good-looking, or powerful people who are happiest—it's those who have loved ones, friends, community, and meaningful work.

At this point I hope you're convinced: Relentlessly trying to boost or maintain self-esteem, whether through proving yourself capable, good, or likable, or trying to live up to some inner standard, winning competitions, or scrambling to avoid feelings of shame or failure is no route to happiness. Fortunately, the most powerful antidote has not only worked for me and my patients, but is supported by hundreds of studies demonstrating a tight correlation between safe social connection and health.

When you ask yourself, "What really matters?," there's a good chance your answer has to do with other people. Almost all of us develop a sense of meaning from our connections to one another. Recall Desmond Tutu's observation that in many African societies people measure their well-being as a group, rather than as individuals. Parents worldwide know this viscerally—we can only be as content as our least-contented child. And research backs it up: When our friends, spouses, siblings, or neighbors are happier, so are we. In fact, the closer we live to a happy person, the stronger the effect.

Sadly, however, we're becoming more disconnected. As the political scientist Robert Putnam documented in his landmark book *Bowling Alone,* in America, at least, participation in community activities has steadily declined over the past decades. We're also living alone more, and less likely to have friends over for dinner, visit neighbors, or have someone close to us with whom we can talk. Being preoccupied with self-evaluation contributes to the problem. It reinforces our sense of being a separate "I" striving to make it in a competitive world.

Redefining "me"

We've already seen that the more we cultivate supportive relationships, practice compassion, and embrace our ordinariness, the more we can connect to others. It's possible, however, to take this a step further, expanding our sense of self to feel less like separate individuals and notice more clearly who we really are—part of a larger human family and the web of life. Shifting our sense of self in this way is a powerful tool for freeing us further from self-judgment. Here, again, we need to engage our heads, hearts, and habits.

How might we change how we think of ourselves? First, recall the thought experiment in Chapter 12 where we saw that the boundary between "us" and the outside world is just a concept, challenged by the exchange of molecules every time we eat, poop, or breathe. Then consider that scientists as early as the 1700s coined the term *superorganism* to describe species in which the idea of a separate "individual" seemed particularly questionable.

Take ants, for example. The colony includes a queen, workers with various roles, soldiers, and so forth. No single ant survives very long without the support of the rest, and they all act for the good of the collective. So early biologists concluded that the "organism" is actually the colony, not the individual ant. As our understanding of ecology has grown, we've learned that all creatures are part of larger interdependent systems, and the idea of separate "individuals" never really made sense.

Rather, all organisms are akin to cells in our body. We don't look at the skin cells of our face and say, "This is Sally, who lives next to Darnell, who's neighbors with Isabel—they all get along and share nutrients, but they're really separate individuals with their own nuclei and mitochondria."

Similarly, when we cut a finger, our other fingers don't react by saying, "Sure glad it didn't happen to me! I better keep my distance from that one to avoid blood-borne pathogens."

In the same way, as we loosen our attachment to our stories about ourselves and our status, we become more inclined to connect to and care for others. We discover that we're not good or bad, worthy or not, winners or losers, nor meaningless specks of dust in an impersonal universe, but rather part of an evolving human family and, beyond that, an amazing web of life.

As much as we may forget it, we're inextricably interconnected. Are you a subsistence farmer? Me neither. That means you and I are dependent on one another for food, not to mention shelter, electricity, medical care, and all of our other needs. The more we notice our interdependence, the more our tend-and-befriend system comes online, so we feel more love, while our fight-or-flight and achievement systems become quieter, so we feel less afraid, stressed, angry, and driven.

The joy of generosity

> No act of kindness, no matter how small, is ever wasted.
> —AESOP, "THE LION AND THE MOUSE"

Most approaches to spiritual development involve realizing that we're part of something larger than ourselves: We're all God's children, members of the human family, or otherwise parts of nature and the wider universe. And virtually all the world's religious and wisdom traditions extol service to others as a way to honor, express, and reinforce this understanding.

Modern science concurs. Psychologists studying human flourishing have found that generosity is a particularly effective path to well-being. While it's true that money can't buy happiness (once basic needs are met), giving it away can. Researchers approached people on a university campus in Canada and gave them cash. They instructed half of them to spend the money on themselves and half to spend it on someone else. Guess which group felt better?

A different study involved people who received stem-cell transplants to treat cancer. One group was asked to write about the emotional challenges of the experience—a well-established practice for working through trauma. Another group was asked to write about the experience, but also to imagine that someone scheduled for the procedure was going to read their story and benefit from it. Guess which group had greater relief? Just *imagining* helping others was psychologically healing.

After controlling for factors like household income, researchers at Notre Dame found that people who were the most generous financially, with their time, and in personal relationships, were significantly happier, physically healthier, and felt more purpose in life than those who were less generous.

The relationship between service or generosity and well-being is so predictable that we can sum it up in a pair of equations:

selfish action = greater material riches + less well-being

unselfish action = fewer material riches + greater well-being

Or as the Dalai Lama often says: *Be selfish; love one another.* I once saw him put this into practice in a very touching way:

A colleague and I had the privilege of personally inviting the Dalai Lama to an event at Harvard Medical School. After 6 long hours of discussing research with clinicians and neuroscientists at a conference, he was ushered into a back hallway where he graciously met us and accepted our invitation. His next stop was a room where a dozen undergraduates—members of Students for a Free Tibet—were waiting. Clearly exhausted, he nonetheless took the time to present a prayer shawl to each student and to personally thank them for their efforts, like a loving grandfather. It was inspiring to witness.

MOTIVATION MATTERS—BUT FORGET ABOUT PERFECTION

The consensus is clear: Generosity helps us feel more connected to others and happier as a result. But do our motivations matter? After all, there are many types of giving. Sometimes we give with the hope that we'll get something back in return. This is the biologically based reciprocal altruism discussed earlier. It makes sense for our joint survival if I share when I have more in the hopes that you'll share when you have more.

Another kind of giving involves our self-image. We want to think of ourselves, and be seen by others, as generous. In lab experiments, economists have demonstrated that not only do we give more when we think others are watching, but our private concerns about self-image play a role even when they're not. This kind of giving connects us to others but risks further trapping us in self-evaluation concerns, even if it's better than trying to look good through self-promoting behavior.

The third kind of giving springs from recognizing another's need and sensing our common humanity—getting it that *there but for the grace of God go I.* Compassion arises spontaneously, and we feel moved to give, neither expecting something in return nor buffing up our self-image.

While it would be nice to be sufficiently saintly or enlightened to always give in this selfless, wise way, I suspect it's unusual in its pure form. When I'm generous, there's often a part of me hoping for some sort of reciprocity someday, and I almost always think more highly of myself. While these other elements might invite trouble (perhaps I'll be upset if my friend doesn't reciprocate, or my self-esteem will plunge the next time I see my greed), giving helps us connect anyway.

In some Buddhist traditions selfless generosity is represented by *bodhisattvas*—individuals who have attained enlightenment but instead of blissfully entering nirvana deliberately stick around to alleviate the suffering of others. What if we were to live as though *our* central purpose was helping others? Psychologist Charles Styron designed a simple habit change practice to inch us in this direction:

Exercise: A bodhisattva to-do list*

Make a to-do list of things that you are going to do for others on each day of the week. You may do things for many people or for only a few. They can be big things or small things that you routinely do for someone else. Aim for two or three items per day. If you have more free time available on the weekend, see if you might schedule something more involved then.

Take a few minutes to draft the to-do list now. What thoughts and feelings arise as you make your list? Are you concerned about being too generous or not generous enough? Do negative feelings toward others get in the way? Try to be open to all of your reactions.

Once you've made your list, put it into action. Do the generous acts as consciously as possible over the next week, so you notice how you feel doing them and how others respond. Check things off the list as you would with any other to-do list.

Before bed each day, reflect for a few moments on your generous activities of the day. How did it feel to do them? Try to be self-compassionate—forgiving yourself for whatever you didn't manage to do.

Ashley, a single woman in her mid-20s, had been driving an Uber after quitting her retail sales job and breaking up with her

---

*Adapted from "Positive Psychology and the Bodhisattva Path" by Charles Styron.

boyfriend. She wanted to go back to school but didn't know what kind of work to train for. Her self-image was pretty shaky. Every time she spoke to a friend on a solid career track or in a good relationship, she had a sinking feeling of failure and inadequacy.

Then her favorite aunt was diagnosed with cancer. "When I spoke with her and heard how scared she was, a light bulb went off in my head—I've been completely focused on myself." Tired of being unhappily self-preoccupied, Ashley decided for the next week to focus her attention on helping others. As it turned out, a surprising number of her rides were going through tough times and wanted to talk. She started each trip with the intention to be as kind and supportive as she could—listening compassionately to passengers' stories. Sometimes the conversations were really moving, and she felt like she had made a friend, however briefly. Ashley also made a point to keep in touch with her aunt. "It really worked. Instead of being stuck in self-pity, I felt engaged and alive again."

Gratitude

> Who is rich? One who is happy with his lot.
> —Mishnah (Jewish oral law)

Of all the interventions to enhance well-being that psychologists have studied, gratitude practices have proven to be the most powerful. Gratitude boosts our capacity to deal with and recover from life's challenges. It's linked to having more energy, sleeping better, feeling less lonely, having improved physical health, and experiencing more joy, enthusiasm, and love. But why?

First, gratitude is an antidote to desire. Anytime we want things to be other than they are, we experience desire. And as sages throughout history have pointed out, this causes a lot of suffering. Recall a recent moment of distress (so many to choose from). Were you wishing for something to be different than it was in that moment? Are you still wishing for that now? When we're grateful, we notice instead ways that things *are* as we'd like them to be—noticing ways that our glass is half full rather than half empty. Gratitude therefore naturally softens our cravings for achievement, status, recognition, or worth.

The other way that gratitude works is, like generosity, by fostering connection to something larger than ourselves, shifting our sense of self in the process. When we feel gratitude, we feel it *toward* something or someone. We might feel grateful toward a person who has been helpful, or toward nature, fate, or God. In moments of gratitude, we feel connected to someone or something outside of ourselves and experience the other as *good*—perhaps loving, generous, or kind. Gratitude also supports generosity. We naturally want to "pay it forward" and give to others when we're grateful for what we have. And we've seen how connection lightens our self-evaluative concerns.

Mindfulness as gratitude practice

A great way to cultivate gratitude is through mindfulness practice. The Zen master Suzuki Roshi famously said, "In the beginner's mind there are many possibilities; in the expert's mind there are few." Mindfulness practices help us see with fresh eyes, to not habituate or become jaded. Whether it's the taste of a tangerine, the color of a sunset, or the warmth of a smile, mindfulness sensitizes us to what is actually happening in the moment and helps us experience it more fully.

As we practice being aware of what's actually happening now with loving acceptance, we become more inclined to appreciate what *is* rather than being lost in our wishes for things to be different than they are. Little, ordinary experiences become full, rich, and valuable. We also notice how fleeting everything is, which reminds us to savor each moment. We discover that gratitude for simple, everyday experiences is much easier to renew than are the highs that come from winning the lottery, falling in love, or getting a promotion.

Mindful awareness also helps us transform lemons into lemonade. Instead of ruminating on how annoying the other cars are when we're stuck in traffic, we might appreciate the song on the radio, the colors of the leaves, or the shape of the clouds. Instead of complaining about the pile of dishes, we might get into the sensations of the soapy water and the collage of plates in the sink. We can only be grateful for things we notice—and mindfulness practices help us notice everything.

Fredricka, a 48-year-old administrative assistant at an investment firm, had fallen into a slump. She hated her job. "It's *soul crushing*—what's the point of just helping rich people get richer?" She had become a wellspring of negativity: nothing felt like it mattered anymore, the world was really messed up, and she was only a cog in the machine.

Aware that her attitude wasn't optimal, Fredricka signed up for a meditation class. As she started meditating regularly, the cloud began to lift. She still didn't like her job, but she began to notice and appreciate little things. "I love the way the light looks when the sun comes through the window." "I actually tasted an apple for the first time in months." "I love the coziness of my bed at the end of the day." These were small moments, but they gave her hope that there was a way to appreciate being alive.

Learning from loss

In some wisdom traditions students are encouraged to wish for difficulties. Ask yourself, "When have you developed more compassion? When has your heart grown wiser? When have you appreciated what you have? Was it during good times or when things fell apart?" Indeed, many of our growth spurts are triggered by pain. As they say in some Christian circles, "Suffering is grace."

Researchers tested this notion. Since people often express more gratitude for their lives after near-death experiences or life-threatening illnesses, they examined whether deliberately contemplating our mortality would increase gratitude—and it did. So we can use the exercise in the previous chapter, *The Future of Our Social Self,* not only to appreciate our ordinariness and impermanence, but also to cultivate gratitude for still being alive.

Noticing others' suffering

Another effective way to cultivate gratitude is by noticing how hard life is for others. In the developed world, most of us have electricity, refrigeration, central heating, running hot and cold water, toilets, and access to antibiotics. We sleep in comfortable beds, free from rodents and insects. Many of us actually struggle *not to eat* all the wonderful food at our disposal.

We live so much better than the wealthiest people in the olden days, not to mention all the impoverished people today. According to the World Bank, some *689 million people* live on less than $1.90 per day. You can see how your income compares to the rest of the world at *https://howrichami.givingwhatwecan.org/how-rich-am-i*. Noticing what we have can help a lot when we're feeling deprived.

Another easy-to-access path to gratitude is to compare our current state to our own past. Thich Nhat Hanh invites his students to try a simple experiment: Recall the last time you had a toothache. Remember your pain, your worry, and your wishes for relief? I have excellent news for you today—no toothache!

Counting your blessings

Researchers have tested a wide range of other exercises to cultivate gratitude. One of the most widely validated approaches is keeping a gratitude journal. It's a great habit to develop. In various studies, compared to control groups, people who kept gratitude journals exercised more regularly, reported fewer physical symptoms, and felt better about their lives. They also reported greater alertness, enthusiasm, determination, and energy, and were more likely to report having helped someone with a personal problem. Sound good? Here's how to do it:

Exercise: Gratitude journal

Once a week, take a few minutes to reflect on gifts that you've received in your life. These gifts could be simple everyday pleasures, people in your life, personal strengths or talents, moments of natural beauty, or gestures of kindness from others. An item might be a conversation, a lovely view, an event at work, a treasured possession, a beloved friend, connection to God—whatever occurs to you.

Jot down several gifts. As you write, try to be specific and open to feelings that arise as you bring each gift to mind. Let yourself relish or savor the gifts and be aware of the depth of your gratitude. Some items may repeat from week to week, but try to keep the list fresh, reflecting on recent experiences and taking the time to mindfully explore the feelings associated with each one.

You may find it helpful to consider different realms in which you might feel gratitude and see if you can recall a gift in each category. Write these gifts on the blanks below if you like (if you need more space, go to *giftofbeingordinary.com* or *guilford.com/siegel4-materials*).

Work: _____

_____

Family and friends: _____

_____

Nature: _____

_____

Health: _____

_____

Uplifting moments: _____

_____

Material comforts: _____

_____

If writing doesn't suit you, feel free to speak or silently contemplate your gifts instead; express gratitude for your gifts as part of an evening reflection or prayer; or find a "gratitude buddy" with whom to share your reflections in person or by phone, text, or email.

Research on gratitude practices suggests that they're most effective if we note as much detail as possible, include gratitude toward other people, and savor surprises—unexpected opportunities or gifts. An additional trick for increasing appreciation is to imagine life without any one of our everyday blessings. As my wife's grandmother used to point out, "If you lost everything you had today and got it back tomorrow, that would be happiness."

Connecting through gratitude

One of the most famous research studies in positive psychology tested five different interventions to see which would have the most powerful effect on well-being. The clear winner was a *gratitude letter*. Subjects who participated in the exercise had a dramatic increase in happiness scores and a decrease in depression, and the benefits lasted for a full month. The exercise focuses on using gratitude to connect with others:

Exercise: A gratitude letter*

Begin by calling to mind someone in your life who made a positive difference and whom you never properly thanked. It can be anyone—a parent, another relative, a friend, a mentor, a coworker.

Next set aside some time and write a one- to two-page letter to that person.

Make it clear and concrete, telling the story of what the person did, how it made a difference to you, and where you are in life now as a result. Share with them your feelings as you write the letter.

If the person you've chosen is still alive, and you're feeling courageous, once you've completed your letter, contact the person and say that you'd like to come for a visit. If they ask why, suggest that you would rather not say—it's a surprise. Finally, visit the person and read your letter slowly, sharing your feelings and making eye contact if you can.

---

*Adapted from "Positive Psychology Progress" by Martin Seligman, Terry Steen, Nansook Park, and Christopher Peterson.

This exercise is not usually easy. Even imagining doing it can feel overwhelming. If the person has passed away, we might feel regret that we never properly thanked them when alive. If the person is alive, we might encounter our fears of vulnerability, of showing how much they mean to us. The exercise can also trigger thoughts of all the other people we haven't thanked properly. See if you might try it anyway and open to whatever feelings arise.

An alternative approach is to express our gratitude to someone in conversation. My good friend Michael died a few years ago. While we had been close since high school, we had had a typical guy relationship—sharing experiences and ideas, joking around, ribbing one another, but not talking much about our mutual affection or what our friendship meant to each of us.

As his death neared, I realized that I had been afraid to really tell him, with an open heart, how grateful I was to have had him in my life and how much I was going to miss him. It felt too intimate, too vulnerable, and out of character from our usual way of being together. One day he said to my wife, "Ron's been a great support, but he doesn't really tell me how he feels." Hearing that was a wake-up call. Facing the great leveler of death, and not wanting to let him down or miss out on the opportunity to connect, I pushed past my fear. I shared with Michael how much I appreciated him, how much I learned from him, and what an important influence he'd been on my life. We had some of the most important conversations of our friendship after that, for which I'm deeply grateful.

Cultivating gratitude isn't always intense and deeply moving, however. Sometimes it involves little, lighter experiments:

o Stay in bed an extra moment when you wake and gratefully consider the possibilities a new day brings.

o Give thanks before or after a meal.

o Smile at a stranger knowing that just as you want to be happy, so do they.

o Take time to say "thank you" and notice how your kindness affects you and others.

o Identify something that you've learned from a challenge.

- o Express your gratitude to someone.
- o Be grateful for the fruits of gratitude practice!

Forgiveness

We talked about how anger can screw up relationships in Chapter 9. Holding on to anger, endlessly reviewing how we were good and the other person was bad, is a particularly troublesome form of self-preoccupation. Studies document all sorts of mental and physical health problems arising from this sort of chronic resentment. And while we might bond with someone who felt similarly mistreated, chronic resentment reinforces our sense of separate self, blocking us from feeling fully a part of humanity and the web of life.

A powerful antidote is forgiveness. It gives us a way to let go of our grievance stories, reconnect with others, and reunite the human family. Not surprisingly, research finds that forgiveness is linked to reduced anxiety, depression, physical symptoms, and even mortality. But for forgiveness to be effective, we can't just paper over our negative feelings, since as we've discussed before, when we bury feelings, we bury them alive. Rather, we need to connect with our hearts, to feel our feelings fully before we can let them go. This usually starts with recognizing the pain beneath our anger:

Exercise: Pain beneath the anger

Spend a few minutes practicing mindfulness to open your heart and become aware of thoughts, images, and sensations. Then take a moment to call to mind someone or something that makes you angry. (There are so many candidates—just pick one.) Can you identify the vulnerability, hurt, or fear beneath your anger? It's usually not buried too deeply.

You can try using the RAIN technique from Chapter 11 to stay with and explore the hurt (**R**ecognize, **A**llow, **I**nvestigate, rest in **N**atural awareness) and then use self-compassion practices from Chapter 10 to self-soothe, allowing the pain to be. Of course it hurts. It's only natural, and you're only human. Notice any urges that arise to distance from the pain, to make it go away. Use your judgment—if you feel you're able to stay with it, spend some time with the hurt or fear.

You may notice during this practice that anger arises and provides some distance from the pain. If you feel ready, see if you can let it go and return to the underlying hurt.

Connecting with the pain beneath our anger is an important first step toward releasing it. We can't rush this—sometimes the pain is too great to bear for long periods; sometimes we don't feel sufficiently safe to let go of the anger. But we can experiment to see what our hearts can tolerate.

Remember Tom, the guy who stormed out on his boss rather than take any crap? Tom eventually got that it was the pain of being put down by his father, and picked on by other kids in school, that fueled his current anger. He had to feel it to heal it. The same is true for all of us. It's only by connecting with our tender hurt, tolerating it, and investigating it lovingly that we can begin to let go of anger. And we need to be able to let go of anger to move toward forgiveness and connection with others.

Every once in a while, we come across stories of extraordinary acts of forgiveness. I recall hearing about a couple who lost their daughter to neighborhood violence—she was an innocent bystander caught in the crossfire between rival gangs. After a period of intense mourning, the couple raised money to start a program to help gang-involved kids. They actually stayed in contact with the young man who shot their daughter and did what they could to help him get rehabilitated.

Or consider Nelson Mandela. Coming to power after decades of incarceration at the hands of the apartheid government in South Africa, he had the wisdom to create a pathway for his former oppressors to be integrated into a new democratic society.

How do people forgive those who have hurt them so deeply? How do they come to the perspective that the perpetrator isn't an evil other? One way is by seeing how all of our behavior is actually the result of factors and forces.

Remember the discussion of blame in Chapter 10? When we

blame another person, or think of them as bad or evil, we're usually not seeing the factors and forces that made the person act as they did. We're implicitly assuming that if we had their DNA and life history, we wouldn't have acted the same way. But since then we'd actually *be* the other person, we of course would have done exactly what they did.

As a psychotherapist, seeing the factors and forces that drive our behavior is central to my work. If a patient behaves in a certain way, or has certain feeling, reactions, or beliefs, I want to understand *why*—both to help my patient be more self-compassionate and to see how we might work together to change future behavior.

This is not, however, how I see things when I'm angry. Instead, I'm a good person pissed at the bad, unfair, selfish %&#$ (fill in your favorite swear). Understanding why people do what they do is an essential element in forgiveness. It's what allows us to see that we're all ordinary human beings, buffeted about by our fears, desires, past hurts, and misunderstandings. Here's an exercise that can help shift our perspective when we find it difficult to forgive:

Exercise: Forgiving a %&#$

Start with a few minutes of mindfulness practice to become aware of your thoughts and feelings. Then bring to mind someone who has wronged you, toward whom you feel anger or resentment.

Now imagine that you're this person's psychotherapist and they're explaining to you what they did. You become curious. What do you imagine prompted the behavior? What aspects of their temperament— which may be inherited—contributed to the process? What past hurts, or patterns of reward, might have prompted the person to go down that path?

Now imagine for a moment being the person who hurt you. Ask yourself, "Why did I do it?" Let yourself be in their shoes, feel what they might feel, think what they might think.

Amy had been angry with her older sister for years. She felt put down by her all the time. "I hope you enjoyed your vacation in

Florida. Where's your next trip?" The comment seemed innocent enough on the surface, but underneath was a dig—Amy had the resources to go away while her sister didn't.

It was holiday time, and Amy realized that she had to do something about her anger or it would ruin the family gathering. So she decided to try to put herself in her sister's shoes. She realized that her sister had always compared herself to Amy. "It must've really been hard that I was Dad's favorite." "It's gotta be a bummer that my marriage is pretty good but hers fell apart." The more Amy was able to see and understand her sister's pain, the easier it was to forgive her (though she still didn't like the digs).

FORGIVING ISN'T CONDONING

As we consider another person's motivations and begin to soften our resentment, we may think, as Amy did, "Yeah, but it's still not right!" No argument there. Forgiving someone for their transgressions isn't the same as condoning behavior. A jury of our peers may well agree with us—what the other person did was *wrong*. Perhaps they should face consequences, either to learn a lesson or as a warning to others. But imposing a consequence is very different from holding on to anger and self-righteousness. It's even possible to feel love and connection while punishing someone (we do it with kids and pets all the time).

APOLOGY

Sometimes it's best to work on forgiveness by ourselves. The other person may have passed away, or it may not be emotionally safe, or wise, to have them in our life. But if we're hurt and angry with someone with whom we want to have an ongoing relationship, we need to address the problem together in order to reconnect. This can be a delicate process, since anger or resentment activates everybody's self-evaluative concerns. If I'm mad at you, I believe that I've been good and you've been bad. You hear this and immediately respond that no, actually, *you've* been good and *I've* been bad. Not a great foundation for feeling part of the web of life together.

When we feel wronged, we usually can forgive another person more readily if they understand how their behavior hurt us and sincerely express remorse. The same is true for people that we've injured. Countless books and articles have been written about how to apologize effectively. Most suggest a few basic principles:

o Acknowledge what you did to hurt the other person and try to explain in as much detail as possible your understanding of why your behavior was hurtful.

o Apologize only if you actually feel bad about hurting the other. Don't say, "I'm sorry *if* I hurt you" or "I'm sorry *but* . . ." Wait until you actually feel remorse before trying to express it.

o Ask for forgiveness, and if it's not forthcoming, try to understand why. It might be that the other person doesn't feel that you really understand why they're in pain or doesn't really feel that you're sincere.

o Try to place your self-esteem concerns aside—debates over who was right or wrong or who hurt whom more don't usually work out well. Similarly, pointing out that the other person is "too sensitive" probably won't soften their heart. Stick to the emotional reality that your behavior hurt the other person.

o Don't blame the other person for your behavior. Telling someone that "you provoked me" or "you were mean first" usually doesn't go over well.

o Be patient. The other person may feel too hurt to be able to let you in right away, so you may need to approach them several times. Saying that you've already apologized and they should drop it already usually isn't a great strategy.

o Make a commitment to try not to do it again and then try to follow through.

These guidelines can also be useful to consider if you're seeking an apology from someone who has hurt you. If the apology isn't softening your heart and allowing you to reconnect, it may be because you were hurt too deeply and need time to recover, or it may be that one of these elements is missing. If you can identify and communicate what's missing, the person who hurt you may be able to give you what you need.

However we cultivate forgiveness, whether on our own or through open and caring communication, when we forgive, we choose to let go of our grievance and open our hearts and risk being vulnerable again. In the end, it's a gift to ourselves, since the more we forgive, the less preoccupied we'll be with being right, good, lovable, or other self-evaluative concerns, and the more connected we'll be to others.

Shifting from feeling like a separate "me" worried about how I'm doing to feeling part of not only the human family, but also the magical, ever-changing web of life is perhaps the ultimate antidote to self-evaluation worries. Cultivating gratitude, generosity, and forgiveness all can help. There are also countless other overlapping pathways from diverse spiritual and secular traditions, including prayer, yoga, sacred art and dance, and even psychedelic medicines. I invite you to experiment and explore whatever helps you most feel like a part of this amazing world that is so much bigger than us.

o   o   o

As it turns out, I was wrong about something. While most of us are ordinary, *you* are indeed a very special person—you made it to the end of a nonfiction book (which statistically, most people don't do).

Hopefully it has been a helpful journey. But we've all inherited powerful tendencies to compare ourselves to others, to want to feel loved or included, and to get addicted to self-esteem boosts. And we live in a world full of messages that insist if only we could be better and do better, we'd be happy.

It's therefore possible that simply reading this book and trying the exercises within it hasn't yet completely transformed you into a fully awakened being, able to see the folly of pride, ego, popularity, self-righteousness, and status seeking while boundlessly loving yourself and all the other beings on our planet. I'm certainly nowhere close myself, and striving too hard to be such a person can quickly become yet another self-evaluation trap.

Rather, I hope that this book has brought to life the proposition suggested at the beginning: We can use each new disappointment, failure, or moment of self-doubt as an opportunity to learn and grow. That means each time you feel terrible about yourself, fret about what other people are thinking, or see yourself as below others, you can use it as a chance to see the absurdity of these judgments, to love yourself and others more deeply, and to turn your attention to what matters to you most.

Every time we use a painful self-judgment this way, we feed our more wholesome inner wolf. Because of the strength of our biology and conditioning, it's a lifelong project. We need repeatedly to work with our heads—noticing each time we get sucked into pursuing some boost to our self-image; work with our hearts—opening to our hurts, to others' suffering, and to love; and work with our habits—choosing activities that reflect our values and enrich our relationships. Practicing mindfulness, loving-kindness, and compassion toward ourselves and others can provide important support, as can practicing gratitude, generosity, and forgiveness. You may also find it helpful to revisit other exercises in this book whenever you find yourself getting bogged down in one or another self-evaluative trap.

Working this way, I hope that you'll continue to experience some of the fruits that I've tasted from writing this book—seeing more clearly the seductive allure and limitations of self-esteem boosts, nurturing your loving, compassionate nature, celebrating your ordinariness and common humanity, and engaging more in meaningful activities. I also hope you'll find it a bit easier to relax into safely connecting with others as we all try to help one another inch toward sanity, however elusive this may be at times.

It's not easy to be a human being. May your efforts bring you peace, joy, and fulfillment, benefiting all the lives you touch, as you increasingly enjoy the extraordinary gift of being ordinary.

notes

ACKNOWLEDGMENTS

Page xiii   **As the astronomer Carl Sagan put it, "If you wish to make an apple pie from scratch, you must first invent the universe."**
    Sagan, C., Druyan, A., & Soter, S. (1980). Cosmos: A personal voyage. *The Lives of the Stars* (Episode 9), PBS. Retrieved April 7, 2021, from *www.youtube.com/watch?v=lMc3WqkSWKI.*

CHAPTER 1: ARE WE DOOMED?

Page 3   **Sometimes I lie awake at night, and I ask, "Where have I gone wrong?" Then a voice says to me, "This is going to take more than one night."**
    Cubillas, S. (2019, October 14). Peanuts: Charlie Brown's 10 saddest quotes. Retrieved March 19, 2021, from *www.cbr.com/ peanuts-charlie-brown-saddest-quotes.*

Page 7   **William Masters and Virginia Johnson, the famous sex researchers, described how our "internal spectator" interferes with sexual functioning.**
    Masters, W. H., & Johnson, V. E. (1970). *Human sexual inadequacy.* New York: Bantam Books.

Page 8   **Researchers studied the interactions that preceded schoolyard scuffles in Great Britain. Turns out they were usually arguments over *who is superior* or *who was right*.**
    Blatchford, P., & Sharp, S. (Eds.). (1994). *Breaktime and the school: Understanding and changing playground behaviour.* London: Routledge. (p. 43)
    Blatchford, P. (1998). *Social life in school: Pupils' experience of breaktime and recess from 7 to 16 years.* London: Routledge. (p. 156)

Page 15   **"If you desire glory, you may envy Napoleon, but Napoleon envied Caesar, Caesar envied Alexander, and Alexander, I dare say, envied Hercules, who never existed."**

Russell, B. (2019). *The conquest of happiness.* Snowballpublishing.com, 2019. (p. 84)

Page 16   **Indeed, there is also some evidence that people who feel good about themselves often are living lives that have gone reasonably well.**

Baumeister, R. F., Campbell, J. D., Krueger, J. I., & Vohs, K. D. (2003). Does high self-esteem cause better performance, interpersonal success, happiness, or healthier lifestyles? *Psychological Science in the Public Interest, 4*(1), 1–44.

Page 16   **Particularly high self-esteem is linked to problems like arrogance, conceit, overconfidence, and aggressive behavior.**

Baumeister, R. F., Smart, L., & Boden, J. M. (1996). Relation of threatened egotism to violence and aggression: The dark side of high self-esteem. *Psychological Review, 103*(1), 5.

Page 18   **Neurosis is the manure of bodhi.**

Trungpa, C. (2002). *The myth of freedom and the way of meditation.* Shambhala Publications.

CHAPTER 2: IT'S DARWIN'S FAULT

Page 21   **All animals are equal. But some animals are more equal than others.**

Orwell, G. (1945). *Animal farm.* Toronto: Penguin. (Chapter 10)

Page 22   **Birds have "pecking orders," as do fish, reptiles, and even some crickets.**

Buss, D. (2012). *Evolutionary psychology: The new science of the mind* (4th ed.). Boston: Allyn & Bacon. (p. 349)

Page 22   **Robert Sapolsky concluded after years of primate study hiding behind blinds of vegetation in Africa, "it turns out that it's very bad for your health to be a low-ranking male in a baboon troop."**

Interview with Terry Gross, *Fresh Air,* NPR, August 17, 1998. Retrieved from *www.npr.org/templates/story/story.php?storyId=1110280.*

Page 23   **Evolutionary psychologists have spent the past several decades trying to discern which aspects of human nature are universal instincts that evolved because of their survival value.**

Buss, D. (2017). *Evolutionary psychology: The new science of the mind* (5th ed.). New York: Routledge.

Pinker, S. (2003). *How the mind works.* London: Penguin.

Page 25   This observation led to a famous wisecrack by the biologist J. B. S. Haldane, who was once asked if he would lay
down his life for his brother: "No, but I would for at least
two brothers or sisters, four cousins, or eight nephews or
nieces."
    Ricard, M., Mandell, C., & Gordon, S. (2015). *Altruism: The
power of compassion to change yourself and the world*. New York: Little,
Brown & Company. (p. 161)

Page 26   In addition to our proclivity to look out for our families,
evolutionary psychologists identify an instinct called *reciprocal altruism*.
    Buss, D. (2015). *Evolutionary psychology: The new science of the
mind* (5th ed.). London: Routledge. (p. 269)

Page 26   There's a popular contemporary story often presented as a
Cherokee legend (though its origins are unclear) that sug-
gests a path forward.
    This story appears in many variations. The best accounting
I've found of its origins is at *https://en.wikipedia.org/wiki/Two_Wolves*.

Page 28   It's a powerful instinct—the word for *leader* in most foraging
societies means "big man."
    Pinker, S. (2003). *How the mind works*. London: Penguin.
(p. 495)

CHAPTER 3: THE LIBERATING POWER OF MINDFULNESS

Page 33   You can observe a lot by watching.
    Kaplan, D., & Berra, Y. (2008). *You can observe a lot by watching:
What I've learned about teamwork from the Yankees and life*. Hoboken,
NJ: Wiley.

Page 39   The Buddhist monk Bhante Gunaratana put it well: Somewhere in this process, you will come face to face with the
sudden and shocking realization that you are completely
crazy.
    Gunaratana, B. H. (2010). *Mindfulness in plain English*. Somer-
ville, MA: Wisdom Publications. (pp. 69–70)

Page 41   In a now classic study, researchers randomly assigned people either to eight weeks of mindfulness training or to a
control group that received no training.
    Farb, N. A., Segal, Z. V., Mayberg, H., Bean, J., McKeon,
D., Fatima, Z., & Anderson, A. K. (2007). Attending to the present: Mindfulness meditation reveals distinct neural modes of self-
reference. *Social Cognitive and Affective Neuroscience, 2*(4), 313–322.

Page 42   You can also listen to a variety of mindfulness practices on
my website, *DrRonSiegel.com*, and can find more detailed
suggestions about how to establish a mindfulness practice in
my book *The Mindfulness Solution: Everyday Practices for Everyday Problems*.

Siegel, R. D. (2009). *The mindfulness solution: Everyday practices for everyday problems.* New York: Guilford Press.

CHAPTER 4: DISCOVERING WHO WE REALLY ARE

Page 44   **"Who are you?" said the Caterpillar. This was not an encouraging opening for a conversation.**
Carroll, L. (2015). *Alice's adventures in wonderland.* London: Puffin Books. (p. 27)

Page 46   **The psychiatrist Carl Jung noticed that we tend to identify with some parts of ourselves, which he called our *persona*, and reject others, which he called our *shadow*.**
Jung, C. G. (2014). *Two essays on analytical psychology.* Mansfield Center, CT: Martino Publishing.

Page 47   **Dr. Richard Schwartz developed a form of psychotherapy called internal family systems (IFS), which helps people integrate their various parts.**
Schwartz, R. C. (2021). *No bad parts: Healing trauma and restoring wholeness with the internal family systems model.* Boulder, CO: Sounds True.
Schwartz, R. C., & Sweezy, M. (2019). *Internal family systems therapy.* New York: Guilford Press.

Page 48   **Perhaps you've heard a version of this popular European fairy tale.**
Von Franz, M. L. (1978). *An introduction to the psychology of fairy tales.* Irving, TX: Spring Publications, (p. 33)

Page 50   **Archaeologists speculate that humans didn't have anything like our conventional sense of self until some 40,000 to 60,000 years ago. That's when the Middle to Upper Paleolithic transition happened—our *cultural big bang*.**
Leary, M. R., & Buttermore, N. R. (2003). The evolution of the human self: Tracing the natural history of self-awareness. *Journal for the Theory of Social Behaviour, 33*(4), 365–404.

Page 50   **As the psychologist Mark Leary points out, it's "unlikely that cats or cows or butterflies think consciously about themselves and their experiences as they sit quietly, graze, or flit from flower to flower."**
Leary, M. R. (2004). *The curse of the self: Self-awareness, egotism, and the quality of human life.* Oxford: Oxford University Press. (p. 27)

Page 50   **It was only during the cultural big bang that we suddenly began making sophisticated tools, adorning ourselves with beads and bracelets, creating representational art, and planning for the future by building boats.**
Leary, M. R., & Buttermore, N. R. (2003). The evolution of the human self: Tracing the natural history of self-awareness. *Journal for the Theory of Social Behaviour, 33*(4), 365–404.

Page 52   **"We don't see the world as it is. We see it as we are."**
Nin, A. (1961). *Seduction of the minotaur*. Athens, OH: Swallow Press. (p. 124)

Page 55   **They're the result of a brain that, as the neuroscientist Wolf Singer put it, is like "an orchestra without a conductor."**
Singer, W. (2005). The brain: An orchestra without a conductor. *Max Planck Research, 3,* 14–18.

Page 57   **In fact, the English word *ecstasy* comes from the Greek meaning roughly "to stand outside of oneself."**
Oxford Online Dictionary. Retrieved March 19, 2021, from *https://en.oxforddictionaries.com/definition/ecstasy.*

Page 57   **Einstein, who was decidedly secular and scientific in his understanding of the universe, saw self-transcendence as our most important project.**
Sullivan, W. (1972, March 29). The Einstein papers: A man of many parts. *New York Times.*

CHAPTER 5: THE FAILURE OF SUCCESS

Page 63   **There is perhaps nothing worse than reaching the top of the ladder and discovering that you're on the wrong wall.**
Retrieved March 19, 2021, from *www.goodreads.com/quotes/429115-there-is-perhaps-nothing-worse-than-reaching-the-top-of.*

Page 65   **Instead of lasting, we find that self-image boosts are particularly subject to what psychologists call the *hedonic treadmill.***
Brickman, P., & Campbell, D. T. (1971). Hedonic relativism and planning the good society (pp. 287–302). In M. H. Apley (Ed.), *Adaptation level theory: A symposium.* New York: Academic Press.

Page 65   **As studies of lottery winners attest, it usually doesn't take us long to return to our previous level of happiness.**
Frederick, S., & Loewenstein, G. F. (1999). Hedonic adaptation. In D. Kahneman, E. Diener, & N. Schwarz (Eds.), *Wellbeing: The foundations of hedonic psychology* (pp. 302–329). New York: Sage.

Page 73   **Or, as the poet Mary Oliver asks, "Tell me, what is it you plan to do with your one wild and precious life?"**
Oliver, M. (1992). The summer day. *New and selected poems,* 22–23. Boston: Beacon Press.

Page 76   **There's one way to find out if a man is honest: ask him; if he says yes, you know he's crooked.**
Finn, A. (2021, February 26). *80 Mark Twain quotes on life.* Quote Ambition. Retrieved from *www.quoteambition.com/mark-twain-quotes.* (Less often attributed to Groucho Marx.)

Page 76   **This particular form of deception is called *illusory superiority*, or more colorfully, the *Lake Wobegon effect*.**

Cannell, J. J. (1988). The Lake Wobegon effect revisited. *Educational Measurement: Issues and Practice, 7*(4), 12–15.

Page 76 **In a large study, 70% of high school students rated themselves as above the median in leadership ability, 85% rated themselves as above the median in ability to get along with others, and a full 25% rated themselves in the top 1%.**

College Board. (1976–1977). Student descriptive questionnaire. Princeton, NJ: Educational Testing Service.

Page 76 **College students were asked to rate themselves and "average college students" on 20 positive and 20 negative traits. Typical students rated themselves as better than average on 38 out of the 40 traits.**

Alicke, M. D., Klotz, M. L., Breitenbecher, D. L., Yurak, T. J., & Vredenburg, D. S. (1995). Personal contact, individuation, and the better-than-average effect. *Journal of Personality and Social Psychology, 68*(5), 804–825.

Page 77 **87% of MBA students at Stanford rated their academic performance as above the median.**

It's academic. (2000). *Stanford GSB Reporter,* pp. 14–15.

Page 77 **96% of university professors think that they're better teachers than their colleagues.**

Cross, P. (1977). Not can but will college teachers be improved? *New Directions for Higher Education, 17,* 1–15.

Page 77 **In one study, 93% of American drivers rate themselves as above average for safety.**

Svenson, O. (1981). Are we all less risky and more skillful than our fellow drivers? *Acta Psychologica, 47*(2), 143–148.

Page 77 **A study of 1,000 Americans asked them to say whether they themselves or certain well-known individuals were more likely to go to heaven.**

New science suggests a "grand design" and ways to imagine eternity. (1997, March 31). *US News and World Report,* 65–66.

Page 77 **Most of us think that our capacity to evaluate ourselves accurately is better than average!**

Pronin, E., Lin, D. Y., & Ross, L. (2002). The bias blind spot: Perceptions of bias in self versus others. *Personality and Social Psychology Bulletin, 28*(3), 369–381.

Page 77 **My favorite observation in social psychology, the Dunning-Kruger effect, helps predict when our self-evaluations will be most inflated. Researchers have found repeatedly that across all sorts of human domains and activities, *actual competence is inversely proportional to perceived competence.***

Kruger, J., & Dunning, D. (1999). Unskilled and unaware of it: How difficulties in recognizing one's own incompetence lead to inflated self-assessments. *Journal of Personality and Social Psychology, 77*(6), 1121.

Page 77   **If, for example, we encounter someone who is more talented than us in some area, we assume that he or she must
be extraordinary (because there's *no way* that we could be
below average).**

Alicke, M. D., LoSchiavo, F. M., Zerbst, J., & Zhang, S.
(1997). The person who outperforms me is a genius: Maintaining
perceived competence in upward social comparison. *Journal of Personality and Social Psychology, 73*(4), 781.

Page 78   **If we're told by experimenters that we did better than average on a test, we conclude that we're smart or skillful. But
if we're told that we did poorly, we surmise that the test was
unfair or excessively difficult, test conditions were bad, or
we were just unlucky.**

Blaine, B., & Crocker, J. (1993). Self-esteem and self-serving
biases in reactions to positive and negative events: An integrative
review. In R. F. Baumeister, *Self-esteem: The puzzle of low self-regard*
(pp. 55–85). New York: Plenum Press.

Page 78   **When we behave immorally, we tend to attribute this to
external conditions: "Everybody does it" or "I was just following orders."**

Forsyth, D. R., Pope, W. R., & McMillan, J. H. (1985). Students' reactions after cheating: An attributional analysis. *Contemporary Educational Psychology, 10*(1), 72–82.

Page 78   **In group activities, when the outcome is positive, we overestimate our contribution; but when the outcome is nega-
tive, we underestimate it.**

Schlenker, B. R., & Miller, R. S. (1977). Egocentrism in
groups: Self-serving biases or logical information processing? *Journal of Personality and Social Psychology, 35*(10), 755.

Page 78   **Here's a brief experiment from the data scientist Seth
Stephens-Davidowitz you can try to see the pull toward
deceiving ourselves and others.**

Stephens-Davidowitz, S., & Pabon, A. (2017). *Everybody lies:
Big data, new data, and what the Internet can tell us about who we really
are.* New York: HarperCollins. (p. 106)

CHAPTER 6: RESISTING SELFIE-ESTEEM

Page 82   **"Nonstop You"**

"Nonstop you"—Lufthansa launches new ad campaign. (2012,
March 13). *Travel Daily News.* Retrieved March 19, 2021, from *www.
traveldailynews.com/post/%E2%80%9Cnonstop-you%E2%80%9D---
lufthansa-launches-new-ad-campaign-48206.*

Page 82   **The forward-looking governor of California and members
of the legislature created the California Task Force to Promote Self-Esteem and Personal Responsibility. The idea was
that feeling good about yourself could be a kind of "social
vaccine" that could prevent all sorts of problems.**

Baumeister, R. F., Campbell, J. D., Krueger, J. I., & Vohs, K. D. (2005). Exploding the self-esteem myth. *Scientific American, 292*(1), 84–91.

Page 82   **After spending over a quarter of a million dollars, the task force found that associations between social ills and self-esteem were either mixed, insignificant, or entirely absent—and there was no scientific evidence that poor self-esteem actually caused *any* social problems.**

Smelser, N. J. (1989). Self-esteem and social problems: An introduction. In A. M. Mecca, N. J. Smelser, & J. Vasconcellos (Eds.), *The social importance of self-esteem* (pp. 1–23). Berkeley: University of California Press.

Page 83   **Parents were told, "Don't be afraid to tell your child over and over again how bright and talented they are."**

Folkins, M. J. (1988, May). Can do: Tips for helping your child. *Parents, 63,* 70.

Page 83   **Schools offered courses called "Self-Science: The Subject Is Me."**

Stone, K. F., & Dillehunt, H. Q. (1978). *Self science: The subject is me.* https://eric.ed.gov/?id=ED165056.

Page 83   **Management consultants told entrepreneurs that they should create organizations where "everyone feels great about themselves."**

Tracey, B. (1986). I can't, I can't: How self-concept shapes performance. *Management World, 15*(April–May), 1, 8.

Page 83   **Farmers were told that there was one skill that would determine their success, and it wasn't information about "weeds, seeds, breeds, and feeds," it was knowing how to "develop and maintain a positive self-image."**

Brown, J. (1986). How to rekindle confidence and esteem. *Successful Farming, 84*(March), 11.

Page 83   **Kim Jong-il, the late "dear leader" of North Korea, apparently had very high self-regard. His official biography states that he was born on top of the highest mountain in the country, a glacier opened to emit mysterious sounds, and a double rainbow appeared at the time of his birth. He learned to walk at 3 weeks, spoke by 8 weeks, and wrote 1,500 books as a university student.**

Ricard, M., Mandell, C., & Gordon, S. (2015). *Altruism: The power of compassion to change yourself and the world.* New York: Little, Brown, & Company.

Page 84   **It turns out that people who think highly of themselves are no smarter, more attractive, or otherwise superior to those with lower self-regard—they just think they are.**

Baumeister, R. F., Campbell, J. D., Krueger, J. I., & Vohs, K. D. (2003). Does high self-esteem cause better performance, interpersonal success, happiness, or healthier lifestyles? *Psychological Science in the Public Interest, 4*(1), 1–44.

Page 84   **In children, high self-esteem makes it more likely that they will be uninhibited, willing to disregard risks, and prone to engage in sex at a younger age. Bullies also tend to be surer of themselves and have less anxiety than other children.**

Baumeister, R. F., Campbell, J. D., Krueger, J. I., & Vohs, K. D. (2005). Exploding the self-esteem myth. *Scientific American, 292*(1), 84–91.

Page 84   **In video games designed by political scientists to simulate real-world geopolitical conflicts, the more certain players were of themselves, the more often they lost. Overconfident "leaders" often launched rash attacks leading to reprisals that were devastating for both camps.**

Johnson, D. D., McDermott, R., Barrett, E. S., Cowden, J., Wrangham, R., McIntyre, M. H., & Rosen, S. P. (2006). Overconfidence in wargames: Experimental evidence on expectations, aggression, gender and testosterone. *Proceedings of the Royal Society B: Biological Sciences, 273*(1600), 2513–2520.

Page 86   **The Pew Center for People and the Press reached out to hundreds of young adults, asking millennials, who were raised when the self-esteem movement took off, about their generation's goals in life. The results, and the contrast with the generation before (in parentheses), were striking: 81% (vs. 62%) said they wanted to get rich; 51% (vs. 29%) to be famous; but only 10% (vs. 33%) said they wanted to become more spiritual.**

Twenge, J. M., & Campbell, W. K. (2009). *The narcissism epidemic: Living in the age of entitlement.* New York: Simon & Schuster. (pp. 162–163)

Page 86   **A poll in Great Britain asked teenagers what was "the very best thing in the world." Their top three answers were "being a celebrity," "good looks," and "being rich."**

Twenge, J. M., & Campbell, W. K. (2009). *The narcissism epidemic: Living in the age of entitlement.* New York: Simon & Schuster. (p. 94)

Page 87   **In the 1890s, young women typically resolved to take more interest in others and refrain from focusing only on themselves. By the 1990s, their goals were to lose weight, find a new hairstyle, or buy new clothes, makeup, and accessories.**

Brumberg, J. J. (1998). *The body project: An intimate history of American girls.* New York: Vintage.

Page 87   **In 1951, only 12% of 14- to 16-year-olds agreed with the statement "I am an important person." By 1989, 80% did.**

Newsom, C. R., Archer, R. P., Trumbetta, S., & Gottesman, I. I. (2003). Changes in adolescent response patterns on the MMPI/MMPI-A across four decades. *Journal of Personality Assessment, 81*(1), 74–84.

Page 87 **In 2012, 58% of high school students expected to go to graduate or professional school—twice the number in 1976. Yet the actual number attending remained unchanged at 9%.**

Twenge, J. M. (2014). *Generation me: Why today's young Americans are more confident, assertive, entitled—and more miserable than ever before* (rev. ed.). New York: Simon & Schuster. (p. 109)

Page 87 **A full two-thirds of high school students expect themselves to be in the top 20% in job performance.**

Twenge, J. M., & Campbell, W. K. (2009). *The narcissism epidemic: Living in the age of entitlement.* New York: Simon & Schuster. (p. 36)

Page 89 **On Facebook, the most common phrases people use to describe their husbands are "the best," "my best friend," "amazing," "the greatest," and "so cute." In anonymous Google searches, the most frequent words that people type along with "my husband" are "mean," "annoying," "a jerk," and "gay."**

Stephens-Davidowitz, S., & Pabon, A. (2017). *Everybody lies: Big data, new data, and what the Internet can tell us about who we really are.* New York: HarperCollins. (p. 160)

Page 89 **The highbrow *Atlantic* magazine and lowbrow *National Enquirer* have similar circulations and similar numbers of Google search inquiries. Yet the *Atlantic* has 27 times more Facebook likes.**

Stephens-Davidowitz, S., & Pabon, A. (2017). *Everybody lies: Big data, new data, and what the Internet can tell us about who we really are.* New York: HarperCollins. (p. 151)

Page 89 **In Facebook world, the average adult seems to be happily married, vacationing in the Caribbean, and perusing the *Atlantic*.**

Stephens-Davidowitz, S., & Pabon, A. (2017). *Everybody lies: Big data, new data, and what the Internet can tell us about who we really are.* New York: HarperCollins. (p. 153)

Page 90 **_Selfie_ was the 2013 word of the year.**

Brumfield, B. (2013, November 20). Selfie named word of the year for 2013. Retrieved March 16, 2021, from *www.cnn.com/2013/11/19/living/selfie-word-of-the-year/index.html*.

Page 90 **Increased communication over Zoom and FaceTime has led to an explosion of *Zoom dysmorphia disorder*.**

Rice, S. M., Siegel, J. A., Libby, T., Graber, E., & Kourosh, A. S. (2021). Zooming into cosmetic procedures during the COVID-19 pandemic: The provider's perspective. *International Journal of Women's Dermatology, 7*(2), 213–216.

Page 90 **Roy Baumeister, arguably the world's foremost researcher of self-esteem, concluded in a review of the scientific literature, "After all these years, I'm sorry to say, my recommendation is this: forget about self-esteem and concentrate more on self-control and self-discipline."**

Baumeister, R. (2005, January 25). The lowdown on high self-esteem. Retrieved March 17, 2021, from *www.latimes.com/archives/la-xpm-2005-jan-25-oe-baumeister25-story.html*.

CHAPTER 7: CONSPICUOUS CONSUMPTION AND OTHER STATUS SIGNALS

Page 95 **We buy things we don't need with money we don't have to impress people we don't like.**

Retrieved March 19, 2021, from *https://quoteinvestigator.com/2016/04/21/impress*.

Page 95 **"In 1899 Thorstein Veblen wrote a book called *The Theory of the Leisure Class*. He was the first economist to use the term *conspicuous consumption*."**

Veblen, T. (1912). *The theory of the leisure class: An economic study of institutions*. New York: B. W. Huebsch.

Page 97 **Feathers are actually a form of conspicuous consumption. They signal to the peahens, "I'm so extraordinarily strong and healthy that I can afford to put all of these resources into my tail feathers and nevertheless survive."**

Zahavi, A., & Zahavi, A. (1999). *The handicap principle: A missing piece of Darwin's puzzle*. New York: Oxford University Press.

Page 97 **Before breeding season, the males collect edible prey such as snails and useful objects like feathers and pieces of cloth—90 to 120 such items in total. They then hang them on thorns and branches in their territories to show off their wealth.**

Yosef, R. (1991). Females seek males with ready cache. *Natural History, 6*, 37.

Page 97 **It's therefore not surprising that historically, fishermen told tales about fish they caught, male farmers bragged about the size of their vegetables, and male hunters boasted about the large animals they killed.**

Hill, K., & Hurtado, A. M. (2017). *Ache life history: The ecology and demography of a foraging people*. London: Routledge.

Holmberg, A. R. (1950). *Nomads of the long bow: The Siriono of Eastern Bolivia*. Washington, DC: Smithsonian Institution.

Page 97 **In a recent study of over 3,000 subjects from 36 countries, women still placed a higher value on good financial prospects in choosing a mate, while men placed a higher value on appearance, whether or not they lived in a more gender-equal society where women have greater earning capacity.**

Zhang, L., Lee, A. J., DeBruine, L. M., & Jones, B. C. (2019). Are sex differences in preferences for physical attractiveness and good earning capacity in potential mates smaller in countries with greater gender equality? *Evolutionary Psychology, 17*(2), 1–6.

Page 101 **Social psychologists tell us that we make judgments about other people's social class within a few minutes of meeting them.**

Kraus, M. W., Park, J. W., & Tan, J. J. (2017). Signs of social class: The experience of economic inequality in everyday life. *Perspectives on Psychological Science, 12*(3), 422–435.

Kraus, M. W., Torrez, B., Park, J. W., & Ghayebi, F. (2019). Evidence for the reproduction of social class in brief speech. *Proceedings of the National Academy of Sciences, 116*(46), 22998–23003.

Page 105 **We attract sexual partners, impress potential clients, customers, or employers, and even try to avoid persecution (if we're members of a marginalized group) with our choice of garments.**

Bell, Q. (1948). *On human finery.* London: Hogarth Press.

Page 105 **Trend-setters are members of upper classes who adopt the styles of lower classes to differentiate themselves from middle classes, who wouldn't be caught dead in lower-class styles because they're the ones in danger of being mistaken for them.**

Pinker, S. (2003). *How the mind works.* London: Penguin. (p. 502)

Page 107 **In the late 1800s, the industrialist J. P. Morgan said he'd never invest in a company where directors were paid more than six times the average wage of employees.**

Piketty, T., & Saez, E. (2001). *Income inequality in the United States, 1913–1998* (updated to 2000). Cambridge, MA: National Bureau of Economic Research.

Page 107 **By 1982, the average CEO in the United States made 42 times the average worker's income.**

Twenge, J. M., & Campbell, W. K. (2009). *The narcissism epidemic: Living in the age of entitlement.* New York: Simon & Schuster. (p. 52)

Page 107 **More recently the CEO of JPMorgan Chase earned *395 times* the salary of a typical worker at his company.**

Kilgore, T. (2021, April 8). JPMorgan CEO Jamie Dimon's total pay in the year of COVID-19 was the most since the 2008 financial crisis. Retrieved July 15, 2021, from *www.marketwatch.com/story/jpmorgan-ceo-jamie-dimons-total-pay-in-the-year-of-covid-19-was-the-most-since-the-2008-financial-crisis-11617887608.*

Page 107 **When income differences are bigger, social distances become larger and social stratification plays a bigger role in our lives. When there's more inequality, we also feel less connected to one another, have less feeling of common humanity, and have more need to signal where we are in the hierarchy.**

Wilkinson, R., & Pickett, K. (2011). *The spirit level: Why greater equality makes societies stronger.* New York: Bloomsbury. (pp. 27, 43)

Page 109   **In a survey of American 18- to 23-year-olds, 91% indicated that they had no or only minor problems with mass consumerism.**

Smith, C., Christoffersen, K., Davidson, H., & Herzog, P. S. (2011). *Lost in transition: The dark side of emerging adulthood.* New York: Oxford University Press.

Page 109   **In another study, 93% of teenage girls reported that shopping was their favorite activity.**

Twenge, J. M., & Campbell, W. K. (2009). *The narcissism epidemic: Living in the age of entitlement.* New York: Simon & Schuster. (p. 163)

Page 109   **Studies show that when we focus on material values, we have more conflict with others, engage more in social comparisons, and are less likely to be motivated by the intrinsic joy of our activities.**

Kasser, T. (2002). *The high price of materialism.* Cambridge: MIT Press.

Page 109   **People were asked to imagine being in a poorer society where they'd be less well off than they are today but where they'd be one of the richer individuals. Fifty percent of subjects said that they'd trade up to half of their income to be better off than others.**

Solnick, S. J., & Hemenway, D. (1998). Is more always better?: A survey on positional concerns. *Journal of Economic Behavior & Organization, 37*(3), 373–383.

Page 109   **Some 6–7 million years ago our evolutionary tree split and led to two species of ape: chimpanzees and bonobos. We're close to both genetically.**

de Waal, F. B., & Lanting, F. (1997). *Bonobo: The forgotten ape.* Berkeley: University of California Press.

Page 110   **Chimpanzees go through elaborate rituals in which one individual communicates its status to the other.**

de Waal, F. B., & Lanting, F. (1997). *Bonobo: The forgotten ape.* Berkeley: University of California Press. (p. 30)

Page 110   **As de Waal put it, "Sex is the glue of bonobo society."**

de Waal, F. B., & Lanting, F. (1997). *Bonobo: The forgotten ape.* Berkeley: University of California Press. (p. 99)

Page 110   **The good news is that humans actually have the bonobo rather than the chimp pattern.**

Hammock, E. A., & Young, L. J. (2005). Microsatellite instability generates diversity in brain and sociobehavioral traits. *Science, 308*(5728), 1630–1634.

Page 110   **Yet another way to relax our status judgments—including those signaled through conspicuous consumption—is based on an observation by Ram Dass, the Harvard research psychologist who became a well-known spiritual teacher.**

Dass, R. (2020, August 4). Ram Dass on self judgment. Retrieved March 17, 2021, from *www.ramdass.org/ram-dass-on-self-judgement.*

CHAPTER 8: TREATING OUR SELF-ESTEEM ADDICTION

Page 113   **Quitting smoking is easy; I've done it hundreds of times.**

March 19, 2021, from *www.quotes.net/quote/1624.* (Most often attributed to Mark Twain.)

Page 113   **They only have about 20,000 nerve cells, compared to the 100 billion or so in humans.**

Dobbs, D. (2007). Eric Kandel. *Scientific American Mind, 18*(5), 32–37.

Page 114   **A basic principle of animal learning has been known for well over 100 years: If a behavior is followed by a pleasant experience, an animal will tend to repeat it; if followed by an unpleasant experience, it will be avoided.**

Thorndike, E. L. (1913). *The psychology of learning* (Vol. 2). New York: Teachers College, Columbia University.

Page 114   **James Olds and Peter Milner of McGill University planted electrodes in the septal regions deep within rats' brains. They crafted an experiment in which the rats could send a little electricity to this region by pressing a lever. The rats quickly learned to do this enthusiastically, presumably because it felt so good.**

Olds, J., & Milner, P. (1954). Positive reinforcement produced by electrical stimulation of septal area and other regions of rat brain. *Journal of Comparative and Physiological Psychology, 47*(6), 419.

Page 115   **The neurotransmitter *dopamine* is released into a related reward center, the nucleus accumbens, in response to all sorts of addictive behavior—from romantic love to taking drugs like amphetamines, cocaine, and morphine. The area is also activated by positive reinforcements such as food, water, sex, and, of particular interest here, *self-esteem boosts.***

Brewer, J. (2017). *The craving mind: From cigarettes to smartphones to love: Why we get hooked and how we can break bad habits.* New Haven: Yale University Press.

Page 115   **Psychologists find that by age 4 children can reliably identify their most popular peers.**

Prinstein, M. J. (2017). *Popular: The power of likability in a status-obsessed world.* New York: Penguin. (p. 33)

Page 115   **As one kid put it recently, "If you're popular, if everyone is talking about you, you can go out with whoever you want. You can be friends with anyone. It just, like, feels good."**

Prinstein, M. J. (2017). *Popular: The power of likability in a status-obsessed world.* New York: Penguin. (p. 61)

Page 115   **According to social psychologists, there are two paths to popularity.**

Prinstein, M. J. (2017). *Popular: The power of likability in a status-obsessed world.* New York: Penguin. (p. 44)

Page 116   **To add to our "adolescence can be hell" theme, likability matters much more for younger kids than it does for teens, when status becomes more important.**

Prinstein, M. J. (2017). *Popular: The power of likability in a status-obsessed world.* New York: Penguin. (p. 33)

Page 116   **Those who seek close, caring relationships, pursue personal growth, and enjoy helping others—intrinsic rewards and qualities associated with likability—tend to be happier and physically healthier.**

Sheldon, K. M., Ryan, R. M., Deci, E. L., & Kasser, T. (2004). The independent effects of goal contents and motives on well-being: It's both what you pursue and why you pursue it. *Personality and Social Psychology Bulletin, 30*(4), 475–486.

Page 116   **In the early 2000s a sophomore at Harvard wrote the software for a site called Facemash. Using photos of undergraduate students available through the university's computer system, he posted pairs of pictures and asked users to choose the "hotter" person. The site attracted 450 visitors and 22,000 photo views in its first 4 hours online.**

Kaplan, K. (2003, November 19). Facemash creator survives Ad Board. *Harvard Crimson.* Retrieved March 17, 2021, from *www.thecrimson.com/article/2003/11/19/facemash-creator-survives-ad-board-the.*

Page 117   **For example, in 2016, psychologists at UCLA examined teen brains while they viewed a simulated Instagram feed.**

Sherman, L. E., Payton, A. A., Hernandez, L. M., Greenfield, P. M., & Dapretto, M. (2016). The power of the like in adolescence: Effects of peer influence on neural and behavioral responses to social media. *Psychological Science, 27*(7), 1027–1035.

Page 117   **As one kid said when asked why a successful social media presence is so important, "It's like being famous. . . . It's cool. Everyone knows you, and you are, like, the most important person in the school."**

Prinstein, M. J. (2017). *Popular: The power of likability in a status-obsessed world.* New York: Penguin. (p. 61)

Page 117   **After all, everyone else is checking their phones all day long (96 times for the average American).**

Asurion Research (2019, November 21). Americans check their phones 96 times a day. Retrieved March 17, 2021, from *www.asurion. com/about/press-releases/americans-check-their-phones-96-times-a-day/*.

Page 120   **Alan Marlatt, an addictions specialist at the University of Washington in Seattle, invented a great practice for this called urge surfing.**

Bowen, S., Chawla, N., Grow, J., & Marlatt, G. A. (2021). *Mindfulness-based relapse prevention for addictive behaviors: A clinician's guide.* New York: Guilford Press.

Page 121   **Adapted from *Reclaim Your Brain* by Susan Pollak.**

Pollak, S. M. (2018, March 28). Reclaim your brain. Retrieved April 11, 2021, from *www.psychologytoday.com/us/blog/the-art-now/201803/reclaim-your-brain*.

Page 126   **"What others call happiness, that the Noble [Awakened] Ones declare to be suffering. What others call suffering, that the Noble Ones have found to be happiness."**

Dvayatanupassana Sutta: The Noble One's happiness. In *The discourse collection: Selected texts from the Sutta Nipata.* Retrieved March 17, 2021, from *www.accesstoinsight.org/tipitaka/kn/snp/snp.3.12.irel. html*.

CHAPTER 9: MAKE A CONNECTION, NOT AN IMPRESSION

Page 129   **You can make more friends in two months by becoming interested in other people than you can in two years by trying to get other people interested in you.**

Carnegie, D. (1998). *How to win friends & influence people.* New York: Pocket Books. (p. 52)

Page 130   **It's the central ingredient in successful parenting, as well as the secret sauce in therapy, predicting good outcomes much more robustly than anything else.**

Miller, S. D., Hubble, M. A., Chow, D. L., & Seidel, J. A. (2013). The outcome of psychotherapy: Yesterday, today, and tomorrow. *Psychotherapy, 50*(1), 88–97.

Page 130   **Our nervous system evolved pathways by which safe social connection can quiet our stress response.**

Porges, S. W., & Dana, D. (2018). *Clinical applications of the polyvagal theory: The emergence of polyvagal-informed therapies.* New York: Norton.

Page 133   **A dopamine-producing reward region connected to the nucleus accumbens (the center activated by likes on social media and drugs like cocaine) had increased activation. The more attractive the partner, the more activation occurred.**

Aron, A., Fisher, H., Mashek, D. J., Strong, G., Li, H., & Brown, L. L. (2005). Reward, motivation, and emotion systems associated with early-stage intense romantic love. *Journal of Neurophysiology, 94*(1), 327–337.

Page 134   **When people are engaged in passionate romantic love relationships, they show more activation in a brain region associated with self-evaluative thinking called the *posterior cingulate cortex* (PCC).**

Aron, A., Fisher, H., Mashek, D. J., Strong, G., Li, H., &
Brown, L. L. (2005). Reward, motivation, and emotion systems
associated with early-stage intense romantic love. *Journal of Neurophysiology, 94*(1), 327–337.

Page 134   **Studies have shown that both mothers caring for their
children and nonobsessed lovers have less PCC activation
when thinking about their kids or partners. And when
people practice loving-kindness meditation, in which they
generate loving feelings by wishing others well, the reward
pathways activated by passionate romantic love are quieted.**

Brewer, J. (2017). *The craving mind: From cigarettes to smartphones
to love: Why we get hooked and how we can break bad habits.* New Haven:
Yale University Press. (p. 129)

Page 142   **"People will forget what you said, people will forget what
you did, but people will never forget how you made them
feel."**

Retrieved April 3, 2021, from *https://quoteinvestigator.
com/2014/04/06/they-feel/#note-8611–16.* (Widely attributed to
Maya Angelou, though it has other sources as well.)

Page 142   **Other animals get angry for good reason. They respond
with aggression when they, their children, or their relatives
are physically attacked; when competing for food or a mate;
or when another animal encroaches on their turf.**

Leary, M. R. (2004). *The curse of the self: Self-awareness, egotism,
and the quality of human life.* Oxford: Oxford University Press. (p. 88)

Page 143   **In Buddhist traditions, anger is described as being seductive, having *a honeyed tip and poisoned root.***

Ghatva sutta: Having killed (T. Bhikkhu, Trans.). (2010, June 2).
Retrieved March 17, 2021, from *www.accesstoinsight.org/tipitaka/sn/
sn01/sn01.071.than.html.*

Page 144   **The Bible itself points to this danger: "Judge not that ye be
not judged."**

King James Bible (Matthew 7:1–3). (2008). New York: Oxford
University Press. (Original work published 1769)

Page 144   **A powerful Chinese prime minister asked a meditation
master for the Buddhist perspective on egotism.**

Leary, M. R. (2004). *The curse of the self: Self-awareness, egotism,
and the quality of human life.* Oxford: Oxford University Press. (p. 88)

Page 144   **Research studies suggest that people with elevated self-
esteem (who rate themselves highly) are actually *more* likely
to become aggressive when symbolically threatened than
are people with average or low self-esteem.**

Baumeister, R. F., Smart, L., & Boden, J. M. (1996). Relation of threatened egotism to violence and aggression: The dark side of high self-esteem. *Psychological Review, 103*(1), 5.

Page 149   **They call the process *identity recategorization*.**

Dovidio, J. F., Gaertner, S. L., & Saguy, T. (2008). Another view of "we": Majority and minority group perspectives on a common ingroup identity. *European Review of Social Psychology, 18*(1), 296–330.

CHAPTER 10: THE POWER OF COMPASSION

Page 150   **If you want others to be happy, practice compassion. If you want to be happy, practice compassion.**

Dalai Lama. (2010, December 27). Retrieved September 14, 2021, from *https://twitter.com/dalailama/status/19335233497210880?l ang=en*.

Page 153   **We do this in part by activating *mirror neurons* that allow us to experience in our own bodies the feelings that we imagine are occurring in someone else's.**

Iacoboni, M. (2009). Imitation, empathy, and mirror neurons. *Annual Review of Psychology, 60,* 653–670.

Page 159   **He also tells a story about a senior Tibetan monk who was released after years of incarceration in a Chinese concentration camp.**

Dalai Lama. (2009, May 1). *On compassion*. Presentation, Harvard Medical School Conference, Meditation and Psychotherapy, Boston, MA.

Page 160   **Psychologists Kristin Neff and Chris Germer developed the popular 8-week mindful self-compassion (MSC) program that teaches how to develop compassion for ourselves instead (see *https://centerformsc.org*).**

Neff, K., & Germer, C. (2018). *The mindful self-compassion workbook: A proven way to accept yourself, build inner strength, and thrive.* New York: Guilford Press.

Page 162   **In one study, the wire mother held a bottle with food, while the cloth mother had no bottle. Overwhelmingly, the baby monkeys preferred spending their time clinging to the cloth mother, visiting the wire monkey only briefly to feed.**

Harlow, H. F., & Zimmermann, R. R. (1958). The development of affective responsiveness in infant monkeys. *Proceedings of the American Philosophical Society, 102,* 501–509.

Page 162   **In humans, specialized nerves in our skin are actually programmed to respond to stroking at the rhythm that most of us instinctively use when we're being affectionate. And the nerves respond only to a hand at body temperature—not to one warmer or colder.**

Ackerley, R., Wasling, H. B., Liljencrantz, J., Olausson, H., Johnson, R. D., & Wessberg, J. (2014). Human C-tactile afferents are tuned to the temperature of a skin-stroking caress. *Journal of Neuroscience, 34*(8), 2879–2883.

Page 162   **Exercise: Affectionate hugging and stroking**

Germer, C., & Neff, K. (2019). *Teaching the mindful self-compassion program: A guide for professionals.* New York: Guilford Press. (p. 171)

Page 163   **Exercise: Affectionate breathing**

Germer, C., & Neff, K. (2019). *Teaching the mindful self-compassion program: A guide for professionals.* New York: Guilford Press. (p. 181)

Page 164   **Exercise: Self-compassion letter**

Neff, K. (2015, May 15). *Mindful self-compassion.* Workshop at FACES Conference, May 15. Another version of this exercise can be found in Neff's 2011 book *Self-Compassion* (p. 16).

Page 166   **Exercise: Sweetened Tonglen**

Germer, C., & Neff, K. (2019). *Teaching the mindful self-compassion program: A guide for professionals.* New York: Guilford Press. (pp. 251–252)

CHAPTER 11: YOU HAVE TO FEEL IT TO HEAL IT

Page 169   **Kathy Love Ormsby had it all.**

Demak, R. (1986, June 16). "And then she just disappeared." *Sports Illustrated.* Retrieved March 18, 2021, from *https://vault.si.com/vault/1986/06/16/and-then-she-just-disappeared.*

Page 176   **As Proust put it, "One is cured of suffering only by experiencing it to the full."**

Proust, M. (1982). *Remembrance of things past* (Vol. 3, *Time regained*). (Trans. C. K. Scott Moncrieff, Terence Kilmartin, & Andreas Mayor). New York: Vintage. (p. 546)

Page 180   **The ancient Greeks had shaming down to a science. Each year the citizens of Athens were asked whether they wished to hold an ostracism—the democratic process of throwing someone out of the city.**

Forsdyke, S. (2009). *Exile, ostracism, and democracy: The politics of expulsion in ancient Greece.* Princeton, NJ: Princeton University Press.

Page 182   **There's a wonderful poem by Daniel Ladinsky, based on the writing of the 14th-century Persian poet Hafez, that can encourage us.**

Ladinsky, D. (Ed.). (2002). *Love poems from God: Twelve sacred voices from the East and West.* New York: Penguin.

Page 184   **Dr. Richard Schwartz developed internal family systems (IFS) therapy to help people befriend these diverse parts of themselves.**

Schwartz, R. C. (2021). *No bad parts: Healing trauma and restoring wholeness with the internal family systems model.* Boulder, CO: Sounds True.

Schwartz, R. C., & Sweezy, M. (2019). *Internal family systems therapy.* New York: Guilford Press.

CHAPTER 12: SEPARATING THE DOER FROM THE DEED

Page 189   **Why are you unhappy? Because 99.9% of everything you think, and everything you do, is for yourself. And there isn't one.**

Wei, W. W. (2002). *Ask the awakened: The negative way.* Boulder, CO: Sentient Publications.

Page 190   **Ellis called the troublesome, addictive kind of self-appraisal we've been discussing throughout this book *conditional self-esteem.***

Ellis, A. (2010). *The myth of self-esteem: How rational emotive behavior therapy can change your life forever.* Amherst, NY: Prometheus Books.

Page 192   **We assume, as Ellis put it back in 1957, "A person should be thoroughly competent, adequate, talented, and intelligent in all possible respects; the main goal and purpose of life is achievement and success; incompetence in anything whatsoever is an indication that a person is inadequate or valueless."**

Ellis, A. (2010). *The myth of self-esteem: How rational emotive behavior therapy can change your life forever.* Amherst, NY: Prometheus Books. (p. 278)

Page 192   **Almost all encouraged parents to communicate a simple but remarkably elusive idea to their kids when they misbehaved: "You're not bad—your behavior is inappropriate."**

Ginott, H. G. (2003). *Between parent and child* (rev. ed.). New York: Three Rivers Press.

Page 193   **Carl Rogers identified self-acceptance as a central ingredient in psychotherapy: "By acceptance . . . I mean a warm regard for [the client] as a person of unconditional self-worth—of value no matter what his condition, his behavior, or his feelings."**

Rogers, C. R. (1995). *On becoming a person: A therapist's view of psychotherapy.* Boston: Houghton Mifflin Harcourt. (p. 34)

Page 195   **Navajo weavers, who are famous for their rugs, routinely include at least one incorrect knot in every carpet to temper the egotism of perfectionism.**

Landry, A. (2009, March 16). Navajo weaver shares story with authentic rugs. Retrieved March 18, 2021, from *www.nativetimes. com/archives/22/1217-navajo-weaver-shares-story-with-authentic-rugs*.

Page 198   **Cognitive scientists tell us that most of us locate our awareness or consciousness somewhere in the head, behind the eyes.**
Barbeito, R., & Ono, H. (1979). Four methods of locating the egocenter: A comparison of their predictive validities and reliabilities. *Behavior Research Methods & Instrumentation, 11*(1), 31–36.

Page 199   **What or where is the unified center of sentience that comes into and goes out of existence, that changes over time but remains the same entity, and that has a supreme moral worth?**
Pinker, S. (2003). *How the mind works*. London: Penguin. (p. 558)

Page 200   **We begin to glimpse the insight suggested in the title of psychiatrist Mark Epstein's book *Thoughts Without a Thinker*.**
Epstein, M. (2013). *Thoughts without a thinker: Psychotherapy from a Buddhist perspective*. New York: Basic Books.

Page 204   **The Cloud in the Sheet of Paper**
Hanh, T. N. (2005). *Being peace*. Berkeley: Parallax Press. (p. 51)

CHAPTER 13: YOU'RE NOT THAT SPECIAL—AND OTHER GOOD NEWS

Page 205   **When the game is over, the pawns, rooks, knights, bishops, kings, and queens all go back into the same box.**
Steen, F. F. (2003, November 8). Italian proverbs. Retrieved April 05, 2021, from *http://cogweb.ucla.edu/Discourse/Proverbs/Italian. html*.

Page 205   **Do you know who the king of England was in 1387?**
Richard II. The fact that most of us don't know, despite his once-great importance, was shared in a personal communication from Dr. Robert Waldinger, April 4, 2021.

Page 205   **By many estimates, in only 50,000 years the earth will enter another ice age. In 600 million years, as the sun gets hotter, CO2 will disappear from the atmosphere, and all the plants will die. In a billion years, the oceans will evaporate, and all remaining life on earth will be annihilated.**
Future of earth. (2021). *Wikipedia*. Retrieved March 18, 2021, from *https://en.wikipedia.org/wiki/Future_of_Earth*.

Page 206   **In America in 1950, one out of three boys was given one of the 10 most common names, as was one in four baby girls. Being "normal" was prized. By 2012, fewer than one out of 10 boys, and one out of 11 girls, received a common name.**

Twenge, J. M., Abebe, E. M., & Campbell, W. K. (2010). Fitting in or standing out: Trends in American parents' choices for children's names, 1880–2007. *Social Psychological and Personality Science, 1*(1), 19–25.

Page 206 **Martin Seligman quipped, "It's as if some idiot raised the ante on what it takes to be a normal human being."**

Seligman, M. E. (1988). Boomer blues. *Psychology Today, 22,* 50–55.

Page 206 **Joel Osteen, pastor of America's largest evangelical church, says, "God didn't create any of us to be average."**

Osteen, J. (2007). *Become a better you: 7 keys to improving your life every day.* New York: Simon & Schuster. (p. 109)

Page 206 ***God Wants You to Be Rich.***

Pilzer, P. Z. (1997). *God wants you to be rich.* New York: Simon & Schuster.

Page 207 **"Blessed are the meek: for they shall inherit the earth"**

King James Bible (Matthew 5:5). (2008). New York: Oxford University Press. (Original work published 1769)

Page 207 **"The Lord will destroy the house of the proud"**

King James Bible (Proverbs 15:25). (2008). New York: Oxford University Press. (Original work published 1769)

Page 207 **"Humility, modesty . . . absence of ego; this is said to be knowledge."**

Mitchell, S. (2000). *Bhagavad Gita: A new translation.* New York: Three Rivers Press. (Chapter 13)

Page 207 **Mike Robbins, who teaches leaders how to be more authentic, invites us to complete this sentence: "If you really knew me, you'd know that _____ ."**

Robbins, M. (2009, May 12). Express yourself. Retrieved March 18, 2021, from *https://mike-robbins.com/express-yourself.*

Page 208 **The father of American psychology, William James, reflected in 1882 on how freeing it can be: "Strangely, one feels extremely lighthearted once one has accepted in good faith one's incompetence in a particular field."**

André, C. (2012). *Feelings and moods.* Cambridge: Polity Press. (p. 88)

Page 208 **Psychiatrist Michael Miller suggested a corollary: "I know many people who have been ruined by success, but few by failure."**

Personal communication, August 22, 2019.

Page 209 **Research studies suggest that when we think we're superior, we become self-righteous and judge others more harshly for their faults, seeing them as less forgivable.**

Bushman, B. J., & Baumeister, R. F. (1998). Threatened egotism, narcissism, self-esteem, and direct and displaced aggression: Does self-love or self-hate lead to violence? *Journal of Personality and Social Psychology, 75*(1), 219.

Page 209   **In fact, one clever experiment that made subjects feel superior to peers demonstrated that this diminished their ability to even identify, much less care about, others' feelings.**

Galinsky, A. D., Magee, J. C., Inesi, M. E., & Gruenfeld, D. H. (2006). Power and perspectives not taken. *Psychological Science, 17*(12), 1068–1074.

Page 209   **A wonderful new application of big data is to alleviate shame by showing us how ordinary we all are.**

Stephens-Davidowitz, S., & Pabon, A. (2017). *Everybody lies: Big data, new data, and what the Internet can tell us about who we really are.* New York: HarperCollins. (p. 161)

Page 210   **I'm fond of a story I heard from Barry Magid, a psychiatrist and Zen priest in New York.**

Magid, B. (2012). *Ordinary mind: Exploring the common ground of Zen and psychoanalysis.* New York: Simon & Schuster. (p. 177)

Page 215   **Psychiatrist Bob Waldinger directs the Harvard Longitudinal Study, the longest running study of human well-being (it began in 1938).**

Mineo, L. (2018, November 26). Over nearly 80 years, Harvard study has been showing how to live a healthy and happy life. Retrieved March 18, 2021, from *https://news.harvard.edu/gazette/story/2017/04/over-nearly-80-years-harvard-study-has-been-showing-how-to-live-a-healthy-and-happy-life.*

Page 215   **Some 30 years ago I was traveling in Krabi, Thailand, and came across a fascinating Buddhist monastery.**

Wat Tham Suea (Tiger Cave Temple). Retrieved from *www.watthumsua-krabi.com.*

Page 216   **"For dust you are, and to dust you shall return."**

King James Bible (Genesis 3:19). (2008). New York: Oxford University Press. (Original work published 1769)

Page 216   **We "all go to one place."**

King James Bible (Ecclesiastes 3:20). (2008). New York: Oxford University Press. (Original work published 1769)

Page 216   **During the American Civil War, when death was ever present, it became customary to remind oneself of mortality every day so as to better appreciate being alive.**

Faust, D. G. (2009). *This republic of suffering: Death and the American Civil War.* New York: Vintage.

Gross, T. (2008, October 24). In a "Republic of Suffering," death's unifying effect. Retrieved March 18, 2021, from *www.npr.org/transcripts/96076929.*

CHAPTER 14: BEYOND I, ME, MINE

Page 221   **All you need is love.**

Lennon, J. (1967). All you need is love. *Yellow Submarine* [audio recording]. EMI Parlophone.

Page 221   **Back in 1895 Sigmund Freud wrote that the most we could expect of psychoanalysis was to transform "hysterical misery into common unhappiness."**

Freud, S. (1955). *The standard edition of the complete psychological works of Sigmund Freud, Volume II (1893–1895): Studies on hysteria.* London: Hogarth Press. (p. 308)

Page 221   **As the psychologist Chris Peterson, one of the founders of the positive psychology field, put it near the end of his life: "Other people matter!"**

Peterson, C. (2008, June 17). Other people matter: Two examples. Retrieved March 18, 2021, from *www.psychologytoday. com/us/blog/the-good-life/200806/other-people-matter-two-examples.*

Page 221   **Feeling safely connected to others turns out to be the central ingredient in human flourishing, while being disconnected is a risk factor for all sorts of ills.**

Eisenberger, N. I., & Cole, S. W. (2012). Social neuroscience and health: Neurophysiological mechanisms linking social ties with physical health. *Nature Neuroscience, 15*(5), 669.

Cacioppo, J. T., & Patrick, W. (2008). *Loneliness: Human nature and the need for social connection.* New York: Norton.

Page 221   **It's not the rich, privileged, good-looking, or powerful people who are happiest—it's those who have loved ones, friends, community, and meaningful work.**

Pinker, S. (2003). *How the mind works.* London: Penguin. (p. 393)

Page 222   **Fortunately, the most powerful antidote has not only worked for me and my patients, but is supported by hundreds of studies demonstrating a tight correlation between safe social connection and health.**

Holt-Lunstad, J., Smith, T. B., & Layton, J. B. (2010). Social relationships and mortality risk: A meta-analytic review. *PLoS medicine, 7*(7).

Page 222   **When our friends, spouses, siblings, or neighbors are happier, so are we. In fact, the closer we live to a happy person, the stronger the effect.**

Fowler, J. H., & Christakis, N. A. (2008). Dynamic spread of happiness in a large social network: Longitudinal analysis over 20 years in the Framingham Heart Study. *BMJ, 337.*

Page 222   **As the political scientist Robert Putnam documented in his landmark book *Bowling Alone*, in America, at least, participation in community activities has steadily declined over the past decades.**

Putnam, R. D. (2000). *Bowling alone: The collapse and revival of American community.* New York: Simon & Schuster.

Page 222   **We're also living alone more, and less likely to have friends over for dinner, visit neighbors, or have someone close to us with whom we can talk.**

McPherson, M., Smith-Lovin, L., & Brashears, M. E. (2006). Social isolation in America: Changes in core discussion networks over two decades. *American Sociological Review, 71*(3), 353–375.

Page 223   **Scientists as early as the 1700s coined the term *superorganism* to describe species in which the idea of a separate "individual" seemed particularly questionable.**

Wilson, E. O. (1988). The current state of biological diversity. *Biodiversity, 521*(1), 3–18. (Chapter 56)

Page 224   **No act of kindness, no matter how small, is ever wasted.**

Aesop, A. (2016). *Aesop's fables.* Xist Publishing. (The Lion and the Mouse)

Page 224   **Researchers approached people on a university campus in Canada and gave them cash. They instructed half of them to spend the money on themselves and half to spend it on someone else.**

Dunn, E. W., Aknin, L. B., & Norton, M. I. (2008). Spending money on others promotes happiness. *Science, 319*(5870), 1687–1688.

Page 224   **A different study involved people who received stem-cell transplants to treat cancer.**

Rini, C., Austin, J., Wu, L. M., Winkel, G., Valdimarsdottir, H., Stanton, A. L., . . . & Redd, W. H. (2014). Harnessing benefits of helping others: A randomized controlled trial testing expressive helping to address survivorship problems after hematopoietic stem cell transplant. *Health Psychology, 33*(12), 1541.

Page 224   **After controlling for factors like household income, researchers at Notre Dame found that people who were the most generous financially, with their time, and in personal relationships, were significantly happier, physically healthier, and felt more purpose in life than those who were less generous.**

Smith, C., & Davidson, H. (2014). *The paradox of generosity: Giving we receive, grasping we lose.* New York: Oxford University Press.

Page 225   **Or as the Dalai Lama often says: *Be selfish; love one another.***

Ricard, M., Mandell, C., & Gordon, S. (2015). *Altruism: The power of compassion to change yourself and the world.* New York: Little, Brown & Company. (Quoted by André Comte-Sponville, p. 240)

Page 225   **In lab experiments, economists have demonstrated that not only do we give more when we think others are watching, but our private concerns about self-image play a role even when they're not.**

Tonin, M., & Vlassopoulos, M. (2013). Experimental evidence of self-image concerns as motivation for giving. *Journal of Economic Behavior & Organization, 90,* 19–27.

Page 226   **Exercise: A bodhisattva to-do list**

Styron, C. W. (2013). Positive psychology and the bodhisattva path. In C. K. Germer, R. D. Siegel, & P. R. Fulton (Eds.), *Mindfulness and psychotherapy* (2nd ed., pp. 295–308). New York: Guilford Press. (p. 307)

Page 227   **Who is rich? One who is happy with his lot.**

Pirkei Avot 4:1. Retrieved April 5, 2021, from *www.chabad.org/library/article_cdo/aid/2032/jewish/Chapter-Four.htm.*

Page 227   **Gratitude boosts our capacity to deal with and recover from life's challenges. It's linked to having more energy, sleeping better, feeling less lonely, improved physical health, and experiencing more joy, enthusiasm, and love.**

Davis, D. E., Choe, E., Meyers, J., Wade, N., Varjas, K., Gifford, A., . . . & Worthington, E. L., Jr. (2016). Thankful for the little things: A meta-analysis of gratitude interventions. *Journal of Counseling Psychology, 63*(1), 20.

Emmons, R. A., & Stern, R. (2013). Gratitude as a psychotherapeutic intervention. *Journal of Clinical Psychology, 69*(8), 846–855.

Page 228   **The Zen master Suzuki Roshi famously said, "In the beginner's mind there are many possibilities; in the expert's mind there are few."**

Suzuki, S. (1973). *Zen mind, beginner's mind.* New York: John Weatherhill.

Page 229   **Researchers tested this notion. Since people often express more gratitude for their lives after near-death experiences or life-threatening illnesses, they examined whether deliberately contemplating our mortality would increase gratitude—and it did.**

Frias, A., Watkins, P. C., Webber, A. C., & Froh, J. J. (2011). Death and gratitude: Death reflection enhances gratitude. *Journal of Positive Psychology, 6*(2), 154–162.

Page 230   **According to the World Bank, some *689 million people* live on less than $1.90 per day.**

World Bank. (2020). *Poverty and shared prosperity 2020: Monitoring global poverty.* Washington, DC: World Bank. (p. 28)

Page 230   **Thich Nhat Hanh invites his students to try a simple experiment: Recall the last time you had a toothache. Remember your pain, your worry, and your wishes for relief? I have excellent news for you today—no toothache!**

Hanh, T. N. (2011). *Making space: Creating a home meditation practice.* New York: Parallax Press. (p. 3)

Page 230   **One of the most widely validated approaches is keeping a gratitude journal.**

Davis, D. E., Choe, E., Meyers, J., Wade, N., Varjas, K., Gifford, A., . . . & Worthington, E. L., Jr. (2016). Thankful for the little things: A meta-analysis of gratitude interventions. *Journal of Counseling Psychology, 63*(1), 20.

Page 230   **In various studies, compared to control groups, people who kept gratitude journals exercised more regularly, reported fewer physical symptoms, and felt better about their lives. They also reported greater alertness, enthusiasm, determination, and energy, and were more likely to report having helped someone with a personal problem.**

Emmons, R. A., & Stern, R. (2013). Gratitude as a psychotherapeutic intervention. *Journal of Clinical Psychology, 69*(8), 846–855.

Page 232   **Research on gratitude practices suggests that they're most effective if we note as much detail as possible, include gratitude toward other people, and savor surprises—unexpected opportunities or gifts.**

Marsh, J. (2011, November 17). Tips for keeping a gratitude journal. Retrieved March 19, 2021, from *https://greatergood.berkeley.edu/article/item/tips_for_keeping_a_gratitude_journal.*

Page 232   **One of the most famous research studies in positive psychology tested five different interventions to see which would have the most powerful effect on well-being. The clear winner was a *gratitude letter.***

Seligman, M. E., Steen, T. A., Park, N., & Peterson, C. (2005). Positive psychology progress: Empirical validation of interventions. *American Psychologist, 60* (5), 410–421.

Page 234   **Studies document all sorts of mental and physical health problems arising from this sort of chronic resentment.**

Toussaint, L. L., Worthington, E. L. J., & Williams, D. R. (2015). *Forgiveness and health.* Dordrecht: Springer Netherlands.

Page 234   **Research finds that forgiveness is linked to reduced anxiety, depression, physical symptoms, and even mortality.**

Toussaint, L. L., Worthington, E. L. J., & Williams, D. R. (2015). *Forgiveness and health.* Dordrecht: Springer Netherlands.

Page 238   **Countless books and articles have been written about how to apologize effectively.**

Lazare, A. (2005). *On apology.* New York: Oxford University Press.

Page 239   **You made it to the end of a nonfiction book (which statistically, most people don't do).**

Heyman, S. (2015, February 4). Keeping tabs on bestseller books and reading habits. Retrieved March 19, 2021, from *www.nytimes.com/2015/02/05/arts/international/keeping-tabs-on-best-seller-books-and-reading-habits.html.*

index

about the author

RONALD D. SIEGEL, PsyD, is Assistant Professor of Psychology, part time, at Harvard Medical School, where he has taught since the early 1980s. His books include *The Mindfulness Solution: Everyday Practices for Everyday Problems*. Dr. Siegel teaches internationally about the application of mindfulness practices in psychotherapy and other fields, and maintains a private practice in Lincoln, Massachusetts. He regularly uses the practices in this book to work with his own ever-fluctuating self-esteem.

list of audio tracks

Title	Run time
What Matters to Me?	07:10
Riding the Self-Evaluation Roller Coaster	05:10
Mindfulness of Breath	20:45
Identifying Emotions in the Body	06:40
The Joys of Self-Transcendence	04:10
Urge Surfing	05:00
Embracing a Self-Esteem Injury	04:10
Loving-Kindness Practice	15:35
RAIN for Self-Esteem Injuries	06:15
It All Changes	18:25
The Future of Our Social Self	08:20